MW00563989

Happiness is a skill
you can develop!

Are you tired of self-help books that offer fuzzy anecdotes of inspiration, but leave you wondering what are science-based ways you can improve your life starting today?

Then this book is for you.

Jim McCarthy had a Stanford MBA and a successful career in Silicon Valley. But a cancer diagnosis suddenly changed his life, forcing him to ask questions such as

- **How much longer will I live?**
- **What do I need to repair in my relationships?**
- **How can I use my work to help others?**
- **What, after all, would make me happy?**

Since then, Jim has spent years studying the latest in neuroscience and psychology in an effort to understand what helps people thrive with abundant pleasure, purpose, and peace. His conclusion: Happiness is a skill you can develop.

Wanting to share his findings, Jim developed an innovative and highly acclaimed "Happiness Workshop," which he has presented to organizations of all sizes across the U.S. and internationally. His talks aren't just inspirational — participants take away proven strategies, science-based insights, and daily practices to lower their stress, boost their confidence, and find greater meaning.

Jim delivered the talk "What Cancer Taught Me About Happiness" at TEDx Oakland in November, 2018. You can watch the video here: https://www.youtube.com/watch?v=x0pulJf7Fl0.

He has distilled what he's learned from his research and his workshop experiences into the new book, *Live Each Day: A Surprisingly Simple Guide to Happiness*. It's an intriguing, enjoyable, immediately applicable blueprint for anyone seeking to live more fully. Throughout *Live Each Day*, Jim encourages readers to explore intriguing questions through focused, thought-provoking writing activities, with the ultimate aim of helping each person design their own path to happiness.

Praise for
Live Each Day

"We all face challenges. Some of us know how to respond intelligently and bounce back. For the rest of us, we need Jim McCarthy. Jim's teachings will help you reset your life, so you become more resilient, make wiser choices, and enjoy a more balanced, meaningful journey. Backed up by real world experience, *Live Each Day* is a practical guide that truly works. Gift a copy to anyone you love."

Tony Surtees
Serial Entrepreneur, ex-Yahoo VP, Co-founder of Laava.id

"With a healthy dose of humility and sense of humor, Jim McCarthy presents a roadmap to help us find meaning in life, live in the present, and connect with people and projects that matter to us. Jim does a terrific job translating complex psychological research into accessible but powerful action steps that can drastically improve your emotional well-being."

Dr. Daniele V. Levy
Clinical Psychologist

"Jim McCarthy uses a Silicon Valley approach to 'hack' happiness. Innovative and practical, science-based but also personal — *Live Each Day* gives you the strategies and daily tactics to be both successful and happy. His Happiness Workshop was amazing, and this book is even better. Highly applicable for smart, hard-working people everywhere."
Anil Sethi
Serial Entrepreneur, Founder and CEO at Ciitizen

"In *Live Each Day*, Jim expertly marries more esoteric happiness concepts with real-world tactics, weaving a highly-readable tapestry that not only inspires, but demands action. Ideal for the modern professional who sees the benefits of happiness in life and work, but needs a blueprint for how to make it happen."
Chris Butsch
Author, *The Millennial's Guide to Making Happiness*

"Jim's Happiness Workshop helped me achieve a major breakthrough in my life a few years ago. Thanks to the writing and discussion activities, I found a greater sense of clarity on a vital decision I needed to make. I am delighted to see him expand his workshops with this book — sharing practical tools with a greater audience, while guiding readers to develop lasting habits in key areas of personal growth."
Judith Duval
CEO, Media & Education Startup

"I've read many books on happiness and living a better life, but *Live each Day* is different — providing the ideal balance of research, personal stories and practical insights. Jim is unique as a writer, showing deep authenticity and relatability, that brings out the humanity in all of us. I recommend this book to anyone who is tired of pursuing a happier life and who simply wants to remember the power to choose to be happy, right now, in the midst of real life."

Ariane de Bonvoisin
Bestselling Author of *The First 30 Days*, Speaker and
Executive Coach

"*Live Each Day* is an ambitious achievement. Jim McCarthy takes fascinating anecdotes from his intriguing career, and provides the reader with a robust framework to understand happiness. He is a Modern Elder, sharing his hard-earned wisdom while also asking the right questions. A must-read for anybody who seeks to find more pleasure and purpose in their life — at any age."

Chip Conley
Strategic Advisor to Airbnb and Bestselling Author of
Wisdom@Work: The Making of a Modern Elder

"For happiness books it is one stop shopping … combining the common happiness activities with practices of depth, wisdom and profound insight. Written with humor, clarity, and humility, I know this great book will help many people live significantly better lives."

Frederick Luskin, Ph.D.
Senior Consultant, Wellness and Health Promotion,
Stanford University

"It would be hard to overstate the incredible value I got from this book. More than just a thoughtful read, *Live Each Day* is an action-provoking, life-changing vehicle. I highly recommend doing the activities with a close friend or loved one, as you will help each other uncover and implement changes to make your life more fulfilling, peaceful … and even fun."

Heidi Roizen
Partner, DFJ Venture Capital

"Captivating storytelling, intriguing questions, pioneering research, and deceptively doable daily practices — *Live Each Day* has something for everyone. Grounded in science, but coming from the heart, this book shows you not only how to be authentically happier; it's a wake-up call to living your life to the absolute fullest."

Randy Taran
Founder of Project Happiness and author of *Emotional Advantage*

"I invited Jim McCarthy to give a TEDx talk. His talk was simply phenomenal — inspiring yet practical. I'm so happy to see that he's taken his wealth of knowledge and condensed it into this book. A must-read for anybody seeking to lead an intentional life!"

Christopher Ategeka
Serial Entrepreneur, Founder/CEO UCOT Inc.

Live Each Day

A Surprisingly Simple Guide to Happiness

Jim McCarthy

PUBLISHER'S NOTE:

This publication is designed to provide accurate and authoritative information in regard to the subject matter covered. It is sold with the understanding that neither the publisher nor the author is engaged in rendering psychological, financial, legal, medical, or other professional services. If expert assistance or counseling is needed, the services of a competent professional should be sought.

TO MY PARENTS, ED AND JOAN McCARTHY

who have always loved and encouraged me, even when they did not understand what I was trying to do.

AND TO MY WIFE, STACY

who has taught me more about happiness than anybody.

CONTENTS

PART TWO
What Is "Happiness"?

PART THREE
Presence

PART FOUR
Practices

Introduction:
How to Use This Book

Would you like to be *less* stressed out?
Would you like to be *more* focused and confident?
Would you like to *enjoy* your life more?
Great! You've come to the right place.
Because *all* of these are skills you can develop.

Most of us are mercilessly bombarded with the message, "Work harder. Work longer hours. Make more money. The stuff you buy will fulfill you. Do your job, whether you like it or not. Keep up with everyone else. This is what's important. If you just accomplish that next goal, you'll be sexy, successful, and eventually happy ..."

But according to what you will read in this book, that approach will *not* bring you happiness.

Instead, there is another way, which will.

By the time you finish this book ...

- You will have reflected upon the quality and purpose of your relationships and your work.
- You will have gained knowledge of a simple framework for

how to be happy.

- You will have absorbed a variety of practical ways to boost your presence in the here and now.
- You will have followed an easy process for reflecting upon and writing about the choices you make in your life. You will have come up with very specific action items on what you want to affirm, what you need to stop doing, and what you need to start doing.
- You will have learned multiple scientifically proven practices, which you can do daily, starting now, to help you create your pleasure, purpose, and peace. I call the time you invest in these practices "the Magical 1 Percent."

I've tried to organize this book in an intuitive yet methodical way. But each of the chapters can stand alone in its own right. So you might be in the middle of reading the chapter on Relationships, then jump to the chapter on Affirmations.

The Process: Writing and Exploration

I've always loved this quote from Socrates: "The unexamined life is not worth living."[1]

After all ... who are you? How did you get here? What are you doing ... and why?

Dr. Rick Hanson, a San Francisco Bay Area neuropsychologist, reminds us of the value of self-reflection. In his outstanding book, *Just One Thing*, he writes, "There are three fundamental phases to psychological and spiritual growth: *being with* difficult material (e.g., old wounds, anger); *releasing* it; and *replacing* it with something more beneficial. In a nutshell, you let be, let go, and let in."[2]

I've always found diary writing, or journaling, an excellent way to sort through my thoughts, feelings, and behaviors. When I was a student in Europe, I wrote in my diary to not only record my travels, but also to process and make sense of different people and cultures. At times of real crisis in my career, I've written "Important note to self" emails, which have helped me sort out my plan of action going forward. Whenever I've had major problems in my relationships, I've found that journaling helped me calm down and see the situation more clearly. Writing has been not only cathartic, but also practical.

A *New York Times* article notes that "while writing doesn't solve every problem, it can definitely help people cope." In that same article, University of Virginia Psychology Professor Timothy D. Wilson goes on to say, "Writing forces people to reconstrue whatever is troubling them and find new meaning in it."[3]

When I first started formulating and conducting my "Happiness Workshop: Create Your Pleasure, Purpose, and Peace," I would tell my story, then ask participants to think about various questions and write out their answers. People found this helpful, but they wanted more discussion, so they could think out loud, learn from others, and gain further insight.

At the same time, they asked for a lot more scientific research, so they could believe my claims about what makes people happier in relationships and at work. Understandably, they wanted a solid, credible framework for defining and achieving happiness.

I'm glad I received that feedback from the skeptics, because I tend to be a skeptic as well. I raise an eyebrow whenever anybody makes big assertions with vague, undefined terms such as "attraction," "energy," and "laws." For the purposes of this book, I leverage the wisdom from various spiritual traditions, but I have no religious agenda. My emphasis is on verifiable methods that people can apply to their daily lives. I've spent years tracking down and confirming a wealth of rigorous research to support the practices in this book.

Based on user feedback, the master classes I teach have evolved to follow variations on this process:

- I share scientific research, anecdotes, observations, and frameworks with you.
- I distribute a handout, with questions.
- You think.
- You write on the handout. I usually give a very short period of time, such as four minutes or seven minutes. This gives you no time to procrastinate. The best answers often come when you have no time to filter, edit, or censor your thoughts and feelings.
- I ask you to pair up — one-on-one, with another person — and share what you wrote. It's a bit like speed dating.
- I bring the whole group together, so you can ask questions, share epiphanies or insights, and discuss.
- I give you a few more minutes to write out your individual action items.
- If you want, you can make a public commitment as to what you plan on doing next to improve your life.

This is serious emotional work.

I always bring tissues to my workshops, because many times someone ends up crying. The tears are a positive sign that people are going deep and getting real. My master class participants often tell me that they're amazed at how quickly we are able to explore fundamental life issues — and gain actionable insights. In other words, they realize what important changes they need to make. It may not be easy, but it's worth it.

I've tried to take the best aspects of my Happiness Workshop and replicate them in this book. Better yet, because a book is not the same as a workshop or a keynote address, we're able to delve deeper into many topics.

On the other hand, what I *can't* do is force you to do the writing activities. In a master class, if I look around the room and see that someone is frozen with writer's block, I can gently nudge or encourage them. But I can't do that with you.

Instead, I have to persuade you right here that you will definitely get the most out of this book when you actually do the writing activities, share your responses with others, and follow through on your action items. Couples who've been married 25 years have told me that after my workshop, they went out, had a glass of wine, and talked about life-and-death matters they'd never addressed before. With my corporate clients, people have said they got to know their colleagues on a deeper, more personal level thanks to the master class. One of the many benefits was that they developed trust within their team.

So here are some ways to get the most out of the writing activities:

Do them by yourself.

- Write them in the easiest way possible. Open a document and just start writing. Send yourself an email. Or grab a pen and a piece of paper.
- Do them quickly, if that helps. Set the timer on your smartphone for five minutes and see how much you can write. (When the timer rings, you'll probably have built so much momentum that you won't want to stop — which is great! Just keep going.)
- Give yourself a full hour, if not more, to ruminate and explore your feelings while doing the exercise.
- Do them when you tend to feel more contemplative, such as first thing on a weekend morning. Or before you go to bed on a Sunday night, as you reflect on the week

ahead. Or while watching the orange sunset on a beach, when you're feeling relaxed and inspired. (I like fireplaces and snow outside.)

Do them with a loved one.

- Tell your husband, wife, or partner that you'd like to have fun doing an activity that could help you think about life and get to know each other better. (Yes, even if you've been together 30 years, you have room to get to know each other better.) Whether you have a partner or not, you might get a lot out of doing the writing with a parent, child, sibling, or trusted friend.

- You can take one question at a time, once per week, or do several at a time. Ideally, both of you can formally write out your answers. But it's also worthwhile if you simply discuss the answers — say, while you're on a long car ride or flight. Or as part of your "pillow talk" at the end of the day.

Do them in a group.

- Your family might enjoy doing the writing activities together. Or the questions could simply be a springboard for conversation around the dinner table, or over drinks at the neighborhood bar.

- When you're having lunch with your colleagues, ask them how they'd answer some of these questions. You might be surprised at their answers, and all of you might feel a lot closer to each other afterwards.

- If you'd like me to conduct my master class or deliver a keynote for an event, please contact me and we can discuss (jim@jimmccarthy.com). I've found that the writing activities and discussion work exceptionally well, even in settings where the audience is used to just sitting and listening.

Execute your action items.

- Insights are most powerful when you put them into action.

As part of your writing, I ask you to come up with specific things you are going to start doing, stop doing, or continue doing.

- To help you make sure this happens, I've written a short chapter at the end of this book on how to create and stick with useful habits. It was tempting to not include it in the book, but then I realized how important it is that you *implement* what you've learned, so that you benefit the most. **Revisit your writings from time to time.**
- Put a reminder in your calendar for every three or six months, to review what you originally wrote. Feel free to revise this document over time. This alone can be a very worthwhile exercise as you see how you are evolving — or how the world is changing around you.

The Process: Practices

Thinking, reflecting, writing, discussing, and implementing changes are all wonderful and useful. But so are a series of practices that, over time, have become a bigger part of my work.

This development began when I started reading my workshop feedback forms. Participants said they loved the writing activities and action items, loved the interaction and discussion, and loved the inspiration. But they sought more specific, daily practices that they could start doing *right now*.

When I once mentioned in passing that forgiveness was essential for being able to enjoy one's life journey, people wanted to know how to forgive. They were stressed, and I said that mindfulness meditation can help. "How do you do that?" they asked. Others said they knew what they wanted to do, but could not find the courage to take that first step. "Affirmations can help," I replied, and they asked, "What's that?" Many workshop participants reported that they were always striving for more, and I suggested they'd be a lot happier with a gratitude practice.

The good news is that I had already spent many years practicing forgiveness, meditation, affirmations, and gratitude, and I gradually incorporated all of these activities into my workshops.

This book will show you how to do a forgiveness practice, how to meditate, how to affirm yourself, and how to be grateful. You will learn why these practices work, and you will be able to incorporate them into your life — immediately.

Getting the Most Out of This Book

You can view this book as an organized collection of anecdotes and research, with some writing activities and practices as optional add-ons. You can simply read and look for best practices and inspiration, without ever doing any deep introspection, without any writing, without any action plans, without changing any of your routines or practices. In fact, most "motivational" books don't ask you to do any more than that.

Yet I'm asking you to do more.

I'd like you to view this book as a how-to guide to change your life. It's a compact, crystallized, high-octane, practical workbook, with step-by-step suggestions and activities — each of which is surprisingly simple to do.

My goal is not to make your growth and transformation amazingly hard.

My goal is to make it ridiculously easy.

But that means you have to do it, one baby step at a time. I'd like to suggest how much you could benefit — more or less — from doing the following:

- **20% benefit** — if you *just read this book*, but never do the writing activities or action items, talk to anyone else, or do any of the practices.
- **40% benefit** — if you just *read this book, do the writing activities and action items*, but never talk to anyone else, or do any of the practices.
- **60% benefit** — if you just *read this book, do the writing activities and action items, talk to someone else*, but never do any of the practices.
- **80% benefit** — if you just *read this book, do the writing activities and action items, talk to someone else, and do all of the practices daily.*
- **100% benefit** — if you *do all of the above, but also keep learning by following me on social media and getting my latest email newsletter updates.*
  (Learn more at www.jimmccarthy.com.) Besides, I'd love to hear from you.

The more deeply you use this book, the more you will benefit. It's up to you how far you want to or need to take these recommendations.

I'm honored that we're spending this time together. I'm delighted to share the absolute best of what I have learned. So that you can live the life you want right now and leave a legacy with no regrets.

Next, I'm going to tell you a bit about my story.

JIM McCARTHY
San Francisco, California

PART ONE

Purpose — Decide What You Want to Do

Chapter One:
Live Like You Have Cancer

"Hello?"

"Mr. McCarthy?"

"Yes?"

It's 12:40 p.m. on Tuesday, February 5, 2013. My doctor calls me up and tells me that I have cancer.

I'm in a strip mall parking lot in Mountain View, California, in the heart of Silicon Valley. Google's headquarters is a mile away. To my right is a Starbucks. To my left is a burrito joint. I've just picked up my dry cleaning. I'm sitting in my shiny blue BMW convertible. And I hear the voice at the other end of my iPhone talking about surgery, radiation, and survival rates.

I drive home, lie down in bed, and cry for a couple of hours. This is the first time in my life that I truly feel my own mortality. I mean, we all know that we're going to die, on an intellectual level. But this is the first time that I realize — on a visceral level — that my skin will someday be as cold as my bathroom's granite countertop.

I call my mom and dad in Omaha, Nebraska. I call my brother Mike in New Jersey. Then my sister Kathy in Omaha. Then my brother Dan in Virginia. It's hard to get out the words. I feel horrible for myself, but even worse for them. They're all really shocked. The conversations are short.

Then, I drink almost an entire bottle of cheap chardonnay wine. I don't normally drink that much, but this time I feel justified.

Next, I do what I almost always do in times of crisis — I start writing in my journal. And out of me flow all sorts of questions I have about my relationships, my career, my legacy, and my regrets.

"How much time do I still have?"

"What do I still want to do?"

"What do I need to repair?"

"What, after all, would make me happy?"

There is never a good moment to get a cancer diagnosis, but the timing of this seemed especially bad. You see, most people would say that I've been very fortunate: I grow up in Omaha, supported by a loving family. I study political science at the University of Iowa. I spend my junior year in Vienna, then win a Fulbright Scholarship to study in Tübingen, Germany. After teaching English to bankers in Frankfurt for two years, I move to Madrid, where I work as a business journalist. I don't have much money, but I have a lot of fun.

In 1991, I move to the San Francisco Bay Area to be with a woman I had fallen in love with. After a few years struggling in sales jobs, I'm lucky enough to get into Stanford for business school, and I earn my MBA there in 1996. Then, I'm fortunate enough to be hired at Yahoo in 1997 as employee number 258. Being part of the Dot-Com Boom is fascinating, exhausting, competitive, and lucrative.

In 2000, I get married and have a daughter. I'm a stay-at-home dad for a year. I have another daughter and then go on to work at other successful internet companies.

So it's fair to say that I'm an ambitious Silicon Valley business guy. My life has been built on privilege, hard work, good timing, risk-taking … and a lot of luck.

In late 2012, I leave the start-up I'm at and start doing leadership consulting — teaching companies how to hire great people and build high-performance teams. At age 49, I am really excited to jumpstart this next phase of my career, playing to my strengths.

And then I get the cancer diagnosis.

About a week after getting the call from my doctor at Kaiser Permanente, I go to their cancer treatment center in nearby Santa Clara. Part of the health provider's protocol is that I speak with various doctors to get their opinions.

I am accompanied by my friend, Gerald, who's there to give me emotional support. I figure that the stress of the situation will make it hard for me to listen accurately.

It turns out I have very early stage prostate cancer. The disease kills about 29,000 men in the United States every year.[1]

My original urologist — the one who called me on February 5 — has already urged me to have surgery.

But today a different urologist explains that this surgery has a 40–50 percent chance of making me impotent for the rest of my life. I've always liked sex. And I don't like those odds at all.

A different doctor — this time a radiation oncologist — mentions that they can place small "radiation seeds" inside my prostate gland. The good news: it should kill the cancer. The bad news: it might trigger a different cancer in my internal organs.

Fortunately, both of these doctors agree that I can do what's called "active surveillance," which means no surgery or radiation yet — just regular blood tests and biopsies to make sure the cancer is not spreading quickly.

We have caught the cancer early. It turns out that I'm lucky, yet again.

Now, you can say, "Hang on, Jim. You have a common form of cancer. You've caught it so early on that you haven't even had to treat it yet. Why all the drama? Why all the talk about life and death?"

These are good questions.

A couple of weeks after I get my cancer diagnosis, I meet with a friend, Diane. Diane was the first head of public relations at Yahoo in the late '90s. She's a very nice, smart, successful Silicon Valley executive.

She also has advanced lung cancer that has spread to the walls of her chest. Sitting in the sunshine around an outdoor table, at an Italian restaurant in Los Gatos, I say, "Diane, I don't even feel like I'm in the same league with you. You've had a lot of chemotherapy. You've lost all of your hair. You have a very serious situation."

Diane looks me in the eye and says, "Jim, it's not about whether you have two months to live, or 20 years. When you get a cancer diagnosis, it changes your life. But when I go to my son's lacrosse games, and I see the blue in the sky, the green in the leaves, and I hear the laugher of the boys running, there are tears running down my face. Tears are streaming down my face, because I'm just savoring the pure simple beauty of the moment ...

"And I wish we all could live like we have cancer."

Now, when Diane says, "I wish we all could live like we have cancer," clearly she doesn't wish on any of us the pain of having cancer. The fear from having cancer. The many losses of having cancer.

But she wishes that each of us *cherish* today. Not hung up on something that happened a week ago, which we can't change. And not freaked out about something that may or may not happen tomorrow. But living as deeply and richly as possible ... *right now*.

Diane taught me the importance of practicing mindfulness, facing life's biggest challenges with courage, and still enjoying the journey. When every moment was precious, that's how she chose to live each day.

I'm sorry to say that Diane passed away, right before Christmas, in 2016. But she lives on in all the lucky people who knew her, as well as in this book and in the workshops that I conduct.

So let me ask you this:

How would *you* live if you had cancer?

Every time I lead a master class, no matter how small the group, there is someone in the room who is a cancer survivor, or who has been touched by cancer in their family, or by some other disease, or some other tragedy. In doing my work, I've realized that you don't have to look far to find real heartbreak in this world. Look out your window. Look around your office. Look around your home.

Maybe you, too, have been driven to think about what life is all about — and how short it can be. Were your reflections prompted by similar events, or something else? Did you ask yourself some big questions, or did you try to put those thoughts out of your mind? My experience inspired me to develop my workshops and this book. I passionately believe that embracing life's impermanence and facing certain questions will help you live each day more fully.

So how would *you* live … if you had cancer?

How would *you* live … if you had a terminal illness?

How would *you* live … if you really felt your mortality — in your gut — the way that I did for the first time on February 5, 2013?

On that day, California wine surging in my blood, I wrote out a lot of questions for myself. And I'm going to ask you many of those same questions throughout this book. I know this topic can be pretty heavy. I mean, this is supposed to be a book on happiness — why are we talking about death?

I understand that the prospect of your mortality may seem dark. But out of darkness comes light. So I'd like to share with you what cancer taught me about happiness, and how I've changed my life as a result:

First of all, I decided to reduce my stress through meditation, affirmations, yoga, exercise, eating well, taking supplements, working less, and getting enough sleep. I get regular blood tests and biopsies, and so far it does not seem like the cancer has spread. So that's great news.

Second, I found the courage to do the things that I'd always wanted to do but had never made happen. I had long dreamt of being a motivational speaker and author. Facing my mortality, I suddenly found the confidence to talk publicly about my diagnosis and the lessons I've learned from it. I hope I can touch your life in a positive way. That's why I wrote this book.

And finally, I gave myself permission to start enjoying my life more. At the time of my diagnosis, I was divorced and living by myself in Mountain View. I had been in the Bay Area for almost 22 years, always dreaming of the opportunity to live in beautiful San Francisco. Within weeks of my diagnosis, I resolved to move to S.F., bought a condo there, and made the move. Six weeks later I met a lovely woman named Stacy, who is today my wife. As a result, I'm investing in family, friends, and community more than ever.

Over the years I've learned a variety of techniques to reduce my stress, boost my confidence, and create my happiness. These are all skills *you* can develop, too. I promise that in the process of reading this book, doing the writing, and implementing these simple practices, you will feel great about yourself and your life.

Let's get started …

Imagine Your Death Day

Writing Activity 1:
Please imagine your death.
When is the exact day, month, and year?
What is your cause of death?
What are your last thoughts, emotions, and sensations?
Who will be with you?

_____

_____

_____

_____

_____

_____

_____

_____

_____

Take as much time as you need, right now, to write out your answer. If you have a printed version of this book, go ahead and write directly in the space provided. If you have an electronic version, you might be able to type notes. Write however you can — using pen and paper, making an entry in your diary, or tapping a few high-level comments on your smartphone.

Write in as much detail as you can. Think about these questions' implications for your career, your relationships, your health, and your legacy.

This is often the first question that I ask in my Happiness Workshop. I hand out the question on an otherwise blank piece of paper, and I give the participants about seven minutes to write their answers. No time to overthink. No time for writer's block. Just hurry up and start writing, now.

I know it's a tough question. As in the workshop, I urge you to just do the best you can. You can manifest whatever you want — if you think you'll live until you're 150, go ahead and write that. If you think you'll die in an earthquake in the next hour, write that.

Why do I pose this question? To shock you into facing your mortality, the way that I had to face mine when I learned of my cancer diagnosis.

Many of us don't want to face the fact that we will die someday — and that avoidance can stand in the way of having a happy, fulfilling, pleasurable life. We are often in denial that — just as you have a birthday — you will also have a death day. Merely writing down a date challenges that denial and helps you grasp your mortality in a way that can start breaking down those barriers to a fuller life.

Will it be
October 6, 2063?

February 17, 2105?
July 4, 2034?

What does that begin to tell you? Powerful, isn't it?

In my master classes, almost all people struggle with this question for the first 30 seconds, and then they start writing. Some are really stuck after a couple of minutes, and then they have a breakthrough. And on rare occasions, a person's fear or denial is so strong that they simply refuse to write anything at all. For those people, I am respectful of their emotions and their struggle. But I think they'll start living a whole lot better when they realize that they don't have forever.

After all, you don't want to be the sort of person who fits the description in the old saying, "Some people die at 25 and aren't buried until 75."

Is the question "morbid"? Well, it's reality:

- You do *not* have forever to live your life.
- You do *not* have forever to start that business or do the work that you've always wanted to do.
- You do *not* have forever to love others, create a family, or be a compassionate father, mother, spouse, son, brother, sister, child, or friend.
- You do *not* have forever to take care of your health. Or do that trip to Italy that you've always wanted to do. Or go to that fancy restaurant that you've been saving for a special day.

In my happiness workshops, it's not uncommon that at least one person in the room starts crying as they respond to this question — because they *are* feeling their mortality, they *are* realizing that their time is precious, they *are* seeing that they need to make some changes to their life, and they need to do so *now*.

Once in San Francisco, I did a workshop for the local Harvard University alumni club. A woman said she visualized dying with her children and grandchildren beside her — and then she realized that she didn't have any kids in the first place! She later told me that she went home that night and decided with her husband to start a family. I'm happy to say they now have a son.

In another workshop, there was a lovely couple from Brazil. He thought he would only live to age 70. She thought she would live to 96. When they discussed this, she started crying because she loves her husband, and she did not like the thought of being a widow for a quarter century. They resolved that he needed to take better care of his health, so that they could envision a long life together.

Lots of participants ask, "Should I write my ideal scenario, or write what I think will really happen?" I say it's up to them. How far apart are the two scenarios? And more important, what would you need to do or change, so that you improve the chances of the ideal scenario actually happening?

Writing Activity 2: Action Plan
What do you need to start doing?
What do you need to stop doing?
What do you need to continue?

_____

_____

_____

_____

_____

_____

_____

_____

_____

_____

_____

_____

_____

_____

Let's assume your life is not perfect. So in doing Writing Activity 1, you probably identified a few things you'd like to improve. Maybe they're huge. Maybe they're pretty trivial. In any case, in Writing Activity 2, get as specific as you can with your Action Plan. Remind yourself *why* you are making these changes. Imagine the better life you can have as a result. Then share your answers with a loved one or a friend. Ask them what they think. Refine your answers, based on an in-depth conversation.

After that, make a public commitment by sharing your new goals or resolutions on social media. Shout it from the rooftops! Research indicates that if you write out a goal, and then give a weekly status report to a friend, you increase the likelihood of accomplishing this goal by a whopping 76 percent! [2] In fact, I'd love it if you sent me an email and told me what you came up with. Just send your thoughts to *jim@jimmccarthy.com.*

Engage others who can and will support you in your quest. Have the courage to live a much better life, knowing that you will not live forever.

In the following chapters, we are going to use mortality as a catalyst for you to think about the legacy you are creating through your relationships and work.

Chapter Two:
Relationships

Family, Friends, and Community

What's on your mind these days? What keeps you up at night? What makes you upset, frustrated, or scared? In the 2017 annual survey from the American Psychological Association, 63 percent of Americans said "the future of our nation" was a "very" or "somewhat" significant source of stress, followed closely by 62 percent citing "money" and 61 percent citing "work."[1]

If you're like me, you've spent huge amounts of your time and energy, throughout your life, trying to maximize your income and optimize your career.

How can I graduate from a good school? How can I get a good job? How can I do well at work and be promoted? How can I be a good manager? Maybe I should start my own business?

And if you're like me, you may also ask: How can I afford to drive a nice car and live in a decent home? How should I furnish my home? Am I into craft beers or artisanal gin? Should I wear collector tennis shoes? Am I into hip-hop or jazz? Do I like to go clubbing in Las Vegas, or do I prefer cycling in Vermont?

In short, what is my "lifestyle"?

It's easy to become seduced and obsessed with your lifestyle. After all, the advertisements that are bombarding you all day — online and in the real world — tell you what sort of lifestyle you should have, so you consume whatever sandals, SUVs, and sectional sofas that Madison Avenue is trying to sell to you. (I confess that I worked for many years in online advertising and e-commerce, for reasons that I describe in Chapter Three.)

So when we're pounded by materialist, consumerist propaganda, all day, every day, for all of our lives, it's easy to lose sight of what Harvard psychologist Daniel Gilbert has found in his research: "We are happy when we have family. We are happy when we have friends. And almost all the other things we *think* make us happy are actually just ways of getting more family and friends."[2]

I love this quote, because it's funny and profound at the same time. When you think about all the effort that you put into your career, it's helpful to ask, "Why am I doing this in the first place?" If the answer is, "So I can improve my relationships with family, friends, and community," then you're on a skillful path. But if your decisions are distancing you from the ones you love and who will bring you happiness, then you might want to reconsider.

For example, your manager comes into your office tomorrow and says, "Great news! I have an awesome opportunity for you! You'll have to start traveling about 30 percent of every month, but you have the opportunity to earn a $5,000 bonus every quarter. Sounds great, huh? Can you start on Monday?"

Now, you and your family might genuinely need the extra money, so you make the trade-off of earning $20,000 more per year, in exchange for 30 percent travel (though often what is promised as 30 percent travel turns out to be 50 percent travel!).

Or, in an alternate scenario, that $20,000 is not really going to make your life or your family's life much better. But you do know that traveling so much will harm the relationships you have with your partner, children, neighbors, and friends.

In my master class, when I first created a PowerPoint slide to address this topic, I wanted to show a nice image of a happy family. I looked online and found a picture of a lovely-looking group — photogenic parents, sage grandparents, adorably cute grandchildren.

The picture was perfect. In fact, it was *too* perfect. And I realized that I was contributing to the kind of ongoing advertising propaganda that hammers us every day. We see images of what "the perfect family" is supposed to look like. And then we feel inadequate, because we know that our own families are very imperfect.

So instead, in my presentation I use a snapshot of some members of my own family, which we took at a family reunion in Florida a few years ago. My brothers are not perfect. Neither are my parents, nor my wife. Our relationships are not perfect. And I'm certainly not perfect — as anyone who knows me will gladly tell you!

But since I got my cancer diagnosis, I realized that this is the only family I have. Getting a cancer diagnosis was like a jolt of electricity, forcing me to return to the most basic, enduring relationships I've had: Mom. Dad. Brother. Sister. Brother.

So now I focus more on family, friends, and community — even if that means I work less and earn less. In the past, if I was working at 2:00 on a Tuesday afternoon and my brother Dan called, I would probably ignore the call because I was busy at work. But these days, I'll much more likely pick up the phone to talk. I have the luxury of working for myself, which makes this easy to do. But that basic decision to work for myself, and not work for others, was part of the lifestyle change I made so that I could do work that I cherish, and at the same time be able to prioritize my loved ones.

Similarly, I now force myself to have relationships that are as positive as possible. I don't claim to be at perfect peace with everyone in my family. But I know that I try a lot harder today than I used to. For example, quite recently I had a fairly unpleasant argument with my brother Mike. We were actually arguing about when we should interact with each other, and how. In the past, I might have simply fumed and let this dispute linger and become a long-standing "falling out." But instead, I realized, "Wow, I have a cancer diagnosis. And just like anybody else, I could die at any time, really. I don't want to have my last interaction with Mike be a fight." So the next day I swallowed my pride, spoke to Mike on the phone, and apologized. We were able to make our relationship *stronger* than it was before the disagreement — thanks to a simple realization that family *is* precious.

All You Need Is ... Kindness

Do you want to get high?

OK, let me rephrase that — do you want to get high in a way that is immediate and legal across the United States, costs you nothing, and does not require inhaling or swallowing?

Then be kind.

In an interview with *Yoga Journal*, Buddhist author and scholar Thupten Jinpa says, "When we help someone out of our genuine concern for her well-being, our levels of endorphins, which are associated with euphoric feelings, surge in the brain, a phenomenon that we call the 'helper's high.'"[3]

If you want to get this emotional high, then be compassionate — which is defined as "concern for the suffering of others," [4] or the empathy we have for others and the desire we have for their suffering to end.

In other words, be "loving" — a word that has become so overused and clichéd that today we're much more comfortable using words like "kind" and "compassionate." I suppose John Lennon could have written "All You Need Is Kindness," but he probably knew that we'd love the title "All You Need Is Love" more.

Being kind has been proven to not only make you happier, but to help your romantic life as well. Early in his career, University of Texas at Austin Psychology Professor David Buss conducted a global study asking, "What is most important to you in a mate?" His finding: "Not only was there agreement across cultures on the top few [universally desired mate characteristics], men and women were statistically identical in nearly all of the 37 cultures on these most valued attributes." What quality ranked highest? A partner being "Kind and Understanding."[5]

Martin Seligman is a psychology professor at the University of Pennsylvania, and is considered one of the key leaders in the positive psychology movement. He has spent his lifetime studying happiness, and says, "Doing a kindness produces the single most reliable momentary increase in well-being of any exercise we have tested."[6]

Other research draws the same conclusion. *Greater Good Magazine* from the University of California, Berkeley's Greater Good Science Center, notes "Compassionate action (e.g., giving to charity) activates pleasure circuits in the brain. Compassion training programs, even very brief ones, strengthen brain circuits for pleasure and reward and lead to lasting increases in self-reported happiness."[7] Compassion benefits include lower risk of heart disease, reduced stress hormones in the blood, a stronger immune system, and many aspects of improved mental health.[8]

How to Practice Compassion

The good news is that we're naturally hardwired to be compassionate. This makes evolutionary sense. As Dacher Keltner, psychology professor and founder of the Greater Good Science Center at the University of California, Berkeley, explains, "our babies are the most vulnerable offspring on the face of the Earth. And that simple fact changed everything. It rearranged our social structures, building cooperative networks of caretaking, and it rearranged our nervous systems. We became the super caregiving species, to the point where acts of care improve our physical health and lengthen our lives. We are born to be good to each other."[9]

No matter how hardwired for compassion we might be, having a daily compassion practice can help us return to our best natural selves in the face of anxiety, fear, threats, and confusion.

It's important to realize that compassion does not always mean you have to try to "fix" everything you encounter today. On the contrary, "Part of compassion is learning to be aware and with the person who is suffering, without going after the urge of wanting to solve the problem," says Dr. Jinpa, who, in addition to his academic work, is also the longtime translator for the Dalai Lama. [10]

Dr. Jinpa suggests that in anticipation of challenging situations, you visualize what your compassionate behavior would look like. The more vividly you can see this, the more likely your response will be successful.

For example, if you expect your partner to come home from work today frustrated and complaining about the same thing they've complained about every day for the last week, you can picture yourself simply sitting, listening, breathing, and making eye contact — without trying to propose solutions or action plans.

You might be amazed that this is the most compassionate response they want from you — whether you think it's "effective" or not.

However, there are also times when you want and need to do more than simply empathize, nod, or give a hug.

Here are just a few examples of compassion in practice:

- You say, "Thank you."
- You hold the elevator door open for others. (It's true — what's called "common courtesy" can also be a form of compassion.)
- Every day, you make it a point to look people in the eye until you can recognize their eye color. If you make eye contact, then you give them a genuine smile. You actually bother to learn the names of the janitor, mail carrier, or barista.
- You decide that the next time someone cuts you off on the freeway, you will simply slow down, take a deep breath, and assume that this other person might be in a hurry for a legitimate reason.
- You call a friend just to say "hi" and see how they are.
- You see yourself being calm, patient, and open-minded as you patch up a disagreement you had with your sister.
- In advance, you visualize having a tough but constructive talk with your manager, and you come to a positive outcome.
- You make it a point to remember that your nemesis at work is probably behaving out of fear, pain, hurt, confusion, or ignorance. They must have somehow suffered to end up acting this way. And you realize that sometimes you're the same way, too, and you would appreciate compassion from others.

In fact, you have received compassion from others countless times.

A lot of compassion is simply remembering that all of us are humans who are suffering and struggling to be happy and successful, every day. Compassion is your heartful response as you recognize this.

Another way you can practice compassion is to perform a daily "five-minute favor." Tech entrepreneur Adam Rifkin developed this concept after witnessing how some of the most successful people in Silicon Valley spent their precious time helping others. You might not have five hours per week to be taking on additional projects to assist strangers, but five *minutes* every day is easy to do and could have a big impact on the person you're helping. Typical quick favors include making introductions, sharing content on social media, giving concise feedback, and writing testimonials. Rifkin has used this method effectively to build an enormous, highly valuable professional and personal network.[11]

Now, a lot of us have been taught to "do unto others" for our entire lives. For example, in 1952, Nobel Peace Prize winner Dr. Albert Schweitzer instructed: "I don't know what your destiny will be, but one thing I know: the only ones among you who will be really happy are those who will have sought and found how to serve."[12]

To me, this sounds noble and benevolent, but also somewhat daunting. Instead, I find it easier to be compassionate when I realize that *I am the one* who benefits the most from my kindness to others. Indeed, the Dalai Lama has called this approach "selfish altruism."[13]

Ever since I saw Dr. Seligman's research on kindness, I've been more likely to give a dollar to some of the homeless people who are all over San Francisco. I no longer try to judge or figure out whether I'm helping them or not. Instead, I'm giving for the reason that I want to feel better about myself.

For you to be a bit happier right now, simply do something kind for another. Never mind whether you're helping the other person (which hopefully you are), but *just for your own sake*, do something kind.

Once you begin with small acts of kindness, you can start a virtuous cycle in your own behavior. In *The Journal of Happiness Studies*, researchers from the University of British Columbia and Harvard Business School provided evidence on how this works: Participants in a study were divided into two groups — those who were asked to recall when they spent money on themselves, and those who were asked to recall when they spent money on others. The group that spent money on others reported greater levels of happiness than the group that spent money on themselves. In turn, that happier group reported that they were more likely to spend money on others in the future. In effect, the more they gave, they more they wanted to give.[14]

Is there an ideal approach to giving? The research suggests you may find it better to do your compassion practice in one big chunk, rather than trying to constantly do compassionate things throughout the day, every day. In his bestselling book, *Give and Take: A Revolutionary Approach to Success*, Adam Grant, a psychology professor at the Wharton School of the University of Pennsylvania, writes that "selfless givers are more inclined to sprinkle their giving throughout their days, helping whenever people need them. This can become highly distracting and exhausting, robbing selfless givers of their attention and energy necessary to complete their own work."[15] Instead, he suggests doing most of your giving one day per week.

Volunteer Work as a Compassion Practice

In early 1992, my biggest goal was to get accepted into a top business school. But it was going to be very hard. I had good grades as an undergrad, but the University of Iowa was not considered an elite school. My work experience could be labelled as "adventuresome," "bohemian," or just plain "weird": English teacher in Germany. Business journalist in Madrid. Struggling phone sales guy in the Bay Area. For me to have any chance at all of getting into a top MBA program, I had to play my hand as well as I could.

Zane, a friend of mine, told me that business school admissions offices looked favorably on people who had a record of community or volunteer work. Maybe this shows you're a nice person. Or it's a great way to develop your leadership skills. Or, perhaps, you even learn how to be around people less fortunate or privileged than you.

After considerable searching, I chose to volunteer Sundays on the hotline of the San Francisco AIDS Foundation. The HIV/AIDS crisis was raging at the time and had decimated a horrifically large part of the gay community worldwide. Gay, straight, or whatever, millions of people had died from the disease. And millions more were going to.

Although I'm straight, I had some very close friends who were gay, and I was doing this out of solidarity with them. At least one, Gary, had already died of the disease.

I may have volunteered with very self-serving intentions, but I was soon caught up in the importance of the work. Because I spoke Spanish, I was trained in Spanish with the Latino volunteers. But when I showed up for my first shift on a Sunday morning, there were really no calls into the Spanish language hotline. Instead, I soon started taking the calls in English, which came in at a steady pace.

"How does a person get AIDS?"

"Where can I get tested for HIV?"

"I just had sex with someone last night. I'm not sure if what I did was risky or not. Can I ask you?"

"I'm a heroin addict. Can I get AIDS from sharing syringes?"

"How can I practice safe sex?"

"My boyfriend just died of AIDS. I feel like killing myself."

This was a very different way to spend Sundays than watching pro football. Fortunately, the S.F. AIDS Foundation's training was excellent. It helped me develop my skills in listening nonjudgmentally. I got quite used to talking with strangers about semen, blood, condoms, dental dams, penetration, death, hospitals, T-cell counts, Kaposi's sarcoma … and love.

I was forced to be in the moment, trying to help callers in whatever way they needed. Meeting them wherever they were intellectually, emotionally, or spiritually. Some calls took 45 seconds. My longest call lasted 3 hours, as one heartbroken man recounted the romance, illness, and loss of his loved one. We were crying together.

But the hotline was not all tears, either. I quickly learned that if you gave yourself permission to cry, you could also give yourself permission to laugh.

And laugh we did. I met amazing people through my volunteer work on the 11:00 a.m. to 2:00 p.m. Sunday shift: Richard, a retired high school teacher who was part of the Free Speech Movement in Berkeley in the 1960s. He was gay and had been fighting for equal rights his entire life. There was Ray, a middle-aged executive at Wells Fargo Bank. There was Sangeeta, a young India-born engineer who happened to be a lesbian. There was Russell, who was sweet and feminine, enjoying his life in the big city. There was our hotline shift leader, James, who died of

AIDS during the course of my time at the hotline.

Oddly, I don't really recall the specific reasons why any of them volunteered. We didn't really talk about it. In a way, it was so obvious that lives were on the line and this work needed to be done. It's sort of like asking, "Why are you pouring water on that burning building?"

When it came time to write my applications to Stanford and Northwestern, I was not shy about describing my experience at the San Francisco AIDS Foundation. And yet, perhaps appropriately, my volunteer experience *did* make me a better leader: I *did* have a better understanding of people — especially those I would not have come into contact with otherwise. I *did* sense others' suffering more acutely. And I learned that in some small way, I *could* make a positive difference in a community.

Research supports the feelings of reward and purpose that I personally experienced. According to a 2013 study from United Health Group, 94 percent of those surveyed said that volunteering improved their mood, 96 percent said it enriched their sense of purpose, and 78 percent said it lowered their stress. [16] In a separate study, Harvard University researchers found that people who contributed either time or money to a charity were 42 percent more likely to be happy than those who didn't. And perhaps best of all, research at the National Institutes of Health showed that "the same area of the brain that is activated in response to food or sex (namely, pleasure) lit up when the participants in the study thought about giving money to a charity."[17]

These mental benefits translate to better health. Researchers from the University of California, Berkeley found that people 55 or older who volunteered for two or more organizations during the five-year study period had a 44 percent lower mortality rate than those who did less volunteering.[18] In effect, the lesson is, "volunteer and live."

How Much Volunteer Work Should You Do?

I was at the AIDS Foundation hotline three hours a week for a couple of years. In another profound but rather different experience, I went door-to-door canvassing for various candidates in U.S. elections. That involved doing nothing for years — then spending 12 hours per day for five consecutive days leading up to election day. Either way, my total involvement amounted to several dozens of hours — not a huge commitment in the grand scheme of things.

Indeed, as Psychology Professor Adam Grant writes in *Give and Take*, "One hundred [hours] seems to be a magical number when it comes to giving. In a study of more than two thousand Australian adults in their mid-sixties, those who volunteered between one hundred and eight hundred hours per year were happier and more satisfied with their lives than those who volunteered fewer than one hundred or more than eight hundred hours annually. In another study, American adults who volunteered at least one hundred hours in 1998 were more likely to be alive in 2000. There were no benefits of volunteering more than one hundred hours. This is the 100-hour rule of volunteering. It appears to be the range where giving is maximally energizing and minimally draining."[19]

As such, "give 'til it hurts" may not be the best advice for long-term, sustainable success as a volunteer. Too much volunteering will probably burn you out and frustrate you. But the right amount — roughly just two hours per week — will make you feel great.

To Live Long … Be Kind

Would you like to not only be happy, but also live a long life? Then consider the findings from research begun in 1921 by psychologist Lewis Terman at Stanford University. The "Terman Study of the Gifted" pioneered the concept of a "longitudinal study," in which scientists track participants on multiple variables over the course of many years.[20]

University of California, Riverside Psychology Professors Howard S. Friedman and Leslie Martin examined the Terman study data and shared their findings in their book, *The Longevity Project:* "We figured that if a Terman participant sincerely felt that he or she had friends and relatives to count on when having a hard time then that person would be healthier. Those who felt very loved and cared for, we predicted, would live the longest. Surprise: our prediction was wrong … Beyond social network size, the clearest benefit of social relationships came from *helping* others [emphasis mine]. Those who helped their friends and neighbors, advising and caring for others, tended to live to old age."[21]

What a remarkable insight! Many of us imagine that if Grandma is simply surrounded by siblings, children, grandchildren, and a large community of friends, she'll live a long time. (It might help if Grandpa is still around, too!) I'm sure those all help. But based on the evidence, these factors are not nearly as important as Grandma believing that she has a *purpose* for getting out of bed in the morning. She has meaning in her life. People need her. And she can use her lifetime of experience, skills, and wisdom to help others.

I've observed thriving longevity in my own family, too. My paternal grandmother, Leona Kappes McCarthy, lived until age 98. Into her 90s, she volunteered regularly at her church, St. Boniface in Sioux City, Iowa. At this writing, both of my parents are still alive, into their early 80s. Their retirement years have been filled with their church group couples' bridge league, volunteering to help with various church activities, and saying prayers at the frequent funerals of their friends.

Do religious people live longer? The authors of *The Longevity Project* found that the religious women in the study lived longer than those who were not religious. But religiosity did not matter for the men. [22] Importantly, they noted that "overall it was not religious involvement per se that was so important to long life, although it helped many women. Rather it was the other characteristics that tended to go along with being religious that explained why these women lived longer. It was not the meditative effect of prayer or the act of regular attendance at religious services that mattered. It was a much broader collection of associated acts and attributes. Those who gradually left their religious involvement were at high risk if they also let their community involvement falter and diminish."[23]

Thus, as long as a person had a community of friends, it did not matter whether that community was based on religion or other common interests.

That's good news for "fallen away" Catholics such as myself. Thank God!

The Wisdom of Age

Think for a second about the older people you know — whether they're your parents, neighbors, colleagues, or friends. Are they happy? The evidence suggests that we can learn a lot about happiness from the older members of our communities.

A massive Gallup Organization telephone survey in the United States sought to understand how respondents' "global well-being," or overall appraisal of their life, might vary over time. This encompassed an "overall judgment of one's life, including one's aspirations, achievements, and current circumstances." Researchers found what is often called a "U-bend" throughout life: Global well-being started very high for the 18- to 21-year-old group, but then continued to drop as life went on, bottoming out at age 50 to 53. (We often label this "midlife crisis.") From that age onward, however, self-reported global well-being continued to go up. By the time people achieved the oldest age in the survey (82 to 85), their global well-being was almost as high as when they were age 18 to 21.[24]

Other research across 72 countries found a similar U-bend of happiness.[25]

Thus, from middle-age onwards, people generally get happier. So what can the most experienced humans in our society teach us about happiness, or how to become happier?

One explanation comes from Psychology Professor Laura Carstensen, who is the founding director of the Stanford Center on Longevity. Interviewed for the "TED Radio Hour from NPR," she says, "Older people are happy. They are happier than middle-aged people and younger people, certainly. Study after study is coming to the same conclusion."[26]

In her TED Talk, she describes that "As we age, our time horizons grow shorter and our goals change. When we recognize that we don't have all the time in the world, we see our priorities most clearly; we take less notice of trivial matters; we savor our life; we're more appreciative; we're open to reconciliation; we invest in more emotionally important parts of life, and life gets better." [27] This makes sense to me. I recently turned 55, and I still have many exciting hopes, dreams, and plans for the rest of my life. But I no longer expect that someday I'll be a journalist on TV's *60 Minutes*, the U.S. ambassador to France, or a U.S. Supreme Court justice. Even though I have an MBA degree from Stanford, I will never be the CEO of a Fortune 500 company, a founder of a cutting-edge Silicon Valley start-up, or a billionaire. Believe it or not, I once considered all of these accomplishments as possible goals for myself.

Instead, after I got my cancer diagnosis at age 49 and hit rock bottom in various aspects of my life, I decided that I would focus much more on family, friends, and community, as well as do work that is really meaningful for me. This meant giving up on a few of the dreams of my earlier life and embracing the beautiful possibilities of the now.

According to research, others feel this way, too. A 2013 study by the National Council of Aging reported, "When asked what is most important to maintaining a high quality of life in their senior years, staying connected to friends and family was the top choice of 4 in 10 seniors, ahead of having financial means (30 percent)." [28]

Celebrated author Tom Wolfe echoed this sentiment. As he approached age 70, he said, "Your soul is your relationships with other people. And that's the part of you that really doesn't die."[29] So, based on your relationships with others, what part of you isn't going to die? What is your legacy going to be? This next activity should help you explore these existential questions.

Writing Activity 3:
A). Imagine you died today. What would other people honestly say about you? How would they feel about you? Include family, friends, community, and colleagues.
B). Imagine you died today. What would you say about yourself?

_____

_____

_____

_____

_____

_____

_____

_____

_____

_____

_____

If we are lucky, we will have adequate time to repair our important relationships, before we leave this world. Unfortunately, not all of us will be so lucky. Instead, some of us will pass suddenly — without having the opportunity to say, "I'm sorry," "Thank you," "You meant so much to me," or, "I have always loved you."

In my master classes, often people find that they get different answers from Part A and Part B. Perhaps more than with any other writing activity in this book, I encourage you to share what you've written with a few family members, friends, or colleagues. It's easy to be harsh with ourselves. Too harsh, in fact. It's very therapeutic to get a sanity check from someone else, who might say, "Hey, I think you're awesome. That's why you're my friend in the first place! Remember that time when …"

Sometimes, we need to forgive ourselves, so that we can more easily forgive others. As the Buddha advised, "You yourself, as much as anybody in the entire universe, deserve your love and affection."[30]

We discuss forgiveness in detail in Chapter Ten.

"Community? I Don't Have a Community."

What community do you belong to? Who's in your community?

In the previous activity, I asked you what your community members would honestly say about you. When I ask this question in my workshops, younger people will often say, "Wow, I just realized that I don't *have* any community."

Growing up in Omaha in the 1970s, I was part of a strong community, whether I realized it or not. My parents were (and still are) devout Catholics, and they made sure my brothers and sister and I all went to Christ the King Grade School, a short 10-minute walk from our suburban home. Many other families in the neighborhood sent their kids there, too. My siblings and I all had daily newspaper routes, so we knew everybody in the neighborhood by name. We would play with other kids in the neighborhood — football, basketball, soccer, baseball, sledding, frisbee football. And then we would also see them in church every Sunday.

On Friday nights I would caddy for my dad in his Knights of Columbus golf league, which was also associated with the church. For many years, my dad played softball on the parish team. My mom and dad played in the church's league for the card game known as bridge. During the winter months, they played in the church bowling league on Sunday nights. Throughout the year there were various fundraisers for the church. We attended church weddings and funerals for people we knew. My brothers and I were all altar boys. We all went to confession regularly. Later, my brothers and I attended the all-boys Jesuit high school in Omaha. The community expanded — but remained tight.

I might be making this parochial life in Omaha sound ideal, but it wasn't. Not by a long shot — for many reasons, including racism, sexism, anti-Semitism, xenophobia, homophobia, and priests I knew sexually molesting boys I knew — although I did not learn of these sexual assaults until decades later. But on the positive side, there were very strong social bonds: kids, parents, grandparents, great-aunts, teachers, neighbors, coaches … and some good priests, too.

There was also tremendous consistency in my parents' jobs. For decades, my dad worked for himself as a solo practitioner lawyer, had the same office on 90th Street, and enjoyed the friendship of others in the firm. My mom was a devoted homemaker for years, and then later taught elementary school. My parents lived in the same house from 1967 until 1981. They've lived in Omaha for the last half-century, relishing a seemingly endless supply of friends and acquaintances, even as many of them are gradually dying out.

Today, this consistency is missing for many people. In a place like Silicon Valley, people arrive from all over the world to get jobs in technology. Housing costs are insanely high. Most people work extremely long hours. Even if you make a good friend, they could move away at any time, as I've repeatedly experienced. (Goodbye, Glenn, John, Jan, Margrethe, Tony, Tony, Mike, and Lauren!) Unlike the world of my upbringing, most people are not part of religious or spiritual communities. Their only "friends" are people they work with. A person can go through an identity crisis if they change jobs or — even worse — get fired.

Many people are lonely.

Nationwide research from Cigna Health, published in 2018, reported that 54 percent of study participants said they always or sometimes feel that no one knows them well. Two out of five felt like "they lack companionship," their "relationships aren't meaningful," and they "are isolated from others." [31] Using the UCLA Loneliness Scale from 20 to 80, the average loneliness score in the U.S. was 44. (The higher the score, the lonelier the person.) The study concluded that "American adults are considered lonely."[32]

This news is sobering. What's perhaps worse is the finding that younger people are lonelier than the older generations. The study reports members of Generation Z, born between the mid-1990s and the early 2000s, had a total average loneliness score of 48.3. Millennials, just a little bit older, scored 45.3. By comparison, baby boomers scored 42.4. The Greatest Generation, people ages 72 and above, had a score of 38.6 on the loneliness scale.[33]

As Generation Z has become the loneliest generation, suicide rates of those aged 13 to 18 in the U.S. increased from 2010 to 2015, especially among females.[34]

Loneliness by Gender

Is your husband, wife, partner, or significant other your best friend? Your soulmate? Your kindred spirit?

If so, I'm happy for you. Really. But it's helpful to remember that in the past, husbands and wives did not look to each other to fulfill all of their physical, psychological, intellectual, spiritual, financial, logistical, and recreational needs. My mom had her circle of friends, her parents, and other moms from the neighborhood. My dad enjoyed time with his colleagues and golf buddies. They did some things as a couple, and some things with us kids, but a lot of things apart. If my mom wanted to talk about her feelings, she would not go to my dad. If my dad wanted to talk about Cold War politics, he would not go to my mom.

And that was OK. Speaking with National Public Radio, Northwestern University Psychology Professor Eli Finkel explains,

"Marriage, for a long time, served a set and relatively limited array of different functions for us. And over time, we've piled more and more of these emotional and psychological functions. So instead of turning to our close friends and other relatives for nights out on the town, or for deep, intimate disclosure, to a larger and larger extent, our spouse has replaced a lot of what we used to look to our broader social network to help us do."[35]

In effect, a lot of today's couples place all of their social eggs in one basket — in the form of their partner or spouse. According to one episode of NPR's *Hidden Brain* podcast, more men than women complain that they don't have enough friends. As one interviewee laments, "I am married. And when my wife and I are together, there are things to do and not enough time in the day to do them with our friends. When she and I are apart for more than a day or two, I turn into a hermit."[36]

When a marriage ends, as it does about half of the time in our society, both people in the relationship may end up scrambling to rebuild their community. Many men, however, never recover from a divorce in midlife. According to a University of California, Riverside study, "the risk of suicide among divorced men was over twice as likely as that of married men. Among women, however, there were no statistically significant differentials in the risk of suicide by marital status categories."[37]

Research finds that unmarried men show vastly higher levels of loneliness than unmarried women.[38] Why would this be?

One explanation is that, sadly, these lonely males tend to be constrained by cultural stereotypes and expectations of what it means to be a man. For example, one study found that "men who display symptoms of loneliness may be regarded more negatively than women who display the same symptoms." Another study found that "both male and female judges were intolerant of depression in men but not in women." And one more study found that "males denied feelings of distress more than females."[39]

Whereas women tend to experience loneliness as depression, men tend to express their loneliness as anger. [40] This may explain why so many American men seem to vent their rage through social media as well as mass media.

Not only can loneliness make you depressed or angry — it can kill you. It has been linked to a variety of health problems: increased risk of coronary heart disease and stroke, gene alterations that can weaken your immune system, and slower recovery from breast cancer.[41] Brigham Young University Psychology Professor Julianne Holt-Lunstad led a research team that examined 148 different studies. Their findings: People with stronger social relationships had a 50 percent lower mortality risk than study participants who had weaker social ties. The negative effect of isolation was even worse for a person's health than physical inactivity or obesity.[42]

If you don't want loneliness to kill you, what should you do?

- **Limit screen time.** San Diego State Psychology Professor Jean Twenge published research in 2017 which found that "adolescents who spent more time on new media (including social media and electronic devices such as smartphones) were more likely to report mental health issues, and adolescents who spent more time on nonscreen activities (in-person social interaction, sports/exercise, homework, print media, and attending religious services) were less likely." [43] I think this is good advice for all age groups.
- **Do volunteer work.** We discussed the benefits of volunteer work earlier in this chapter. No matter how lonely you are, or how unlovable you might feel, I'm sure you can show up at a nearby nonprofit, social, political, or religious

organization, and ask, "How can I help out around here?" They'll be delighted to see you!

- **Take an ongoing class.** Maybe you've always wanted to learn French, dance the tango, do yoga, go for long hikes, or try kayaking. This sort of regular activity will immediately give you a cohort of fellow students, who might quickly become your new friends with a shared passion.

- **Seek therapy.** I'm happy to see that our society is gradually removing the taboos around mental health issues. I recall that when I attended Stanford's business school, many students liked to give the impression that they were happy, smart, and successful. Only later did I learn that a full third of these same students sought some sort of psychological help during their two years there. I was one of them. The therapy helped me a lot.

- **Open your mind about age and gender.** Many men suffer from loneliness but don't feel like they can share their feelings with others. Shankar Vedantam, the host of the *Hidden Brain* podcast, suggests, "Think how much better life could be … if we could be OK with being vulnerable, with being dependent on someone who's not a spouse, if we didn't look suspiciously at older men who are friendly or shame boys who talk about their love for their friends, if we expected friendships to endure, even as our lives change, so they don't have to fade to silence."[44]

- **Create a good work/life balance.** A Cigna study found that people who "work MORE than desired" or who "work LESS than desired" suffered more from loneliness. [45] Never getting out of the house to go to work and see your colleagues can make you lonely. Working constantly and never having time for family or friends can make you lonely as well.

Writing Activity 4: Action Plan

Consider what you wrote about your relationships with
family, friends, community, and colleagues in Writing
Activity 3. What, if anything, do you need to do or change?

_____

_____

_____

_____

_____

_____

_____

_____

_____

Based on what you wrote, I invite you to reach out to others and share your thoughts with them. If you miss their friendship, let them know. If you want to see them more, then schedule a time to get together. If you're sad because you're lonely, they'll appreciate hearing this. They might be sad and lonely, too.

We spend much of our lives at work, so now let's turn our

focus toward relationships in the workplace.

Compassion at Work?

Compassion is not just for relationships outside of work. Compassion can help in the workplace, too, bringing purpose and meaning to what you do and helping you interact better with others. In an interview with *Greater Good Magazine*, University of Michigan Psychology Professor Jane Dutton said that "employees who'd experienced compassion at work saw themselves, their co-workers, and the organization in a more positive light. Statistically, they demonstrated more positive emotions, such as joy and contentment, and more commitment toward the organization."[46]

Indeed, compassion is such an important part of leadership that one of the most popular courses at Stanford's Graduate School of Business is called "Leading with Mindfulness and Compassion." The class integrates traditional contemplative practices such as meditation with current practices and research from psychology and neuroscience.

Ambitious people tend to set the bar high on their own performance, and beat themselves up when they don't succeed. One way to address this is to practice self-compassion. Dr. Leah Weiss, who teaches the Stanford course, suggests the following approaches:

- **"Take it personally."** Acknowledge your emotions and process them, rather than trying to suppress them.
- **"Sit Uncomfortably with Vulnerability."** Take the "good" with the "bad." Expose your weaknesses in order to give compassion to yourself and others.
- **"Remember You're Human."** You are not perfect. Nobody else is, either. Realize that even your greatest heroes have

flaws, pain, and challenges.

- **"Rewrite Negative Scripts."** Talk to yourself the way you'd talk to a dear friend, giving encouragement rather than destructive criticism.
- **"Stop the Worst-Case-Scenario Train."** Instead of obsessing over the worst possible thing that could happen, step back for a second and address the much more realistic challenge at hand.
- **"Self-Soothe."** Instead of whipping yourself, pamper yourself with simple joys such as a cup of tea, a foot massage, or your favorite stroll in nature.[47]

But does all this compassion stuff help a company make more profits?

Yes! "It's hard to think of a way in which compassion is not relevant to leadership, success and well-being" says Dr. Jamil Zaki, director of Stanford's Social Neuroscience Laboratory, in an article about the Stanford course. "People with high empathy and compassion excel themselves. Folks who are managers or leaders who can connect with others succeed, and their bottom line is better." [48]

What does this mean for your own bigger picture? In the next section, we'll explore what you can do to find greater joy, meaning, and happiness in your work.

Chapter Three:
Work

One day in 2004, I was going to go to the funeral of Brian, a neighbor of mine in Cupertino, California. I had known him and his lovely wife for a couple of years. He was a smart, kind, and very successful marketing entrepreneur. Unfortunately, he lost his battle with cancer.

When I woke up the morning of the funeral, my plan was to drive to work, put in a few hours, then leave over the lunch hour to attend Brian's service, which was taking place just 20 minutes away from my office. But suddenly my day became very busy — as was often the case — and at the last minute I decided not to go.

I don't remember what I was working on that day. I barely remember what I was working on that month. But I'll never forget that I missed out on the funeral of a friend, because I thought work was more important.

Of course, work *is* important. But it's not everything. It's helpful to understand what work can and cannot do for you, and how it fits with everything else that's important in your life. This chapter explores the essential role that work contributes to your happiness — or unhappiness.

Your Work ... Viewed from Your Deathbed

Bronnie Ware was an Australian palliative care nurse who helped patients suffer less as they faced chronic or terminal illnesses. She spent many hours with people right before they died. She wrote a blog post, which later became the book, *The Top 5 Regrets of the Dying: A Life Transformed by the Dearly Departing.*

Here's her list:
"Regret 1: I wish I had had the courage to live a life true to myself, not the life others expected of me.
Regret 2: I wish I hadn't worked so hard.
Regret 3: I wish I'd had the courage to express my feelings.
Regret 4: I wish I had stayed in touch with my friends.
Regret 5: I wish that I had let myself be happier."[1]

These regrets all have profound implications for what we're discussing in this book, but right now I'd like to focus on Regret 2: "I wish I hadn't worked so hard." What do you think was the percentage of the men in Ms. Ware's work who mentioned this? According to the author, it was 100 percent! That's right, every single man she cared for at the end of his life — on his actual deathbed — told her that he wished he had worked less.

Granted, Ms. Ware's book is more anecdotal, observational, and inspirational than it is rigorous scientific research. She does not report what percentage of women said they wished they had worked less — or whether she asked this question to women at all. One could seek to isolate variables such as age, social class, country, race, and many other factors. Men and women dying in 2040 might give different answers than men and women dying in 2012. But the fact remains that many people regretted working too much during their lives. Or, as the common sentiment goes,

"No one was ever on their deathbed and wished they had spent more time at the office."

The Importance of Meaningful Work

"*How much* should I be working?" is a basic question for each of us.

"*What work* should I be doing in the first place?" is a related but distinct question. The poet Oliver Wendell Holmes, Sr. (1809–1894) beautifully lamented in *The Voiceless:*

A few can touch the magic string,
And noisy Fame is proud to win them;
Alas for those that never sing,
But die with all their music in them![2]

What is that music which is inside of you? That which is beautiful, amazing, loving, brilliant, smart, compassionate, genius? What talent, skill, gift, experience, or expertise can you give to the world, which is the greatest reflection of your unique essence? Are you in the process of giving your "music" to the world? Have you already done so, and continue to do so every day? Or have you given up on this hope?

Throughout my life, I have always had a deep desire to learn and then share what I've learned. But many times I did not have the courage, conviction, or grit to honor my passions. So for some of the earlier years of my career, I jumped from unfulfilling job to unfulfilling job, somehow thinking that I'd have forever to keep hopping around. I was fortunate to finish my MBA in 1996, just as the internet revolution was taking off in Silicon Valley. Since then, I have been passionate about internet product management, marketing, and leadership — which have all involved a large dose of challenge, learning, and teaching. (This is sometimes called "management.") I've tried to give different "pieces of music" from my soul to the world. At this point in the opera of my life, the song I'm singing, which feels best to me, is to write this book and share it with you. (Thanks for reading!)

What does "meaningful" mean, anyway? Writing in *The New York Times*, journalist Emily Esfahani Smith and Stanford Professor Jennifer L. Aaker say, "Although meaning is subjective — signifying different things to different people — a defining feature is connection to something bigger than the self. People who lead meaningful lives feel connected to others, to work, to a life purpose, and to the world itself."[3]

Finding meaning in your work is closely associated with increased happiness. Sonja Lyubomirsky, a psychology professor at the University of California, Riverside, wrote in her outstanding book, *The How of Happiness: A New Approach to Getting the Life You Want*, that the happiest people "are deeply committed to lifelong goals and ambitions (e.g., fighting fraud, building cabinets, or teaching their children deeply held values)." [4]

Just how important is it that people view their work as meaningful? Wharton psychologist Adam Grant conducted research on this question. He studied a call center — perhaps like the one I worked at in Omaha during my winter holiday breaks from college. The control group did their normal work on the phones, without any special instruction. In contrast, for the test group, Grant brought in a person who had benefited from the work of the call center to speak briefly about its impact.

So, which group did better? That's right — the group that was reminded of the benefits of their work to others.

How much more efficient was the "high meaning" group? According to Grant, the group showed more than a 400 percent spike in weekly productivity. In other words, when people are able to connect their jobs to something meaningful, their productivity increases by as much as five times.[5]

That's an incredible boost in productivity. Many businesspeople spend their entire careers trying to improve efficiency or profitability by 5 percent or 10 percent. Lots of people are given raises and promotions if they work nine hours per day, when all of their colleagues only work eight hours per day.

Find the meaning in your work, and you'll increase your success. Laszlo Bock, the former senior vice president of people operations at Google, notes in his book, *Work Rules! Insights from Inside Google That Will Transform How You Live and Lead*, "Over the coming decades the most gifted, hardworking people on the planet will gravitate to places where they can do meaningful work and help shape the destiny of their organizations."[6]

Meaningful work is not just important for individuals like you and me. It's also vitally important for employers who seek to retain their most talented people. In a 2015 interview with Bloomberg, Bock described what made Google successful. He said, "You want people to feel happy, and motivated, and committed. There's all this data that suggests that when people are enjoying what they do, and when they feel it's *meaningful* [emphasis mine], they're more productive, they stay longer, and they have more impact. And those are all good things for the company, eventually … So all this data and surveying is harnessed with the purpose to first 'How do you make people happier?', and then goodness comes from that."[7]

So what makes a job "meaningful"? And do you have to switch jobs if your job right now isn't meaningful for you? The next section addresses this.

Screw Your "Job" — Define Your "Calling"

Are you employed?
What do you work on?
And *why* do you do this work?

Are you there just to get paid, and for no other reason?
Are you seeking to achieve and advance?
Or does your work fill you with purpose?

You can think of your work as any of these three scenarios, according to Amy Wrzesniewski, a professor of organizational behavior at the Yale School of Management. She describes three types of "work orientation":

- **"A Job"** — you are focused on the paycheck, because it supports other important aspects of your life
- **"A Career"** — you are invested in your work, and you want to experience the trappings of success
- **"A Calling"** — you feel your work contributes to the greater good, draws on your strengths, and gives you meaning[8]

All of us can relate to having a job. And many of us can relate to having a career. But how many of us really feel like we have a "calling"? And if we are not yet working on our calling, what can we do about it?

Dr. Wrzesniewski's amazing finding was this: Your work orientation is *independent* of the sort of work you do. In a Yale School of Management publication, she notes that "I've studied surgeons who have a 'Job' orientation — the work is a paycheck and not much else. I've studied people who scrub toilets for whom it is a 'Calling' and they feel the work is an end in itself and that it makes the world a better place in tangible ways."[9]

Consistent with these findings, author and Harvard lecturer Shawn Achor notes that in one study of 24 administrative assistants performing the same role, roughly one third viewed their work as a job, one third as a career, and one third as a calling. He concludes that "a calling orientation can have just as much to do with mindset as it does with the actual work being done … unhappy employees can find ways to improve their work life that don't involve quitting, changing jobs or careers, or going off to find themselves."[10]

Why is this such good news for you and me? Because it means that how you think about your work is more important than *what* work you do. It means that you can actually bring meaning to your work, as long as you manage how you think.

For example, in 1991 I decided to quit working as a business journalist in Madrid, so I could return to the U.S., gain a few years of corporate experience, and then try to get into a good business school. I moved to the San Francisco Bay Area, where my girlfriend at the time lived. California was in a terrible recession. The first job I got was sweeping the garage of an acquaintance of mine. Then I got a job selling display advertising at *The San Francisco Business Times*, earning about $24,000 per year.

Soon thereafter, I realized that developing sales skills would be helpful for my long-term career, and I could potentially earn a lot more. I got a job selling phone systems and voicemail to businesses door-to-door, because I viewed this as working on what was then called the "Information Superhighway" (which blossomed into the internet we know today). Overall, I disliked the work, but I found meaning in seeing how these phone systems could help my customers. And I found meaning in developing my sales and negotiation skills, which taught me the importance of positive self-talk and positive psychology. (We discuss this more in the chapter on Affirmations.)

Since business school, I have spent most of my career in Silicon Valley working in e-commerce and online advertising. Some people would say "advertising is nonsense" or "I hate online ads because they interrupt my user experience" or "it's creepy how online advertising stalks people." (This was before social media started being used to destabilize our politics.) Honestly, none of those objections ever bothered me. The way I looked at it, products and services need to be sold. Marketing and advertising are part of that sales process. Most online companies can only exist through an advertising revenue model. And it was really challenging, fun, and innovative to figure out how to deliver increasingly effective online ad campaigns. Those reasons were good enough for me to really love the work I did on the internet. For me, at the time, in my own mind, according to my own criteria, the work was highly "meaningful."

As another example, a close friend of mine manages budgets and financial grants for a group of medical researchers and scientists at the University of California, San Francisco. I tend to view her job as "bean counting" — it's not work that I would personally enjoy doing.

But my friend does not see it this way. Instead, she defines her role as enabling world-class scientists to focus on their research, so they can help UCSF in their mission of "advancing health worldwide." My friend might sometimes complain about aspects of her work, but she *always* finds meaning in how her work supports her organization's main goal.

Product managers, software developers, designers, marketers, and salespeople all play an essential role in their companies, building and selling products and services that help others and create jobs. In those same organizations, there are accountants, recruiters, administrative assistants, trainers, and infrastructure and facilities people who keep the business running. Similarly, a bus driver can think that they are helping public transportation and reducing greenhouse gases. Teachers, parents, and home care providers play a vital role in our society.

Every one of these people can define their work as a job. Or a career. Or a calling. It's up to them.

Writing Activity 5:
Do you have a "job," a "career," or a "calling"?
What makes you think this way?

_____

_____

_____

_____

_____

_____

_____

_____

_____

If you have any colleagues you can trust with this kind of inquiry, I encourage you to grab coffee or have lunch with them, and discuss this question. You might be inspired by their answer. Or you might give them sorely needed encouragement. It helps to be part of an organization where people share some common mission.

What Does the World Need from You?

"A man who becomes conscious of the responsibility he bears toward a human being who affectionately waits for him, or to an unfinished work, will never be able to throw away his life. He knows the 'why' for his existence, and will be able to bear almost any 'how'" wrote Dr. Viktor Frankl in his seminal work, *Man's Search for Meaning*.[11]

Frankl spoke with the authority of intense personal agony and courage. Born into a Jewish family in Vienna in 1905, Frankl grew up to become a psychiatrist. The Nazis murdered his father, mother, brother, and wife in concentration camps — just four of the 6,000,000 Jewish people and millions of others killed in the Holocaust.[12]

Frankl wrote, "the prisoner who lost faith in the future — his future — was doomed."[13] While Frankl was himself imprisoned in the death camps, he sought to help his fellow captives. He tells the story of two other inmates who were suicidal, given the horrific loss and suffering which surrounded them.

When Frankl sought to save them, he did not ask, "How can I help you?"

He did not ask, *"What do you need to keep living?"*

Instead, he asked, "What does the world still need from you?"

One man responded by saying he wanted to survive the death camps so that he could be reunited with his beloved child, who was waiting for him in a foreign country. Another prisoner replied that he wanted to keep living so that he could finish and publish a series of scientific books.[14]

Despite the horrible circumstances, these people found a way to define new meaning in their existence, keep hope alive, and survive.

What does this have to do with your work? I certainly don't want to compare your workplace to a Nazi death camp. But it's extremely helpful to be aware of Frankl's advice: "Everything can be taken from a man but one thing: the last of the human freedoms — to choose one's attitude in any given set of circumstances, to choose one's own way."[15]

In the previous section, I described how you can determine your own "work orientation," and how you can bring meaning to your work — independent of the work that you do! Similarly, I encourage you to think "big picture" about the work you do — whatever that may be — so you appreciate the special impact that you already have in this world.

Whether work is "meaningful" or not depends on your unique perspective. For instance, in one of my interactive keynote talks, a middle-aged man said, "I have not been thrilled with the work I've done, but I've earned a good income, which made it possible for my family and me to live in a good neighborhood, and I was able to send my kids to a good college." On the other hand, some people will only find meaning in their work if they're at a nonprofit organization that is doing direct service: helping refugees, fighting malaria, or bringing clean drinking water to places without it.

It's not up to me to tell you what's meaningful in your work. You need to figure it out for yourself.

Writing Activity 6:

Without changing your work at all, how can you bring more purpose or meaning to it?

How can you think about your work differently? What is the most positive way to think about it?

Ask yourself, "How does my work or my organization help people?"

Then, "How does that help people?"

Then, "How does that help people?"

_____

_____

_____

_____

_____

_____

_____

_____

_____

_____

If you keep asking, you'll usually find an answer that excites you. And then, I hope, you'll be able to view your work less as a job just for the paycheck, and more as a calling that contributes to the greater good.

After going through this exercise, if you still can't bring meaning to your work — even for the short term — then what sort of role could you find, which would be more meaningful to you? What sort of trade-offs could you make in order to make your dream a reality?

To make this decision, it helps to know what I call your "nonnegotiables."

Use Nonnegotiables to Overcome FOMO

I've coached and mentored many people who have struggled to decide what to do with their careers and their lives. Sometimes they've been working for a few years and already have hit their "quarter-life crisis," when they realize they're now doing the work that they studied for since the age of four — but they can't see themselves laboring at it for 40 more years. Or even 40 more weeks. In other cases, they're trying to decide if all their problems would be solved if they simply relocated to another neighborhood, city, state, or country.

While many people would be grateful to have any job at all, I'm describing what I call "The Curse of the Well-Educated, Geographically Mobile Person." I've worked with people who have degrees from some of the top schools in the United States. Upon graduation, they can choose to go into investment banking on Wall Street, do management consulting in London, found a tech start-up in San Francisco, or work for a microfinance nonprofit in Bolivia.

Thanks to the internet and social media, it's now easier than ever to switch jobs, careers, and countries. Although immigration laws have been in flux for the past few years, it's still relatively easy for someone to grow up in Poland, study in Paris, and work in Rome. As for myself, I worked as an English teacher in Frankfurt, a business journalist in Spain, a phone salesman in San Francisco, and a McKinsey consultant in Munich — all pre-internet.

Some call this the "digital nomad" lifestyle, which can be truly appealing for many. But having so many options can also be frustrating and paralyzing. As psychologist Barry Schwartz describes in his excellent book, *The Paradox of Choice — Why More Is Less*, a person can feel a lot of stress when they have a huge number of choices on aspects of life — both important and trivial. ("Get the toothpaste that's with or without fluoride? Buy a condo or keep renting? Marry and settle down, or keep dating more and more people you've found on Tinder?")

This is related to what these days we call "fear of missing out" ("FOMO"), the common emotion stoked by social media, when your behavior is driven by the angst that no matter how good this moment may be, there is something better going on somewhere else, and you could actually be doing that right now, if you just managed things better. (We explore this more in the chapter on the Comparing Mind.)

Whether a person is 25 or 75, if they ask me for advice, I first ask them, "What are your nonnegotiables in life?" By "nonnegotiables," I mean the aspects of your life that you absolutely must have to be happy. For example, you could say, "I'll work anywhere in the world, but I have to work in finance," or, "I'll do any job necessary, but I'm not leaving Seattle, because my ailing mom lives here," or, "I have to work in a company with fewer than 100 employees, because I hate big-company bureaucracy," or, "I have to earn at least $50,000 per year to pay off my student loans." Some people find it very useful to combine multiple nonnegotiables: "I'll only work in a finance job in Seattle for a small company, earning at least $50,000 per year."

Why would you intentionally limit your choices on what to do, when you already have FOMO?

So you can shift your focus from "things I can do" to "things I really want to do." Shift from "where I could be" to "where I am," which helps you enjoy the here and now. And instead of chasing 7,369 possible future employers, you're chasing 20 — which is a manageable number for a focused, thorough, and highly successful job search. Instead of the 3,522 women you could be dating in Portland, you focus on the one you're already living with.

Regarding personal relationships, I often suggest investing in family and friends. I recall mentoring a talented young Berkeley engineer who was German, worked in Korea, and ended up in Silicon Valley. He was struggling to decide whether to continue with another high-stress, low-pay, high-upside start-up in San Francisco, or to relocate to Southern California for a much less intense but otherwise excellent job. Once he realized that his nonnegotiable was to start a family and live a balanced life, his career choice became easy. And it turns out that he's now doing very entrepreneurial things — but inside of a large corporation.

Is he missing out on years of the frenzied start-up scene in Silicon Valley? Yes.

Is he a lot happier now, because he's building his life based on the nonnegotiable of investing in "family, friends, and community"? Absolutely.

And he tells me the surfing is a lot better down there anyway.

How to Know Your Nonnegotiables

What must you have, be, or do, in order to be happy? What

is essential for you to experience pleasure, purpose, and peace? And how do you figure this out?

Are nonnegotiables the same as goals? Not really. A goal requires some effort, whose outcome is uncertain. A nonnegotiable is a decision or behavior over which you have a huge amount of control. Often nonnegotiables are not hard to accomplish, as long as you have determination and discipline. Sometimes having a nonnegotiable simply means you say "no" to distractions, which don't make you happy anyway.

For example, when you're age 30, you can have a goal of becoming a millionaire by 40. But that's an aspiration, not a "nonnegotiable." On the other hand, a person living in Chicago can have the nonnegotiable of continuing to live in Chicago.

Can you have too many nonnegotiables? If you come up with 27 nonnegotiables, you might box yourself into such a rigid life structure that you leave no room for spontaneity, creativity, or seizing opportunities. But if you define too few nonnegotiables, then perhaps you're open to everything — which keeps you from focusing on being true to yourself and what really brings you fulfillment.

To define your nonnegotiables, try finishing the following sentence: "The bare minimum circumstances I need to experience pleasure and purpose in life are ..." If you find this hard to do, don't feel bad. Instead, you can break down your nonnegotiables this way:

Spiritual/Philosophical: What process do you have to know yourself and understand your purpose in this universe? You could meditate for 15 minutes daily, or attend services at your mosque, synagogue, or church weekly. You could walk on the beach, write in your diary, or go on a week-long silent retreat. Figure out what works for you, and make this a nonnegotiable for your spiritual life.

Health: Do you have a certain workout routine, which you absolutely refuse to abandon? Vegetarian diet? No smoking? At least seven hours of sleep per night? If you're committed to living healthfully, then maybe you'll pass on that investment banking job, which pays great but destroys your health. As for me, I do 10 minutes of yoga and stretching every morning. Is it hard to do? No. Have I been doing it every day since 1987? Yes.

Geography: A huge number of life decisions are simplified once you define where you are going to live. For some people, they do this all too readily — choosing to live in the town where they grew up or finished college, even when they could honor all their nonnegotiables and perhaps live in a place that is much better for them. In contrast, others flock to the big cities and tell themselves that the only place they could possibly live is San Francisco or London, when in fact they could lead a wonderful life in Costa Rica or Austin.

Family: Would you be willing to live in another city than your spouse or kids? How much are you willing to travel for work, especially in cases where you'll earn more money but see your family less? What does it even mean to be part of your family? For many homemakers, their nonnegotiable is creating the best environment for their children, even if their own income and career suffer as a result.

For couples with kids, many counselors suggest having a weekly "date night" so that you don't get so absorbed by your role as a parent that you lose sight of your role as a spouse. Your nonnegotiable could be putting your marriage first, as the foundation for a happy family.

Social: In Bronnie Ware's *Top Five Regrets of the Dying*, she identifies Regret #4 as: "I wish I had stayed in touch with my friends." So maybe your nonnegotiable is that you have lunch or coffee with two different friends every month.

Work: It can be extremely helpful to identify in your career what you must do (create amazing products, help the least fortunate people in our society, or fight inequality) and what you refuse to do (sell things that make people stupid, apathetic, or sick).

Play/Fun/Travel: Silicon Valley has more than its share of workaholics. Some of them try to "work hard and play hard," whereas others just "work hard and then work some more." Workaholism might be sustainable short term, but not long term. If these people worked a bit less and got more sleep, many of them would be healthier, happier, more creative, more productive, and more successful. I heard one of the most intense, top venture capitalists in Silicon Valley tell a start-up CEO, "Please, take off one day per week to rest and have a life."

Intellectual/Creative/Artistic: Do you love gardening? Fishing? Cycling? Having a hobby or creative outlet can help you fulfill your other nonnegotiables. When I was working my longest hours at Yahoo, back in 1998, I started attending a salsa dancing class on Thursday nights. I wasn't very good at it, but I was completely entranced by the music, movement, and fun. It was about the only time of the week I was able to clear my head and not think about work. So when I got back to the office on Friday morning, I felt like I had rested and was able to enjoy my work again.

Financial: How much money do you want? How much do you need? If you have to make massive sacrifices to keep that big bucks job, then at least be aware that this is your financial nonnegotiable. And recognize all those other things you may be giving up in the Spiritual/Philosophical, Health, Geography, Family, Social, Play/Fun/Travel, and Intellectual/Creative/Artistic categories.

Writing Activity 7:

Write out all your nonnegotiables in the following areas:

- *Spiritual/Philosophical*
- *Health*
- *Geography*
- *Family*
- *Social*
- *Work*
- *Play/Fun/Travel*
- *Intellectual/Creative/Artistic*
- *Financial*

_____

_____

_____

_____

_____

_____

_____

_____

_____

Next, have your spouse or partner do it — and compare lists. Together you may come up with some very creative solutions to your life plans. You might suddenly find that both of you are open to retiring in Portugal, or volunteering with Habitat for Humanity in Indonesia.

Ask, "What Would It Take?"

Here's one way to use your nonnegotiables to help you make an important decision: Imagine you're working as an account manager at an internet start-up in New York City. You'd really rather be a high school math teacher. But you can't afford to live in New York on a teacher's salary.

You could simply ask, "Can I be a high school math teacher?" and answer, "No, I can't."

Or you could ask, *"What would it take* to work as a high school math teacher?"

Then you could revisit all your nonnegotiables in life, and conclude that *it would* be possible if you perhaps moved to a lower-cost city, shared an apartment with someone, used public transportation, spent less money on clothing, and took on an extra job as a tutor in the summers. Then you can imagine what that life would be — especially if you're going to do work that is much more meaningful for you.

You might still decide to stay at your job in New York City — with newfound gratitude and commitment.

Or you might make that move to Colorado to teach calculus — and end up being a lot happier.

If you can truly, honestly, realistically say that another role would be your calling, then you owe it to yourself to figure out how to do that work. The sooner, the better — for your sake. After all, you want a wise, authentic, and passionate answer to the question, *What does the world still need from you?*

The Limits of What Money Can Do for You

Unless you're independently wealthy, at least one of the reasons you work is to earn money. For most of us, this is completely necessary for survival. But over the course of my life, I've seen the popular culture in the United States shift from hippies in the 1960s preaching "peace, love, and understanding," to Wall Streeters in the 1980s asserting "Greed is Good," to today's social media and reality TV stars flaunting their wealth.

A 1966 study of entering college freshmen in the U.S. found that "Being very well off financially" was essential or very important for 43.8 percent of the respondents — far behind "Helping others in need," which received the highest ranking at 68.5 percent. [16] But by 2016, in the same survey, "Being very well off financially" had leapt to the number one spot in importance over all other objectives, cited by 82.3 percent of respondents. "Helping others in difficulty" had also grown in the meantime, but only slightly, cited by 77.5 percent.[17] I can only conclude that young college kids still wanted to save the world and help others — but they needed to get rich in the process.

Perhaps they were inspired by the example of Mark Zuckerberg. He cofounded Facebook and became the youngest self-made billionaire by age 23.[18] In the process, he helped create the social media revolution that has turbocharged "the Comparing Mind" (see Chapter Eight) — our state of suffering when we fear that others are more successful, happier, or having more fun than we are.

According to Dr. Robert Waldinger, a psychiatrist and Zen priest who teaches at Harvard Medical School, a 2015 survey asked Millennials about their major life goals, and found that more than 80 percent wanted to get rich, and 50 percent wanted to be famous.[19] This explains, I believe, part of Donald Trump's appeal — he is apparently rich and famous in a culture that worships fortune and fame. Whether Mr. Trump is happy or not … I don't know.

In any case, it's useful to be aware of the limits of what money can do for you and your happiness. Statistics show that the buying power of Americans almost tripled from the late 1950s until the early 2010s, but the "percentage describing themselves as very happy" remained in the low 30-percent range for almost the entire time.[20]

Nobel prize-winning economists Daniel Kahneman and Angus Deaton published a study in 2010, noting that money and "emotional well-being" were positively correlated — but only up to a point. Their findings, based on 450,000 responses from 1,000 U.S. residents, were that after a person reached $75,000 in annual household income, additional money did *not* make them happier.[21]

They surmised that "Perhaps $75,000 is a threshold beyond which further increases in income no longer improve individuals' ability to do what matters most to their emotional well-being, such as spending time with people they like, avoiding pain and disease, and enjoying leisure."[22] Or, as a Money magazine write-up put it, "richer people have a lot of problems that have nothing to do with a lack of funds."[23]

Now, you might be saying, "Wait a second, Jim! I live in New York (or Washington, D.C., or London …). Our cost of living is higher than the U.S. average!" Fair enough. The most important point of this research is not whether the exact number is $75,000. The key takeaway is that more money has diminishing returns with respect to "emotional well-being": Once you're reasonably comfortable, working your butt off to make a lot more money will *not* make you happier on a day-to-day basis.

In an interview with the *Boston Globe*, Harvard psychologist Daniel Gilbert pithily notes that "we think money will bring us lots of happiness for a long time, and actually it brings us a little happiness for a short time."[24]

What *would* make you happier, after you reach this minimum happiness threshold?

One British researcher examined an increase in frequency of interaction with friends, relatives, and neighbors. He found that "an increase in the level of social involvements is worth up to an extra £85,000 a year [approximately $120,000] in terms of life satisfaction. *Actual changes in income, on the other hand, buy very little happiness.*" [Emphasis mine.][25]

Reflecting on my own experience, this research makes sense to me. When I was in my 20s and living frugally as an English teacher in Frankfurt, a business journalist in Madrid, or a phone salesman in the San Francisco Bay Area, increases in pay from $12,000 per year to $16,000 per year to $25,000 per year were *huge*! I was immediately able to feel the impact on my finances, lifestyle, and sense of accomplishment.

I didn't complain when I was working at Yahoo during the Dot-Com Boom of the late 1990s and became a "dot-com millionaire." I do know that becoming a millionaire helped me "solve" a lot of financial challenges and worries that I had had before. I was able to pay off my student loans, buy a fancy red Volvo convertible, have a gorgeous wedding in Silicon Valley (just as the Dot-Com Bubble started to burst), and buy a lovely home in Cupertino, California for my family.

About a decade later, I was divorced, living by myself in a smaller townhouse in nearby Mountain View. The situation with my ex-wife and two daughters was not good. My last job had not turned out well. And then I received my cancer diagnosis.

I could not help but look at the apartment complex across the
street and see extended families — grandparents, parents, and
grandchildren — having outdoor barbeques and playing in the
swimming pool. At that time, my net worth might have been
easily 200 times or 400 times more than theirs. But I certainly
was not 200 times happier than they were. In fact, based on the
laughter I heard echoing across Rock Street, I was probably not at
all happier than they were.

Of course, it's impossible for me to know for sure. In fact,
I encourage you to avoid "the Comparing Mind," which we
discuss in Chapter Eight. My point is that earning a lot of money
did not make me a lot happier. I don't necessarily subscribe to the
old saying, "People don't own things. Things own people." But
it's worth considering.

According to some research, the more money you earn,
the more you want. Jeffrey Pfeffer is a professor at Stanford's
Graduate School of Business who, with Sanford E. DeVoe of the
University of Toronto and Byron Y. Lee of Renmin University of
China, published a research paper titled, "When Does Money
Make Money More Important?" He notes that money that
comes from the work we do (rather than money we inherit, get
from investments, or win in a lottery) makes that money more
important to us. "The money in that case is a signal of competence
and worth, and that makes it addictive, because the more you
have, the more you want," he says.[26]

Pfeffer says that the paper was inspired by a quote from
Daniel Vasella, the former CEO of Swiss pharmaceutical company
Novartis AG, who was initially offered a $78 million severance
package, but then turned it down after a public uproar. Speaking
to *Fortune* magazine in 2002, Vasella said, "The strange part is,
the more I made, the more I got preoccupied with money. When
suddenly I didn't have to think about money as much, I found

myself starting to think increasingly about it."

Indeed, many of us spend our lives imagining that if we simply had a mountain of cash, then all our worries would go away. But even billionaires get the blues. According to Brad Klontz, a psychologist who works with the superrich, billionaires often feel isolated and have trouble trusting others, because so many of their relationships are based on money. So how great is it to be a billionaire? According to Klontz, the superwealthy have "different problems. But not a lack of problems."[27]

Why am I writing about a "first world problem" or a "top 1 percent" problem? After all, there will probably not be a lot of billionaires reading this book. But whether you're a billionaire or not, you need to understand that financial success does not fix everything. Or, as I like to say, if you think a lot of money will solve all your problems, then you've never had a lot of money.

How to Spend Your Money to Buy Happiness

You might be saying, "OK, Jim, so I accept that money won't fix all of my problems. But how can I squeeze the most happiness out of the assets that I do have?" To accomplish this, you need to pay attention to what you buy, and for whom.

Authors Elizabeth Dunn and Michael Norton wrote *Happy Money: The Science of Smarter Spending* to determine how to get the biggest happiness bang for your buck. Dr. Dunn is an associate professor of psychology at the University of British Columbia in Vancouver. Dr. Norton is a professor at Harvard Business School.

They note the brain's tendency to get used to circumstances (which we will cover later in detail), and cite research that recommends buying a variety of goods and services that boost happiness because they are harder for the brain to adjust to.

Here are their five principles of "happy money":

1. Buy Experiences. The brain does not adapt as well to experiences as it does to things. Over time, experiences grow in value. Even bad experiences can make for a good story. And almost all experiences involve other people — which taps into our human need for social interaction.[28]

2. Make It a Treat. Even the most wonderful thing becomes ho-hum when it becomes routine. But human brains love surprises.[29]

3. Buy Time. Spend money on products and services that will free up some of your time. To get the biggest happiness boost, spend this "extra time" with family and friends — not on TV or commuting.[30]

4. Pay Now, Consume Later. "Because delaying consumption allows spenders to reap the pleasures of anticipation, without the buzzkill of reality," Dunn and Norton write, "vacations provide the most happiness *before* they occur."[31]

5. Invest in Others. The authors cite new research which demonstrates that "spending money on others provides a bigger happiness boost than spending money on yourself."[32]

(For more details on this last point, see Chapter Two on Relationships, and its sections on Compassion.)

My favorite principle on this list is "Buy Experiences" — perfect for anyone who loves travel. Out of the many tremendous travel experiences I've bought in my life, perhaps the best example was when I went to India in 1987. At the time, I was fortunate to have a Fulbright scholarship to study at the lovely university in Tübingen, West Germany.

German universities at that time had very long semester breaks — roughly from late February to late April. The Fulbright organizers had scheduled a week-long "mid-year reunion" in Berlin in March, for the ~200 Americans who were studying in Germany. I was sure it would be fun, and I'd get to see some great people. But I thought hard about how else I could creatively make the best use of my time and money.

I contemplated a few possibilities:

I could go back to visit my parents in Nebraska. But that seemed to be a waste of a tremendous opportunity to see more of the world. I could spend two months of the gloomy, rainy German winter in my dorm room, or at least go check out Berlin. I could try to backpack around the warmer parts of Southern Europe, but I had been to Italy, Greece, and Turkey already. Or, I could ignore the Fulbright mid-year conference entirely and travel the whole time somewhere really cheap and completely out of my comfort zone. I ultimately chose to go to India.

Using the student travel agency, I bought a ticket to Delhi. For the trip home, I had a flight from Mumbai ("Bombay" at the time) back to Frankfurt. Total cost — $600.

I spent six weeks in India, traveling by bus and train from Delhi to Agra, Varanasi, back to Agra, Pushkar, Udaipur, Bombay, Goa, and then back to Bombay. I saw sunrise at the Taj Mahal, witnessed cremations on the Ganges River, rode camels in the desert, visited palaces, and slept on the beach. As time went on, my long blond hair reached my shoulders, I grew a beard, and I jettisoned my jeans in favor of the India *dhoti* pants. If studying in Germany started my transformation into a hippie, then going to India certainly sealed the deal.

But that's all just external stuff. Much more importantly, I met, chatted with, and ate with countless wonderful, kind, hospitable Indians: Hindus. Muslims. Sikhs. Christians. Buddhists. I remember meeting a brother and sister who had an old sewing machine that they used to make clothes for tourists like me. They lived in a very simple hut in Goa, with a view of the glistening ocean. Looking around, it seemed like they had nothing. But they were sweet, fun, funny, and apparently very happy. At that moment, more than any previous time, I realized that a person could live a very joyous life, even if they had very little "stuff."

The entire cost of the trip was $1200 (worth roughly $2677 in today's dollars), for six weeks of life-changing adventures. Looking back, I'm hard-pressed to imagine what else I possibly could have done, on such a limited budget, which would have left such a positive, lasting impression on me.

That's one way to "Buy Experiences."

Write About Your Work

In this chapter on Work, we've discussed your work purpose, calling, nonnegotiables, what money can and cannot do for your happiness, and how to best spend it to maximize your happiness. In order to buy experiences, you have to have a certain level of money in the first place. Which is where work comes in.

How's work been for you? Has it been a great source of energy, passion, joy, and self-expression? Is it something you do as little as possible, just for the money? Has your relationship to work evolved over time, just as your life, your relationships, and your financial situation have evolved as well? Let's explore this more deeply …

Writing Activity 8:
Imagine you died today. How would you feel about the work you did, in terms of compensation, lifestyle, impact, and meaning to you?

I like to ask this question, because it forces you to review the legacy you have, right now, with the "work" you've done. If you got hit by a bus crossing the street today, then you would be finished writing the story of your work and its impact.

You would no longer have time to switch careers or go back to graduate school.

You would no longer be able to actively add value or make a difference.

To help you organize your thoughts on how to answer this broad question, I like to suggest a framework to highlight the different ways to think about your work. Compensation is often thought of as financial, though you could "get paid" in other benefits as well, such as through the pleasure of learning. Lifestyle might allow you to have an excellent work/life balance, even if the other components are suboptimal. Many MBAs that I've known love the idea of "impact," which is sometimes another word for "power." We've already discussed the importance of meaning. "Work" can include working in a typical corporate situation, having your own gig, being a full-time parent or homemaker, or any combination of these.

_____

_____

_____

_____

_____

_____

_____

_____

_____

_____

_____

_____

_____

So what did you come up with in your writing? Any surprises or epiphanies? Was it easy or hard to answer this question? A happiness workshop participant in San Francisco once told me that she enjoyed the intellectual challenge of doing marketing for a giant oil company, but the work lacked any sort of meaning for her. Other people have told me that they loved their lifestyle, even though their work was not challenging. And many have noted that they found great meaning in their work, even if the compensation was low and the lifestyle was tough.

One of the first happiness workshops I did was for Jen, a woman who asked me to speak to her friends from her monthly book club. I thought the evening went great, and I received excellent feedback. About six months later, I ran into Jen, and I asked her if the session had had any lasting impact. She told me that after the workshop, about one third of the participants had decided to change careers. Should I disclose that they were all unhappy lawyers, seeking to do something more fulfilling with their lives? In any case, I viewed this as progress.

Writing Activity 9: Action Plan

Based on what you wrote about your work, what do you need to do or change?

If you are not happy with anything you wrote in Writing Activity 8, I'd like you to use Writing Activity 9 to develop a plan for making some changes. Make sure to take into account everything we've covered in this chapter — defining your calling, asking what the world needs from you, understanding your nonnegotiables, asking, "What would it take?", and understanding the appropriate role for money.

Some possibilities:
- Work longer hours.
- Work shorter hours.
- Work smarter.
- Switch managers.
- Switch departments.
- Switch locations.
- Switch employers.
- Start to work for yourself — even if part time, as a side gig.
- Pursue another career entirely.
- Get additional training, schooling, or certifications, either part-time or full-time.
- Take a few months off.
- Retire.

_____

_____

_____

What can you accomplish in the next 30 to 90 days? Map out a timeline for the things you need to learn and do, the people you need to meet, and the obstacles you need to overcome, so you can get closer to doing work that has more meaning for you. I understand that this might seem like a daunting task, but just getting the ball rolling will start to build momentum that will boost your confidence.

Once you decide what you want to do, it's helpful to make a public commitment to others. Telling one more person about your "secret career desire" is powerful in its own right. But telling a lot of people will make it more real in your mind. You'll get used to putting into words exactly what you mean. You'll have to answer questions and explain in simple language – which forces you to crystallize your thoughts. For me, it was one thing to dream about "writing a self-help book." It was much better when I could put into words, "I'm writing a simple guide on how you can create your happiness, because happiness is a skill you can develop."

Reach out to at least 20 people that you know and tell them of your plans. Even more people will see what you're doing, and almost magically appear to help you, in often unexpected ways. As the German writer Johann Wolfgang von Goethe stated, "At the moment of commitment the entire universe conspires to assist you." [33] He was a Romantic poet. Romantics believe that dreams come true. Make it happen!

Writing Activity 10:

If you knew that you would be healthy for another five years, and then you'd fall over dead, what changes would you make in your life? Why don't you start right now?

_____

_____

_____

_____

_____

_____

_____

———————————————————————————

———————————————————————————

———————————————————————————

———————————————————————————

———————————————————————————

———————————————————————————

I like to ask this question in my master classes, when participants tell me they're not happy with their current work, but they don't know what work they would find *truly* fulfilling. At least sometimes, deep down inside, they know the answer, but they're afraid to say it even to themselves, let alone share it with others.

Death has a wonderful way of helping you focus. In the days after I got my cancer diagnosis, when I was quite unsure whether I'd live another five years or 50 years, I became very clear on what I wanted to do with my remaining time.

I had no more time for excuses.

I had no more time for doubt.

If I was ever going to do certain things, then I needed to start doing them *immediately*. And this insight and urgency led me to start conducting my Happiness Workshop.

I also like this question because I think five years is a good chunk of time to start making an impact on what's meaningful to you. If you had just three months to live before you keeled over and died, then you'd probably spend all that time with family and friends. If you had just a year to live, you'd probably do a lot of fun activities to scratch off your bucket list, in addition to spending time with loved ones.

But if we keep extending out the time further and further (three years? five years? 10 years?), eventually, you'd probably say to yourself, "OK, enough of saying good bye to everyone. And enough of the surfing in Maui, climbing Machu Picchu, raving in Ibiza, and shopping in Paris. Now I'd like to do something meaningful, to create a legacy I can be proud of."

Notice that I did not ask how you would *pay* for the next five years of your life! But what's much more interesting to think about is, "What would I be doing for the next five years, which I could *afford* to do, through my own income, which would be meaningful for me?" For help in answering this question, make sure to look at the sections on "What Are Your Nonnegotiables" and "What Would It Take?"

Facing Your Fate … with Love

I wish that the question above would always be a nice, abstract exercise. Unfortunately, it's the real deal for some people.

In late July of 2018, my wife and I drove from Hacienda Heights, east of Los Angeles, to visit my friend Mary Huffman. Mary and I were classmates at Stanford's business school. I remember having lunch with Mary around 1995, when she told me about growing up in a trailer park, in poverty, in Southern California. Neither of her parents had finished high school. Mary was brilliant, kind, fun, and funny. Her husband Ted was the same. As we made our way to their home north of L.A., I was happy thinking that I could introduce my wife to them.

Mary had been diagnosed with ALS (Lou Gehrig's disease) for almost a year, although her symptoms had begun earlier. Tragically, the average life expectancy from initial symptoms is between two and four years — and Mary had the aggressive form of the disease. (You can learn more about their story here: _https://www.tedandmary.com/_)

As amazingly kind and positive people, Mary and Ted were hoping for the best, but also realistically preparing for the likelihood that she wouldn't be alive in two years or so. Mary's speech had become slurred, as if she were very drunk, and was quite a bit worse than when I had spoken with her on the phone a few months earlier. She was bedridden, mostly fed through a tube going into her stomach, and at that point had to wear adult diapers. She had an iPad propped up on her lap and was tapping at it with a stiff finger. I was able to try out her Tobii Dynavox — the eye-tracking computer that scientist Stephen Hawking (another person with ALS) used to speak. Amazing stuff!

Even more impressive was how I saw Mary and Ted focusing on what's important when one has a lethal degenerative disease. Mary had recently written, "Helping others has always been my guiding passion, and now that I'm unable to even speak clearly anymore, walk, or use my hands, I can look back on a life much larger than I ever could have imagined. Thank you, my friends, for all the laughter and memories."[34]

It gave her a big boost to receive visitors, and she told me she was sad during the weeks when nobody came. She had placed scores of photos all over her walls and on the ceiling, along with rotating images on the TV screen, to remind her of all the loving people in her life. During our visit, they gave us blue "Team Mary" T-shirts with a Wonder Woman theme.

We laughed a lot, but also had tears welling up in our eyes.

Ted explained that for people with ALS, the pH level of their tears tends to burn their skin. So it felt like such a sacred honor to wipe tears of laughter from Mary's eyes.

Stacy, my wife, was especially sweet and loving. Her mom died in 1975, as the family fled Vietnam in boats as refugees. Stacy knows the sorrow of growing up without a mother.

It was sad to imagine what Mary and Ted's 15-year-old daughter and 13-year-old son were going through. Ted said very soberly that the family knew that they were dealing with a tough situation in taking care of Mom, but that it would not be this way forever. I was a bit surprised to hear Ted say this. On the one hand, they needed to hope that Mary would "Steven Hawking the crap out of this" and live for many years. But on the other hand, they understood that the odds were against her surviving long.

Despite the circumstances, Mary and Ted were very grateful to have access to quality care at Cedar Sinai Hospital in Los Angeles, and that they could use technology to communicate, have visitors, and have an intact family. They noted that, given this disease, things could have been worse. I call that "inspiring optimism."

In Mary's case, I suppose you could be angry at God or the universe — but that's not very productive. Indeed, Ted and Mary were able to prepare for Mary's incapacitation and focus on the time she had left.

Less than two months after our visit, somewhere in my Facebook feed I saw this post from Mary:

"If you are reading this post then I have passed away. I wrote this ahead of time because I want you all to know how amazing it has been having you in my life. I am incredibly grateful to all of you for the laughter and the love over the years. Someone recently asked me what my life philosophies are – here you go:

- Don't try to be perfect. Just be the best version of you that you can be.
- Help others when you can
- Don't take your health for granted.
Love to you all…"

She was not yet 50 years old. I remain awestruck by the Huffman family's love and courage.

I wanted to share her story with you because it's a reminder of how short life is — and how wonderful love of life, friends, and family can be.

In my Happiness Workshop, I sometimes ask, "What would you do if you had five years to live?" Ironically, a few years ago, Mary actually attended my Happiness Workshop for the Stanford Business School Alumni Association Chapter in L.A. At the time, she was perfectly healthy. It's likely that in that workshop, I quoted the Christian pastor Charles Swindoll, who said, "Life is 10% what happens to me and 90% how I react to it."[35]

Later Mary would have that quote prominently posted to the frame of her bedroom door.

Seeing Mary and Ted was deeply disturbing and moving, but it filled me with optimism, as well. I told Stacy that I'm not used to having friends my age die. But as we proceed through life, this will happen more and more. Add to that list parents, siblings, and possibly even children. This is the hard part of life — which is nonetheless part of life. All we can do is love others as best we can with the time we have and leave memories and a legacy that will be a positive influence on others.

Mary said that in the future, she would still be here, she just wouldn't "have skin." Stacy noted that she always feels like her mom is watching over her, like a guardian angel. I must admit

I have never gone through my life with that sort of awareness. But I always carry with me the ideas, stories, experiences, and love that I've received from others. We all channel the lessons and legacy of many family and friends, living and deceased.

After my wife and I said goodbye to Mary and Ted that day, we grabbed lunch at a tiny Mexican restaurant in Granada Hills. We ordered fish tacos, ceviche, chips, and guacamole. I asked for extra spicy salsa, even though it makes my eyes water.

I savored the delicious food, but was also deep in thought, absorbing the conversation we had just finished with our friends. I was oblivious to the other patrons in the restaurant. My eyes were welling up with tears.

"This food is perfect for crying," I said to Stacy.

She and I drove north on Highway 5 in my convertible. We crossed the mountains, then navigated California's scorching Central Valley, passing orchards and farmland, and finally returned home to foggy, windy San Francisco.

Behind the wheel of my car, I ruminated on despair and hope, sorrow and joy. This trip through the California landscape felt like we had traversed vast stretches of our emotions and humanity.

It was good to be alive.

Think Long Term So You Have No Regrets

Writing Activity 11:
What work would you do if you had to do it full time for the next 30 years?
Can you start doing it now?

_____

_____

_____

_____

_____

_____

_____

_____

_____

_____

If you are like I was in my late 20s, you might assume that you can just try out a job in a particular company, industry, or career — and if it doesn't work out, sooner or later you can try something else. And if that doesn't work out, then you can switch again. And then again. (Some countries accept this workplace behavior much more than others. For example, in my experience, job-hopping is far more tolerated in Silicon Valley than it is in Germany.)

I understand that you can be desperate to get *any* job, if bills are piling up and you need to support yourself and your family. But for many of us, we're too willing to accept work that is not a good fit for us, rather than being honest, authentic, and courageous enough to pursue a career that would be truly meaningful.

That's where this question comes in. If you had to start a new job first thing Monday morning, and you knew that you'd have to do that job, full time, for the next 30 years, you'd be *crazy* to pick work you didn't love, right? Only an insane person would say, "Sure, this work isn't good for me. It's boring. I'm not learning anything useful. There is no challenge. I don't like the company or the corporate culture, or the mission of the organization. I dislike my colleagues. The commute is horrible, I have terrible work/life balance, and they don't pay me enough. But I'll keep doing this until the middle of this century …"

Instead, if you had to pick a role that you'd have to do full time for the next 30 years, you'd be darned sure that you'd find it fascinating, meaningful, and challenging. Yes, it would need to pay you enough so you could live the life you wanted to lead. You'd ask all your friends and family, seek out the best experts and mentors, do research, and be very creative, asking, "What would it take to do this?"

Take this writing activity and share it with a loved one. What would they answer? Why? What does that say about their hopes and goals? How hard would it be to do this yourself? **Send me an email at** jim@jimmccarthy.com. I'd love to hear what you came up with.

You should be taking this approach to your work anyway, whether you do it for another 30 years — or 30 months.

The next activity offers one way to uncover the path to such rewarding work.

Writing Activity 12:
What gift do you have that puts you in the 99th percentile?

_____

_____

_____

_____

_____

_____

_____

_____

_____

This is a question from my friend, Anil Sethi, who has founded many very successful tech start-ups in his career. (His last start-up was acquired by Apple.) His point is that, if you think very broadly and creatively, you can identify the special skills, talents, or expertise that makes you unique. Often, but not always, your uniqueness can translate into a lucrative and rewarding career.

If you asked five people who know you extremely well, "What special skills or superpowers do I possess?" you'd probably get a quick consensus on something that you take for granted about yourself. You'd probably say to yourself, "Well, I thought *everybody* can do this," when in fact only *you* can do it. Maybe you're amazing at gardening. Or you can spend endless hours doing financial analysis. Or you have great intuition for how smartphone apps should work. Or you're beautifully persuasive and eloquent. If you notice, respect, and honor your superpowers, then you can set yourself up for success in areas that already seem effortless to you. That's a source of competitive advantage.

Earlier in my career, I felt like I had to be constantly challenged by taking on roles and tasks that did not come easily for me — just so I could learn and expand my "toolkit," as we say in MBA parlance. Although I'm glad to have had very diverse work experiences, over time I've come to understand that most people are predisposed to do certain tasks best — and the sooner they end up doing those tasks, the happier and more successful they'll become.

Do what only you can do. For example, I combined my bohemian hippie love of travel and learning languages with an MBA from Stanford, which helped me work on international product rollouts for Yahoo and NexTag, leading Silicon Valley companies at the time. I have a very good friend who got a business degree at a top East Coast school, then graduated from the Culinary Institute of America, one of the best such institutions in the world. Today, he's the CEO of a major restaurant chain in the U.S. No surprise there — who would be better qualified than someone with a strong business background and a serious culinary degree?

You might be a gifted artist who also excels in writing software. Or you have a degree in design and also know a lot about psychology. Any one of these skills can put you in the 90th percentile, which is good. But once you start overlapping them with other skills, you get into the 99th percentile — which is much better.

Don't live a life filled with regrets. Irv Grousbeck is a highly successful businessman and co-owner of the Boston Celtics. He has taught a legendary entrepreneurship class for decades at Stanford's Graduate School of Business. He's spoken to thousands of people who've founded start-ups — and no doubt more who *wanted* to found companies but never did.

Regarding those who never did, Professor Grousbeck notes that by the time these people reach age 45 or 50, "those regrets are palpable." They live with despair for never having even tried. The Stanford professor warns that "the saddest phrase of middle age is 'I wish I had.'"[36]

In contrast, Grousbeck cites others, who at age 30 or 35 attempt to start companies. Some succeed. Some do OK. And some fail. But even the ones who fail are glad that they tried, and they carry that satisfaction with them for the rest of their lives. Grousbeck's observation: "Regret for what you have done can be tempered by time. Regret for what you have not done is inconsolable."[37]

A recent study confirms this. Research by Victoria Medvec, at Northwestern University's Kellogg School, found that the more time that passes after an event, the more a person regrets what they *did not do*, rather than what they *did do*. In an interview with *KelloggInsight*, Professor Neal J. Roese explains the fascinating dichotomy between what we know has happened, and what we imagine could have happened: "Lost opportunities linger in our memory longer … there are so many ways in which you can see different things you could have done."[38]

In related but distinct research, a team of Dutch scientists found that participants overestimated how bad failure would feel, writing, "forecasters predicted to experience more guilt and shame than experiencers actually experienced."[39]

What are you waiting for? Even if you screw up your next big endeavor, you'll be glad that you tried. It's the things you *did not try* that will haunt you. What would you do if you knew you could not fail? What would you try if you had only five years to live?

There are only three Post-It notes on the monitor at my desk. One of them says, "Try and fail, but don't fail to try."

PART TWO

What Is "Happiness"?

Chapter Four:
Happiness Framework

Are You "Happy"? How Happy Are You?

You have probably noticed that you're reading a "Surprisingly Simple Guide to Happiness." I put the word "happiness" in the subtitle, because it's a broadly used and understood word. Just like "health," "freedom," or "justice," pretty much all of us want "happiness" — although your mom, sister, and accountant might have a very different understanding of what the term means to them.

Like a doctor who takes your pulse at the start of a medical examination, I'd like to see just how happy you are, right now.

Writing Activity 13:
On a scale of 1 to 10, with "1" equaling "deeply depressed" and "10" equaling "euphoric or extremely joyful," how would you rate yourself at this very moment?
How would you rate yourself for the past week?
The past month?
The past year?
The past decade?

Live Each Day 99

_____

_____

_____

_____

_____

_____

_____

_____

_____

Is it hard to come up with a number? If this number changes over time, what is the trend? Are you "getting happier" or "getting less happy"?

Do you even trust your own memory? Do you think you're being nostalgic, and rating your past level of happiness higher than it truly was at the time?

Or is it a matter of time healing all wounds, so that the events that seemed very painful in the past don't seem so bad from today's perspective? Have you completely forgotten about that huge challenge or crisis that used to be the main source of your daily suffering, back in 2013, 2002, or 1979? What, if anything, was giving you insomnia last March?

Lots of questions here. Did you notice that I did not even bother to define "happiness" in the first place, other than with the synonyms "euphoric or extremely joyful"? I wanted to see how easy it was for you to answer the question, without giving any definition.

Next, make sure to check in with someone who knows you well — your spouse, children, parents, siblings, work colleagues, or friends. Just ask them: "Hey, I'm doing a little survey ... on a scale of one to 10, how happy do you think I am?"

Then, close your mouth, cover it with your hand, and listen carefully to their response. Just listen and nod. Don't try to refute their answer or explain why they might be "wrong" about you.

Eventually, feel free to give definitions or ask clarifying questions. Share how you would rate yourself. And then you can turn around and ask them, "Would you like to know how I would rate *your* happiness?"

Have fun with this exercise! I just asked my wife this question for the first time, and we ended up having a very insightful 20-minute conversation — touching on some of the most important aspects of our lives.

What Would Make You Happier?

Writing Activity 14:
Regardless of how happy you rated yourself in the previous Writing Activity, what would make you happier going forward?

_____

_____

_____

_____

_____

_____

_____

_____

Take as much time as you want to answer this question. What would have to happen?

What would you have to do, learn, be, or become in order to get happier?

What would you need to add to your life?

What would you need to subtract from your life?

What would you need to keep in your life?

You might want to start with absolutely nothing, then add the essential elements that would bring you happiness. Or you might start with your current life, and then subtract, one by one, whatever is not making you happy, until you can simplify no further.

You can focus on material things, such as having a new car.

You can focus on experiences, such as doing that once-in-a-lifetime trip you've always desired.

You can focus on the sort of work you would love to do — assuming you're not doing it already.

You can focus on relationships — at home, at work, or in your community.

You can focus on your health.

It's not always easy to answer these questions. But they're fundamental for you to understand what would make you happy.

After all, if you don't know what you want to have, how can you get it?

If you don't know how you want to be, how can you be it?

Next, as in the previous Writing Activity, check in with a friend or family member and run this question by them. If their answer is "win the lottery," then you can gently refer them to the section called "Limits of What Money Can Do for You."

A Framework for "Happy"

The word "happiness" gets thrown around a lot. But what does it really mean? Here is one way to think about happiness:

Day 1:

Imagine you're on vacation at a beautiful tropical resort with someone you deeply love. You get a great night's sleep. You have an excellent workout to start the day. After you shower, you have a delicious, healthy breakfast. Next, you do your favorite activity or hobby, be it golf, tennis, swimming, surfing, cycling, shopping, wine tasting, sightseeing, reading, or visiting a museum. After a fabulous lunch, you go to the spa, relax, and get an incredible massage. Back at your room, you have a restful siesta, then dress up and go out for the evening with your loved one. You have an unforgettable meal, listen to live music, then return to your beautiful room for a night of romance and passion. You fall asleep in each other's arms.

Do you think this sort of day would make you happy? (This may not be your sort of ideal day, but it's mine!)

Now, let's compare Day 1 to Day 2.

Day 2:

At the start of Day 2, you are at home. Your alarm clock goes off early. You went to bed late the night before and you are feeling sleep deprived, yet again. You quickly drink a cup of coffee, then commute the long distance to your work at a senior care facility. It's a nonprofit organization, and you do not earn a lot of money, although you do see the direct impact that your work is having on the elderly residents.

At the end of your day, you pick up your two kids at daycare, go grocery shopping and cook dinner for them, help them with their homework, and get them to bed. After that, you answer an email from your mom, text your friend who's sad because of a recent breakup, and then you go to sleep. (No romance for you, because you're a single parent and have no time for dating.)

Now, do you think Day 2 would make you happy? Why? Why not?

Is this a trick question?

In essence, Day 1 is about pleasure. Day 2 is about purpose. Both are extremely different, but very important for creating your own happiness.

HAPPINESS FRAMEWORK

PLEASURE	PURPOSE
Receive	Give
Physical Comfort and Fun	Psychological Comfort, Meaning
Get What You Want and Need	Express and Define Yourself
Love & Take Care of Yourself	Love & Take Care of People Who Need You
	Love Impactful Work You Are Compelled to Do
Do Your Own Thing	Be Part of Something Bigger
Worst Case: Hedonism	Worst Case: Obsession
Best Case: Health, Security	Best Case: True Spirituality
Live in the Now	Make Sense of the Past, Present and Future

Peace and Happiness

This framework is a synthesis of my own thinking, experiences, and research, as well as insights from the 2013 Stanford University Roundtable, "Are You Happy Now?"[1]

The event was hosted by the American journalist and TV host Katie Couric. She interviewed Sonja Lyubomirsky, who is a professor of psychology and director of the Positive Psychology Lab at the University of California, Riverside.

In addition, Couric spoke with the following professors, all from Stanford:

- Jennifer Aaker, marketing professor at the Graduate School of Business;
- Firdaus Dhabhar, associate professor of psychiatry and behavioral sciences;
- Ian H. Gotlib, chair of the Department of Psychology;
- David Kelley, who led the creation of the innovative Design School.

Let's review the framework in detail.

Pleasure is about receiving, such as receiving a foot rub.

Purpose is about giving, such as providing attention and care to the people in the senior care facility.

Pleasure is about physical comfort and fun, such as eating great food, dancing, or playing volleyball.

Purpose is about psychological comfort and meaning, such as teaching your kids to read or have good manners.

Pleasure is about getting what you want and need.

Purpose is about expressing and defining yourself.[2]

Pleasure is about loving and taking care of yourself, such as getting enough sleep and not working too hard.

Purpose is about loving and taking care of people who need

you, which can include any family, friends, or community. It may require significant sacrifice and not be "fun."

Purpose is also about loving impactful work that you feel compelled to do. That could be a career as a social worker, a journalist, or a software engineer.

Pleasure is about doing your own thing, focused on whatever is convenient and enjoyable according to your needs and desires.

Purpose is about being part of something bigger than yourself. You could be a civil rights activist as part of a larger social movement. You could be serving your country in the military. Or you could be an entrepreneur creating an amazing business that provides better services at lower prices for consumers.[3]

Pleasure's extreme is hedonism — the *excessive* pursuit of pleasure and sensual self-indulgence.

Purpose's extreme is obsession. I've seen many entrepreneurs in Silicon Valley who are obsessed with the success of their start-ups. Such intensity might be helpful or even necessary for some businesses to succeed, but don't expect that founder CEO to be available to take you to the hospital for a medical procedure, because they are way too busy building their empire.

Pleasure's best case is genuinely great health and vitality, as well as physical and emotional security and a lack of violence or threats. It can also involve living in the moment, which is quite wonderful, especially as you practice mindfulness and reduce your anxiety.

For purpose, the best case is what I would call a "true spirituality," or deep, wise understanding of your mission or place in the universe. It makes sense of the past, explains the present, and anticipates the future. It gives you a narrative for what you're doing in your life.[4]

Balancing Pleasure and Purpose

It's easy to see the appeal of purpose. Hollywood doesn't make inspirational movies about people sitting on the beach, sipping mojitos. Hollywood makes inspirational movies about people fighting for freedom, justice, or simply survival.

Purpose is what you'd like to have written on your tombstone. It's your legacy.

Purpose is what inspired Nkosi Johnson, the South African AIDS activist who died at age 12, to tell journalist Jim Wooten, "Do all you can with what you have in the time you have in the place you are."[5]

Purpose is what inspired former U.S. Vice President Al Gore to dedicate his life to raising awareness around climate change. He challenged all of us when he said, "Will our children ask, *why didn't you act?* Or [will they] ask, *how did you find the moral courage to rise up and change?*"[6]

Researchers note the difference between pleasure (sometimes called "happiness") and purpose. In *The New York Times*, Stanford Professor Jennifer Aaker and journalist Emily Esfahani Smith wrote, "Although a meaningful life and a happy life overlap in certain ways, they are ultimately quite different. Those who reported having a meaningful life saw themselves as more other-oriented — by being, more specifically, a 'giver.' People who said that doing things for others was important to them reported having more meaning in their lives.

"This was in stark contrast to those who reported having a happy life. Happiness was associated with being more self-oriented — by being a 'taker.' People felt happy, in a superficial sense, when they got what they wanted, and not necessarily when they put others first, which can be stressful and requires sacrificing what you want for what others want. Having children, for instance, is associated with high meaning but lower happiness."[7]

You may have seen how cultures around the world differ in how they try to achieve a balance between pleasure and purpose. One can point to many cultures that value hard work — the Confucianist cultures of eastern Asia, the entrepreneurial people I've known from India and the Middle East, or the hardworking Latinos who do many of the most dangerous and poorly paid jobs where I live — in California. To varying degrees, enterprising individuals in all cultures make time for community, family, and self-actualization.

Looking back on my experiences, I grew up in a middle-class Irish-German-American family in the Midwest of the United States. The U.S., northern Europe, and Scandinavian countries are characterized by their "Protestant work ethic," defined as "a concept in theology, sociology, economics and history which emphasizes that hard work, discipline and frugality are a result of a person's subscription to the values espoused by the Protestant faith."[8] Like many Americans, I was raised Catholic, but I submit to you that even Catholic Americans subscribe strongly to the Protestant work ethic.

I did not give any of this a lot of thought, however, until I spent my junior year of college in Vienna, Austria. During my first semester there, I had an internship at the United Nations' International Atomic Energy Agency. (It was not as sexy as it sounds. But at least the U.N. cafeteria had some pretty good food, especially for a lowly student like me.)

I asked an American career diplomat in my office to describe her experience there. She mentioned the nepotism, cronyism, and corruption that influenced a lot of politics all over the world. And then she said, almost as a given, "Of course, all of the Americans here at the U.N. are workaholics."

A couple of years later, I was visiting a brilliant, fun, French friend of mine in the Marais neighborhood of Paris. I asked him how his job was going at the American advertising agency where he had just started. "Well," Pascal said, "these guys really know a lot about advertising. But they work like crazy! I mean, they don't even go out for lunch! They simply eat at their desks. In France, most people go out for lunch for at least an hour."

I had these admittedly massive cultural generalizations in the back of my mind when I began teaching English to bankers in Frankfurt, Germany — my first real job after college.

One of my very first students, a successful businessman about twice my age, said in his thick German accent, "The Latin countries like Italy, Spain, and France are great when you're a student. You don't need a lot of money to go out at night and have fun. When it comes to your career, the U.S. is the best place to be, because it's a meritocracy and the system allows you to earn a lot of money and not pay a lot of taxes. Then later, when you retire, Germany or the Northern European countries are best, because they're safe, clean, quiet, and well organized."

"Geez!" I thought to my 23-year-old self, as I walked through the German rain back to my dark little studio apartment, "I'm in the wrong country at the wrong time!"

Comments from my colleague and mentor in Frankfurt, Bill McAndrews, only made me feel worse. "Jim," he told me, "you ought to go to Spain! I used to live in Madrid and it was so much fun! People go out all the time, partying until 4:00 a.m. They don't take work so seriously. The weather is great. The city doesn't shut down by 9:00 p.m. like it does here in Frankfurt. In fact, that's when they're just getting started!"

I worked hard in Frankfurt, saved my Deutsch Marks, and later moved to Madrid, thanks to help from Bill's connections. Spain was everything that Bill promised it would be — though I suddenly found a whole new set of things to complain about, such as slow service, bureaucratic inefficiency, and bad infrastructure. (For example, I waited seven weeks to get a telephone line connected in my apartment in the heart of Madrid.) In other words, what I disliked about Spain were all the things which I took for granted in Germany.

I remember one interview while I was working in Madrid as a business journalist. I can't recall the context, but the interviewee, a high-ranking Spanish businessman, noted, "We Latins love everything which is sensual: food, wine, dancing, music, fashion, sex. It's much more a part of the Mediterranean cultures than in Northern Europe."

Are these outrageously huge generalizations?

Yes.

Can you find massive counterexamples?

Sure.

But do I find them true to my experiences of living more than six years in Austria, Germany, Spain, the U.K., and then the rest of my life in Nebraska, Iowa, or California?

Yup.

Why should you care?

Because the Protestant work ethic is filled with purpose — especially related to your job. In contrast, sensual joys are related to pleasure.

In teaching my master classes in the U.S., nobody feels awkward or giggles when I speak about purpose. But some participants get a bit uncomfortable when I mention pleasure — perhaps because they associate it so closely with sex. It's easy to think that purpose is serious, noble, and good. And it is! But pleasure deserves respect and attention, too.

As a psychology doctoral student at Harvard University, Matthew Killingsworth created a smartphone app to track happiness in real-time, daily life. His findings: Out of 22 activities, people were happiest when:

- making love (That's right, sex was the winner!)
- exercising
- talking
- playing
- listening to music
- taking a walk
- eating

What was on the bottom of the list? People were least happy while:

- resting/sleeping (perhaps related to insomnia)
- working
- using a home computer
- commuting[9]

Perhaps unsurprisingly, according to Dr. Killingsworth's findings, people were getting a lot more happiness out of what I'd call their "pleasure activities" than their "purpose activities."

So you should take your pleasure seriously. Take the advice of BJ Miller, a physician who previously headed up the Zen Hospice Center in San Francisco, not far from where I live. At age 19, he lost his left arm and both legs to an accident. He has spent much of his career doing the tremendous work of bringing more compassion, art, and spirituality to end-of-life care. He has comforted the dying, and has also taught many others how to do so.

In Dr. Miller's 2015 TED Talk, "What Really Matters at the End of Life," he discusses the importance of pleasure for his dying patients: "Over Zen Hospice's nearly 30 years, we've learned

much more from our residents in subtle detail. Little things aren't
so little. Take ... Kate -- she just wants to know her dog Austin is
lying at the foot of her bed, his cold muzzle against her dry skin,
instead of more chemotherapy coursing through her veins -- she's
done that. Sensuous, aesthetic gratification, where in a moment,
in an instant, we are rewarded for just being. So much of it comes
down to loving our time by way of the senses, by way of the body
-- the very thing doing the living and the dying.

"Probably the most poignant room in the Zen Hospice guest
house is our kitchen ... We realize we are providing sustenance
on several levels: smell, a symbolic plane. Seriously, with all the
heavy-duty stuff happening under our roof, one of the most tried
and true interventions we know of is to bake cookies. As long
as we have our senses -- even just one -- we have at least the
possibility of accessing what makes us feel human, connected.
Imagine the ripples of this notion for the millions of people living
and dying with dementia. Primal sensorial delights that say
the things we don't have words for, impulses that make us stay
present -- no need for a past or a future."[10]

Finding the Right Balance for You

There are people who have a great deal of purpose in their
lives, but not enough pleasure. They may be stay-at-home
parents, those who take care of their own parents, or people who
work at nonprofit organizations or do volunteer work. In one of
my keynote talks, there was a 20-something woman who had
founded a nonprofit to help the poor in Oakland, California. She
said that although her organization was successful, after about
six years she had had to take a sabbatical, because she had been
simply exhausted from the years of hard work and dedication.

These "high-purpose individuals" might be very committed

to their mission or their families — but they can get burned out. To regain their happiness, they need to take better care of themselves. Give themselves a break. Go to the spa, or take a vacation. Eat better. Get more sleep. Make the time to meditate or do yoga. Otherwise, they run the risk of becoming angry, bitter, self-righteous, self-pitying people. No matter how noble their cause, they can be a real pain to be around. Some literally work themselves to death. Do you know anybody like this?

Having too much purpose and not enough pleasure can be a problem.

Having too much pleasure and not enough purpose can be a problem, too.

A friend of mine from business school (let's call him "Adam") ended up working as an early employee at eBay. (He asked me to join eBay as well, but I was already working at Yahoo, which was at the time a highly successful company.) He ended up making many millions of dollars over several years, retired while he was still in his 30s, and traveled the world. But when he got back to the San Francisco Bay Area, he dropped into a deep, long, clinical depression — so bad that he could not even get himself out of bed in the morning.

How could Adam have become so depressed, right when he had "achieved it all"? According to my Happiness Framework, it's because his life lacked purpose. Sure, he had plenty of pleasure. He could travel anywhere he wanted, eat the best food, drink the finest wine, stay in the most luxurious hotels — and almost certainly be surrounded by lots of beautiful (and potentially romantic) people, as well. He was also able to call "home" the Bay Area — which many people regard as one of the loveliest areas in the United States.

Similar to the Day 1 scenario in my Happiness Framework, Adam's life was filled with pleasure. And I myself might find it very appealing for a month. Or six months. Or even longer. But eventually … sitting on the beach all day and partying all night would feel a little empty for me. I don't know if I'd get "bored," exactly. But my life would lack meaning. And at that point, I'd start looking around to do something — anything — that would have a positive, purposeful impact on others.

Unfortunately, I had lost touch with Adam as he was having his struggles. But his story has a happy ending. Adam eventually found a new purpose in his life — to be a middle school teacher in California — and he's been joyously doing that work for more than a decade. He's also gotten married and raised a family.

Scientific investigations confirm the downside of having more pleasure than purpose. Barbara Fredrickson, a psychology professor at the University of North Carolina, Chapel Hill, found that 75 percent of her study participants were "very high on happiness" but low on "meaning." (I would describe them as very high on "pleasure" but low on "purpose.") As described in the *Atlantic*, the research found that "people who are happy but have little or no sense of meaning in their lives … have the same gene expression patterns as people who are responding to and enduring chronic adversity." This yields an inflammatory response in their bodies, linked to illnesses such as heart disease and cancers. Fredrickson notes that it's OK to be happy, but problems develop when there is happiness without meaning.[11]

A broader study by the Centers for Disease Control found that 41 percent of Americans were either neutral toward or disagreed with the statement, "My life has a clear sense of purpose."[12]

This is unfortunate because, as Emily Esfahani Smith writes in the *Atlantic*, having a sense of purpose in your life "increases overall well-being and life satisfaction, improves mental and physical health, enhances resiliency, enhances self-esteem, and decreases the chances of depression."[13]

I used to call my master class "Happiness: Find Your Pleasure, Purpose and Peace."

And then I realized that you don't suddenly "find" your happiness, the way you'd find a flower on the side of the road, waiting to be picked. Happiness does not land on you from above, either, like the 16-ton weight crushing unsuspecting characters in Monty Python skits.

I would never tell you, "Just be happy!"

Instead, you have to *create* your happiness. You have to actively focus and have the discipline to work on things that increase your happiness. It might be quite straightforward and direct — just like walking five miles is simple and direct, as long as you keep putting one foot in front of the other. Thus, the word "Simple" in the title of this book. In later chapters I'll show you exactly how you can take baby steps to design and develop your happiness, day by day. You have to try. But your effort will be worth it.

Writing Activity 15:
Do you create enough pleasure but not enough purpose in your life?
Enough purpose but not enough pleasure?
Not enough of either?
Or an ideal balance of both?

_____

_____

_____

_____

_____

_____

_____

_____

_____

_____

Once you finish your writing, check in with a loved one and ask them how they would respond.

Happiness, Unhappiness, and Suicide

As I started to write this chapter, the fashion designer Kate Spade and the TV host Anthony Bourdain both took their lives, just days apart. This shocking news forced me to think about the opposite of "happiness." I was reminded of the great author Elie Wiesel, who once commented that the opposite of "love" is not "hate" but apathy. By extension, I suppose the opposite of "happiness" is not "unhappiness," but apathy, despair, hopelessness, and depression.

I believe that many people who cannot find meaning in their lives end up combatting this psychic pain by numbing themselves with alcohol and drugs. This might help us understand how more than 70,000 people in the United States died of drug overdoses in the past 12 months — most from opioids. [14] Another example is the 45,000 people in the U.S. who took their lives in 2016 — a 30 percent increase since 1999.[15]

How does this fit with my framework of happiness? I don't pretend to know everything about the life of Anthony Bourdain, who was an irreverent, funny, and tough-but-compassionate chef and author who traveled the world for his CNN series, "Parts Unknown." But I'm a big enough fan to perhaps draw some lessons from his suicide.

By all appearances, Bourdain had plenty of pleasure in his life. Millions of viewers saw him eating some of the best food, drinking some of the best wine, and visiting some of the most wonderful places in the world. He was famous and probably wealthy. On the opposite side of the "pleasure" part of the equation was that he was on the road 200 days per year, which was a grueling travel schedule. Too much work and sleep deprivation can definitely lead to depression. [16] Similarly, being away on business travel — even if this means eating caviar in Paris — can keep you away from your family, friends, and loved ones.

What about purpose? Bourdain was an incredibly gifted storyteller, who was able to use food as an excuse to probe the humanity of so many people on his episodes. His curiosity, gusto, and empathy showed through, and all of us viewers benefitted from his explorations and explanations. Bourdain's work had a huge positive impact on others.

Unfortunately, my fear is that he ultimately lost sight of how he was touching our lives. I saw an interview with him in which he worried that "Parts Unknown" ruined the tiny restaurants he meant to highlight, created jealousy with the neighbors of the farmers he featured, or even caused a riot in Haiti when his production crew tried to feed hungry children.[17]

Maybe, in the end, Bourdain felt like he was having no positive impact at all. Or that he had seen so much "good" and "bad" in the world, that he became jaded and apathetic.

But the bottom line is that depression and mental illness are *not logical*. If people were perfectly logical, they would not want to kill themselves in the first place. So whether you have enough pleasure, or enough purpose, or both — none of this will register in your mind if you're truly depressed.

I come from a family with our fair share of suicides. Most people I talk with can say the same. I was struck by the comment from Talinda Bennington, the widow of Linkin Park singer Chester Bennington, who died by suicide. She told CNN, "I have not spoken to a single suicide survivor that says they wish they would have succeeded."[18]

A person who is depressed needs expert mental health treatment, just as a person who's broken their leg needs expert physical health treatment. If you feel despair or depression, you can be proud that you have the courage to reach out for help.

In the United States, the National Suicide Prevention Lifeline is 1-800-273-8255
Their website: https://suicidepreventionlifeline.org/

In the U.K. and Ireland, it's 116 123
Website: https://www.samaritans.org/

In Canada, it's 1-833-456-4566
Website: https://thelifelinecanada.ca/

In Australia, it's 13 11 14
Website: https://www.lifeline.org.au/

Chapter Five:
The McCarthy Happiness Matrix

I hope you find my Happiness Framework useful. If you find the right balance of pleasure and purpose, you will have better chances of being happy, more of the time.

And you might have already noticed that pleasure and purpose are not always mutually exclusive. So like all good MBAs, I figured that it might be more nuanced and insightful to think about pleasure and purpose in a 2x2 matrix. Voilà, the McCarthy Happiness Matrix!

THE MCCARTHY HAPPINESS MATRIX

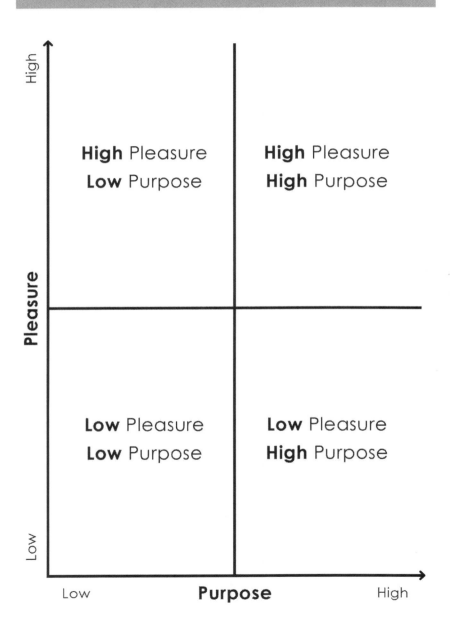

Once I created this matrix, I started searching for examples, to see if the framework still made sense. I think it does — but you need to be the judge of that! Let's look more closely …

Think about the huge range of activities you do or have done. Where would they fit into any of these quadrants?

Below is an example of a wide range of pursuits that quickly came to mind for me. I then tried to see where I would put them in the matrix.

Please know that what I've written here is extremely subjective. My answers will be very different from yours. Whatever you write can easily change over the course of your life.

THE MCCARTHY HAPPINESS MATRIX

How one person might fill this out...

	Low ← Purpose		**High** → Purpose	

High Pleasure

Eating a great meal · Traveling to a favorite destination | Awe in nature · Sex with someone I love

Hearing a favorite song · Watching my favorite sports team | Being "in flow" at work · Disneyland with my kids

Being in great physical shape

Getting a great night's sleep · Kittens | Hanging out with friends · Winning a scholarship

Learning to salsa dance · Hearing a funny joke | Family reunions

---

Low Pleasure

Sex with someone I don't love · Doing a job just for the paycheck | Building a successful product · Visiting a friend in the hospital

Being unemployed | Exercising · Doing volunteer work

Doing meaningless work for a boss I hate · Doing household chores | Changing my baby's diapers

Being in prison | Studying for a big exam

Low ——— **Purpose** ——— **High**

Low Pleasure and Low Purpose

Let's get the worst stuff out of the way first!

Doing meaningless work for a boss you hate would be in this quadrant. You might feel numb, indifferent, detached, or apathetic. Sex with someone you don't love could be pleasurable, but lacking in purpose (precisely because you don't love them).

Doing household chores might not be much fun, but if you do so because you're trying to make life easier for your beloved mom, then that would add a lot more purpose to your tasks.

Doing a job just for the paycheck is more pleasurable if you don't despise your manager, and being able to pay the bills can be a very relevant source of purpose, too.

Initially, I put "Being in prison" in the bottom left corner, because I thought being incarcerated would lack both pleasure and purpose. But then a friend pointed out that a truly guilty criminal might find purpose in paying their "debt to society" and look forward to living a better life once freed. Or, you can imagine a person who was *wrongly* imprisoned due to a miscarriage of justice. For example, Nelson Mandela spent 27 years in South African jails as a result of his leadership in fighting the apartheid regime. His captivity was difficult, but he knew that it was part of a greater, noble struggle. He was ultimately freed and went on to lead the new South Africa.[1]

If you find yourself doing a lot of things with low pleasure and low purpose, then I encourage you to figure out a way to stop doing them. Quit the job you hate and work hard to find a better one. If you can't leave the job, then accept this fact, and assign meaning to the work by acknowledging that you need to do it to pay your bills. (We discussed this earlier in the section, "Screw Your 'Job' — Define Your 'Calling'" in Chapter Three.)

What if you don't have a job in the first place? Being

unemployed can definitely land you in the "Low Pleasure, Low Purpose" quadrant. Not working means you don't experience the rewards of interacting with colleagues. You may get lonely as you stay at home all day long. You don't have the sense of accomplishment of working on a team, adding value, or improving your skills. You may feel the frustration of knowing that you can contribute a lot to the world, but the world does not seem to want you. You may not be able to help with your household's finances, so you worry about not pulling your own weight. Even worse, you may have the real fear of becoming homeless, which afflicted more than half a million Americans on any given night in 2017.[2]

I am fortunate to have never worried about being homeless in my life. However, I've been unemployed on many occasions, including times when my money was running out. If you find yourself in this situation, then I'd encourage you to get work — any work whatsoever — in order to start making money. This will boost your self-worth and confidence, and force you to manage your time more efficiently. Early in my career, I went from being unemployed to sweeping an acquaintance's garage floor, raising money door-to-door for the Democratic Party, selling newspaper advertising for *The San Francisco Business Times*, and selling voicemail and phone systems for a multinational corporation. Less than two years later, I was in business school at Stanford.

Getting out of bed to go to work will give you a sense of purpose. In turn, you can look for better and better jobs, stabilize your finances, and strategically think about how to do work that you love, which will be highly pleasurable and purposeful. This may take years of hard work to bring to fruition. But it's better than the alternative.

High Pleasure and Low Purpose

Moving to the upper left-hand corner of the matrix, I put "Learning to salsa dance." Salsa dancing is festive and joyous, but I must admit I'm not very good at it. (Maybe a year in Cuba would cure that!) It's very fun and sexy — but would be even more pleasurable for me if I developed my salsa skills.

Getting a great night's sleep is becoming increasingly pleasurable, as I get older and my body slows down. It's also becoming a lot more meaningful, because I better understand the importance of sleep for pretty much everything we cherish in our lives, such as health, happiness, analytical ability, creativity, and good relationships.[3]

Hearing my favorite song is wonderful — and would gain in meaning if it suddenly also reminded me of a friend.

Eating a delicious meal is packed with pleasure. In general, though, I don't find a lot of purpose in great food. Rather, the meal is the end in itself. Now, I know that there are lots of foodies who have an almost religious zeal in seeking out the best ramen truck, foie gras, or bottle of Bordeaux. (My wife is one of them, actually, and I love her for that.) In fact, I think part of the reason people become obsessed with food is to create purpose in their otherwise rather unfulfilled lives. ("Bored with your bank job? Then maybe cupcakes should be your new compulsion!") Much of the advertising we see, by the way, is there to convince us that we Gotta Have That Particular Junk Food Right Now!

Maybe I just come from a white, Midwestern American family where the food wasn't so great. (Sorry, Mom! Sorry, Nebraska!) Which might explain why I usually end up asking myself, "What's the big deal about this particular food?" Yes, I love lobster. It tastes delicious. It was hard to get when I was growing up. Most of my life I have not been able to afford it at all. And it enjoys status as a luxury food.

But does that mean that I have to eat lobster at 27 different restaurants in San Francisco, to find "the best"? Do I need to travel nationally or internationally, to find the world's *perfect* lobster?

I don't think so. Because I just don't find eating lobster to be very purposeful. Pleasurable, yes. But deeply meaningful? No.

In contrast, making spaghetti carbonara has meaning for me, because it's one of the few dishes I do well, it reminds me of my first trip to Italy with a dear friend, and it's what I used to make for my two daughters when they were little. I can make a great salad, but the meaning is not there for me — until I remind myself that healthy eating is a great way to fight cancer.

Hearing a funny joke is pleasurable — and will have more purpose if it's satirical or makes an important social or political point.

Kittens are adorable for me — and they could have even more meaning if they remind you of the kitten you had when you were a kid.

Watching your favorite sports team can be exciting, entertaining, and cathartic. It might actually have a lot of purpose for you, if you strongly identify with the team for whatever reason. I'm from Nebraska, where college football has been a key part of the state's identity for my entire life. When I watch a Nebraska football game, I feel like a little kid again — sitting next to my Dad, brothers, and sister as we cheer the Cornhuskers on to another victory.

How does travel affect you? When you travel, do you like to just rest, do yoga, and meditate all the time? Or is clubbing in Miami Beach more your style?

When I was younger, I could not imagine traveling somewhere just to stay at a club and sit on the beach all day long. I figured that there was plenty of local culture to experience, which went way beyond drinking beer and watching the surf. But as I got deeper into my career, and I became exhausted by the intensity of both working in Silicon Valley and raising children, I delighted in the simple pleasure of going to an all-inclusive resort in Mexico and chilling out for a week.

So sometimes there is not a lot of purpose — you're just hanging out at a beach in Maui. But if you return to that same beach, 20 years later, you might realize how you've grown as a person in the intervening years. That's meaningful — making sense out of the past, present, and future. Going to a little village in Ireland might not be terribly fascinating to you — unless you know that your great-grandfather was born there.

As we discussed above, you can gain a lot of happiness by having enough pleasure in your life. But if you find that your life is filled with lots of fun but not enough purpose, then I encourage you to invest more in family and friends, and to do work that is more meaningful to you.

Low Pleasure and High Purpose

This quadrant is full of activities we often call "very rewarding." You could feel motivated, determined, driven, or inspired. Studying for a big exam at school can be grueling. It's even more demanding if you have to dedicate *years* of your life to achieving some sort of milestone, such as finishing your residency to become a physician. If you did not have the burning desire to accomplish this goal — for whatever reason that is meaningful to you — you would probably give up.

I don't find changing a baby's diapers intrinsically enjoyable. But I changed a huge number of my daughters' diapers and I never really minded, because this was an act of love for them. It was very fulfilling to know that they were more comfortable because I was keeping them clean and dry. (For them, having clean diapers was very high on pleasure, but completely lacked any purpose.)

Physical exercise can be onerous for many people, especially if you are not used to it. But even some former couch potatoes find their lives transformed by sticking with a workout program, to the point where they come to enjoy it. That would then put exercise into their "High Pleasure, High Purpose" quadrant.

Doing volunteer work (as I describe in Chapter Two on Relationships) will almost always make you feel better about yourself — so it's high on the Purpose axis. It may not always be a lot of fun, though. I remember participating in "get out the vote" drives in Nevada, Virginia, and Orange County, California for the 2008, 2012, 2016 and 2018 U.S. elections. I spent my own money to get to those places from San Francisco. Most of the time, I did not get enough sleep, because I got up early. I canvassed into the night. It was hot. I was dehydrated. The neighborhoods were often dangerous. People were sometimes hostile. But they were some of the most meaningful experiences I have ever had, because I believed deeply in the candidates and causes that I supported. For the rest of my life, I can feel good about helping my person get elected (three times), and knowing that I did all I could at the time when my candidate lost (once!).

Building a successful product can be fairly purposeful, if you connect the work you do with the positive impact you're having on others. If the product is "successful" but does nothing to help people, then you'll have a lot less purpose.

Visiting a friend in the hospital can be extremely meaningful for you and for them. It might also be disturbing, frustrating, inconvenient, or depressing, so the Pleasure component might be low. Or not.

How do you apply this to your life? The next time you're

grinding away at some activity that is very low on pleasure, ask yourself why you're doing it in the first place. Then, you may concur with the French novelist Honoré de Balzac, who wrote in *Père Goriot*, "Some day you will find out that there is far more happiness in another's happiness than in your own."[4]

High Pleasure and High Purpose

This is the happiest quadrant. This is the optimal, ideal quadrant. Not everything you do will fit here, but the best things in life do: playing soccer with your kids in the backyard during a holiday barbeque, amazing sex with your long-time partner, or being "in flow" at work.

Let's start with family reunions. They could be anywhere on the matrix, really. In my family, they're reasonably fun but not incredible. (We are, after all, an Irish Catholic family from Nebraska — how fun can we actually be?) But I find reunions to have a lot of purpose, especially as we all get older, and I realize that any time I see my family might be the last.

Winning a scholarship can be a thrill, both because it saves you money and it allows you to study something you find purposeful.

Hanging out with friends can be a lot of fun. If they're old friends and you have not seen them for a long time, or you've overcome adversity in the relationship, then the purpose is even greater.

Going to Disneyland can be unforgettable — which is probably why 18.3 million people went there in 2017. [5] Like changing diapers, it's especially purposeful for the parents, and especially pleasurable for the kids. But overall, good theme parks are fun, entertaining, unique, and appealing to kids and parents alike. They make you feel like you're being a great parent by taking your kids there. This one-two punch of pleasure and purpose explains why the marketers at Disney like to call it "The Happiest Place on Earth."

I mentioned that doing physical exercise can be a "Low Pleasure, High Purpose" activity. But a wise person will establish good workout habits with the purpose of living a healthy, long life. (See Chapter Sixteen on habit-building) Each time you do yoga, go for a swim, or visit the health club, it will get easier. You will feel stronger and healthier. You will get sick less often. You will sleep more at night. Even better, as the Harvard Health Letter reports, "Improving heart health is also good for your brain."[6]

This is a wonderful, virtuous cycle!

And as the old saying goes, "When you have your health, you have everything."

It's hard to be happy if you are not in good health. Indeed, research from Dr. Nattavudh Powdthavee at the University of London tried to put a monetary value on the importance of being well. Using a technique called shadow pricing, he found "Improvement in health has one of the largest effects on life satisfaction; a move from having a very poor health to having an excellent health is worth around an extra £300,000 [roughly $389,000] a year."[7]

So vibrant health can greatly add to your happiness, through increased pleasure and purpose.

Before we go on to some of the larger philosophical dimensions of happiness and well-being, take some time to create your own matrix — it could give you a new perspective on many of the things you already do.

Writing Activity 16:
Think of all the things you do, on a regular basis. Put them into this matrix. Evaluate what is purposeful. What is pleasurable. What is both? What is neither?

THE MCCARTHY HAPPINESS MATRIX

How would you fill this out?

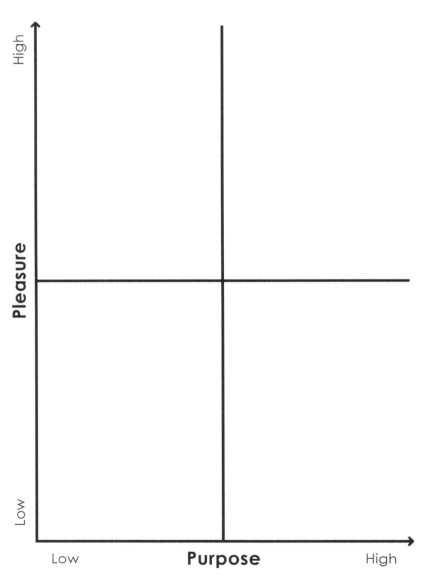

You might have a meaningful conversation with a loved one or close friend as you fill in this matrix together. There are no right or wrong answers, of course. But you can discuss with the other person *why* they would find more or less pleasure or purpose in an activity.

Feeling Awe

Marveling at nature is also one of those "best things in life." I don't even consider myself very outdoorsy, but seeing the Iguazu Falls at the intersection of Brazil, Argentina, and Paraguay was one of the most amazing experiences I've ever had — feeling the roar of hundreds of waterfalls, 20 to 30 stories high, gushing through the jungle and blasting out warm mist. I was engulfed in the enormity of our planet's glory.

Let's look more closely at "awe."

Nature's magnificence literally inspires awe. University of California, Berkeley Psychology Professor Dacher Keltner defines awe as "the feeling of being in the presence of something vast that transcends your understanding of the world."

This can come from nature, art, and individual feats or acts of great skill or virtue. [8] Walking in a redwood forest can inspire awe. So can seeing Michelangelo's "David." Or witnessing the Golden State Warriors' Steph Curry making a ridiculously long three-point shot in an NBA game. (Especially if they're beating Cleveland.)

Keltner writes that "the science of awe suggests that opportunities for awe surround us, and their benefits are profound." He cites research showing that awe increases cooperation and sacrifice for others, reduces the narcissistic instinct, increases kindness towards others, and may even boost your immune system. Perhaps best of all, one study found that people can experience awe through simply being mindful of their daily experiences.[9]

We explore this further in Chapters Twelve and Fourteen on Meditation and Gratitude later in this book.

Experiencing "Flow"

Awe fits nicely into the "High Pleasure and High Purpose" quadrant.

That same quadrant contains a similar but different experience, explained in *Flow: The Psychology of Optimal Experience* by Claremont Graduate University Psychology Professor Mihaly Csikszentmihalyi. (In case you're wondering, his name is pronounced "Me high? Cheeks send me high!") He describes "flow" as "the state in which you are so involved in an activity that nothing else seems to matter; the experience itself is so enjoyable that people will do it even at great cost, for the sheer sake of doing it."[10] You concentrate deeply, forget everything else, and lose track of yourself and time.[11] In turn, you become extremely creative and effective at achieving whatever your goal may be [12] — with your performance simply "flowing" out of you.

Dr. Csikszentmihalyi concludes, "When a person is able to organize his or her consciousness so as to experience flow as often as possible, the quality of life is inevitably going to improve, because ... even the usually boring routines of work become purposeful and enjoyable."[13]

Among the many possibilities, a person can experience flow while:

- working intensely on an important but fascinating marketing plan

- preparing for a major presentation
- coding software to develop a mobile phone app
- cooking in a restaurant kitchen at 8:00 p.m. on a busy Saturday night
- playing drums in a jam session in a Paris jazz club
- learning how to surf in Costa Rica
- having a real conversation in German for the first time after a few beers (The beers were, um, *flowing* ...)

How do you get into a flow state? Dr. Csikszentmihalyi explains that flow is the optimal combination of the challenge and your skill: "Enjoyment appears at the boundary between boredom and anxiety, when the challenges are just balanced with the person's capacity to act."[14] If your skills are low and the challenge is low (such as watching TV all day), then you'll feel apathy. If your skills are low and the challenge is high, then you'll feel anxiety and most likely give up on the task. If your skills are high but the challenge is low, then you'll feel bored. But if your skills and the challenge are commensurate, then you are in the "flow channel," which can lead to ecstasy. (I'll leave it up to you to draw another 2x2 matrix for this.)

Best of all, as you increase your skills, you can increase the challenge, so that you return again and again to the flow channel. You love what you're doing, so you get better at it. You become great at something, so you love it more.[15]

Dr. Csikszentmihalyi advises that, to be happy, you should spend as much of your life as you can in the state of flow. Fitting his theory into my Happiness Matrix, the ecstasy of flow is intrinsically pleasurable. The purpose comes from being challenged while still seeing the opportunity to get better and better. As he states, "The best moments usually occur if a person's body or mind is stretched to its limits in a voluntary effort to accomplish something difficult and worthwhile."[16]

As psychologist Gilbert Brim has said, "One of the important sources of human happiness is working on tasks at a suitable level of difficulty, neither too hard nor too easy."[17]

It turns out that people who work "in flow" generally live longer. Interviewed for the *Atlantic*, Howard S. Friedman, co-author of *The Longevity Project*, said, "Striving to accomplish your goals, setting new aims when milestones are reached, and staying engaged and productive are exactly what those heading to a long life tend to do. The long-lived didn't shy away from hard work; the exact opposite seemed true." He added, "On the other hand, if you hate your co-workers and have many job demands but inadequate resources to accomplish anything worthwhile, then it is time to look for new employment."[18]

Writing Activity 17:
When have you ever experienced "flow"? What would it take for you to spend more of your time in a flow state?

_____

_____

_____

_____

_____

_____

_____

_____

_____

_____

_____

_____

_____

_____

_____

_____

_____

In discussing this question with another, you might ask them, "When have you seen me at my happiest?" or, "What sorts of things do you think I'm absolutely great at?" It's sometimes helpful to get this outside perspective. We also discuss this in the section, "Think Long Term So You Have No Regrets."

Chapter Six:
How Much of Your Happiness Do You Really Control?

I don't want to give you the impression that adopting these techniques — life-changing though they may be — will lead you to complete, uncomplicated happiness. It's totally normal to be sad, frustrated, or disappointed from time to time. That's part of living as a human being. Overall, however, happiness is a skill you can develop.

But just how much of your happiness is within your control, anyway?

How much is *beyond* your control?

Sonja Lyubomirsky addresses this question in *The How of Happiness.* She and her fellow researchers write that "an astounding 50 percent of the differences among people's happiness levels can be accounted for by their genetically determined set points. This discovery comes from the growing research done with identical and fraternal twins that suggests that each of us is born with a particular happiness set point that originates from our biological mother or father or both, a baseline of potential for happiness to which we are bound to return, even after major setbacks or triumphs."[1]

Your happiness set point is like an anchor that doesn't let your boat stray too far. Harvard Psychology Professor Daniel Gilbert reinforces this finding, saying to *The New York Times*, "Things that happen to you or that you buy or own — as much as you think they make a difference to your happiness, you're wrong by a certain amount. You're overestimating how much of a difference they make. None of them make the difference you think. And that's true of positive and negative events."[2]

In Dr. Lyubomirsky's research, she found that in addition to 50 percent of your happiness coming from your genetic set point, just 10 percent was attributed to "circumstances" such as "whether we are rich or poor, healthy or unhealthy, beautiful or plain, married or divorced, etc."[3]

The final part — the part that you control entirely — she calls "Intentional Activity." She writes that "40 percent is that part of our happiness that [is] in our power to change through how we act and how we think, that portion representing the potential for increased lasting happiness that resides in all of us."[4]

How we act.

How we think.

How *you* act.

How *you* think.

This controls 40 percent of your happiness. It may not be 100 percent, but it's still the part you do control. It's how you play the hand you were dealt in the card game of life.

So how do you control your happiness, exactly?

That's the topic for the rest of this book!

PART THREE

Presence

Chapter Seven:
Serenity Prayer

Have you heard of the Serenity Prayer?

God, grant me the serenity
to accept the things I cannot change,
courage to change the things I can,
and the wisdom to know the difference.[1]

This prayer was originally formulated in the 1930s by Reinhold Niebuhr, an American Christian theologian who had graduated from Yale's divinity school. Later, it gained wide use by Alcoholics Anonymous and other twelve-step recovery programs and has given solace and hope to many millions of people around the world.[2]

I first read a version of the Serenity Prayer in Kurt Vonnegut's amazing novel *Slaughterhouse Five*, which deals with his witnessing of the Allies' firebombing of Dresden during World War II. Over time, as I started to recite my daily affirmations (see Chapter Thirteen), I chose to use a nonreligious version:

May I have the serenity to accept the things I cannot change,
the courage to change the things I can,
and the wisdom to know the difference.

But it was only years later, after I had created my Happiness Framework, that I reviewed the original, full text, which I present below.

God, give us grace to accept with serenity
the things that cannot be changed,
courage to change the things
which should be changed,
and the wisdom to distinguish
the one from the other.

Living one day at a time,
Enjoying one moment at a time,
Accepting hardship as a pathway to peace.
Taking, as Jesus did,
This sinful world as it is,
Not as I would have it,
Trusting that You [God] will make all things right,
If I surrender to Your will,
So that I may be reasonably happy in this life,
And supremely happy with You forever in the next.
Amen.
— Reinhold Niebuhr[3]

If you happen to be a Christian, then you might be thrilled with the full version. But the secular version of the first half should work well for you, whether you're an atheist or deeply religious or spiritual. (Remember, I have no religious agenda here at all.) I've always found the Serenity Prayer very powerful, and now I realize that it supports my Pleasure and Purpose Happiness Framework. In fact, Niebuhr literally mentions "happy"!

In the feedback form from one of my workshops, one

participant wrote, "the Serenity Prayer is passé. Can't you find something more current?"

I can understand this feeling about any well-worn saying. Yet for me it has staying power. It might be old. But so is Shakespeare. And the Quran. And the Bhagavad Gita. I really don't care how new or old it is, as long as it works well for me. I've recited the Serenity Prayer to myself every day for decades. I've found its wisdom not just comforting, but also practical and emboldening. Its message has given me courage to press onward when I failed to get jobs I wanted, was fired from work, got cancer, went through a tough divorce, or lost a lot of money through bad investments. It's helped me deal with something as small as the frustration of missing an airline flight, and with something as enormous as the 9/11 attacks.

A friend of mine who was experiencing anxiety attacks sought mental health treatment through Kaiser Permanente, one of the largest health care plans in the U.S. What did I see, printed at the top of the course materials, on how to reduce stress? The Serenity Prayer!

The Serenity Prayer is a great framework for the lessons in the rest of this book. It speaks to living fully, deeply, and richly in the present moment. Next, let's explore various ways to live with more presence.

Chapter Eight:
Beware the Comparing Mind

"CAMDEN, ME—Longtime acquaintances confirmed to reporters this week that local man Michael Husmer, an unambitious 29-year-old loser who leads an enjoyable and fulfilling life, still lives in his hometown and has no desire to leave." The article goes on to mock this content person, because he is "perfectly comfortable being a nobody for the rest of his life."[1]

I love this satire from *The Onion*, because it highlights how some people compare themselves to others and look down on those who might be totally happy, but not very ambitious.

On the other hand, many people compare themselves to very "successful" people. Do you compare yourself to Mark Zuckerberg, Michelle Obama, or Steve Jobs? Does doing so bring you happiness?

Most people compare themselves to others. All the time. It's totally ingrained in how we go through life. Buddhist teachers such as Jack Kornfield call this "the Comparing Mind." This is very similar to the American saying, "keeping up with the Joneses" — making sure that our house, car, education, career, power, image, smartphone, clothes, vacations, food, music, spouse, golf clubs, pets, children, cocktails, health, and handbags are at least as good as those of our neighbors. And in übercompetitive Silicon Valley, the Comparing Mind is everywhere.

You may feel frustrated when you look around and it seems like everyone else is "doing better" than you are — however you might define that. But research indicates that even comparing yourself to others who are "doing worse" than you can have negative effects. Psychologists Robert Emmons from the University of California, Davis, and Michael McCullough from the University of Miami have studied the benefits of gratitude. In a discussion of research on the subject, they say: "Because of its potential for eliciting pride and/or envy ... we cannot recommend downward social comparison [comparing to those apparently less fortunate than you] as a general strategy for inducing feelings of gratitude when more direct routes are available. Downward social comparisons have also been shown to have negative implications for the self and to lead to negative affect."[2]

People tend to compare on things an outsider can easily observe. About 95 percent of all postings on Facebook address the sorts of things we love to compare!

But in a *Time* magazine poll, 60 percent of respondents said they do not feel better about themselves after spending time on social media.[3] A 2017 poll of teens and young adults in the U.K. gave negative marks to YouTube, Twitter, Facebook, Snapchat, and Instagram for their impact on sleep quality, bullying, body image, and "fear of missing out," or FOMO. All of the social media outlets except YouTube increased depression and anxiety.[4]

No surprise here — your Facebook friends most likely share their lives' highlights, not the lowlights. For example, after my separation, when I was newly single, I was very careful not to post anything on Facebook at 10:00 p.m. on a Saturday night, lest people realize that I was lonely at home at that time. Some time later, however, I made sure that all my Facebook friends saw when I was dancing the samba in Rio de Janeiro.

Why Don't Comparisons Bring Happiness?

"Keeping up with the Joneses" is a great recipe for unhappiness, no matter how hard you try to manage your "personal brand" to show off your fun life. It's not that trying to keep up is ethically or morally wrong — it just won't bring you happiness. If you choose to play the comparison game, you're choosing a game that you will always lose, as long as you play it long enough — which most of us do.

You will keep "raising the bar" for your comparison group. As USC economist Richard A. Easterlin explains, "When people think about the effect of having more money, they implicitly assume that their own income increases while everyone else's stays the same, and hence conclude that they'll be happier. What actually happens, of course, is that when their own income increases, so too does that of everyone else."[5]

The comparisons you're making are probably not even fair to yourself. I'm guilty of this as well — I don't compare myself to my classmates from high school in Nebraska or college in Iowa. Or even the people I studied with at business school. No, I tend to compare myself to some of the most successful people who've ever attended Stanford's business school. (Though to be really fair to myself, I *am* satisfied with my career.) Yes, amazingly successful businesspeople do exist, and I know seven billionaires personally, but it's silly for me to feel inadequate because I have not created a global company worth billions.

It's hard to compare on the criteria that really matter. If you're going to compare yourself to someone else, at least compare on matters such as:

Is this person a "good human being"?

Are they happy?

Are they a loving spouse/parent/sibling/son or daughter?

Are they ethical in their business practices?

Is the world a better place because they are here?

It's very hard for one person to be able to make any sort of fair judgment on another person, anyway, precisely because we don't know the other person's journey. Can you really know for sure that your next-door neighbor is a good mother? How would you possibly gain enough information to make such a judgment?

The Comparing Mind is futile. The judging mind is, too.

Why Is It Hard to Avoid "the Comparing Mind"?

For most people, life is full of real and intense competition. This starts in our educational systems, where students are often "graded on a curve." Later, in the workforce, managers have to compare multiple people vying for a promotion and decide who gets the better job. There are real consequences to determining who gets hired, who can afford the condo, who gets to buy the fancy convertible. And whose company succeeds or goes bust.

Heroes, leaders, and role models often inspire us with their amazing courage, skill, dedication, and luck. You become motivated and say to yourself, "If she can do it, so can I!" That's great, but don't let this other person become your obsession. Instead, find your own truth, on your own path. After all, even though Mark Zuckerberg set out to become Bill Gates, he ended up becoming Mark Zuckerberg![6]

Our popular culture encourages it. I have worked in a wide variety of advertising roles, ranging from video production in Spain in 1990 to mobile advertising at a Silicon Valley start-up in 2012. I can say with confidence that almost all advertising is designed to make us feel inadequate. *The New York Times* cites research indicating that we are bombarded every day with up to 5,000 advertising messages — all of which encourage us to have a Comparing Mind.[7] Or, to put it another way, advertising follows the adage I learned doing sales, long ago: "Make the customer sick, and then sell them medicine." So the more ads you see, the more you have the Comparing Mind, the more inadequate you feel, and the more you consume.

But consumption will not bring you more happiness. At least, not for long.

Do you think you have the Comparing Mind? Answer these questions to notice how your mind and emotions work:

Writing Activity 18

Who do you compare yourself to, either in your career or your personal life?

How long have you been comparing yourself to these people? Why do you compare yourself to these people, and not somebody else?

Are you "winning" the competition? According to what criteria? How would you know? When would you know? Is it even possible to win?

How do these comparisons make you feel? Are they making your life better? Or worse?

_____

_____

_____

_____

_____

_____

_____

_____

_____

_____

_____

_____

_____

It's fun to compare your "Comparing Mind" questions with someone else. If you happen to compare yourself to a trusted friend, then you might even reach out to them and say, "Hey, you might find this funny, but I often compare myself to you, because I think you're so good at X." They might be flattered by your comment, explain that they worked hard at their skill, or admit that they're not nearly as talented as they look. They might share tips with you on how you can achieve at this level, too. And they'll probably remind you of some wonderful ability that you have that you take for granted.

An Alternative Path

Don't let comparisons get you down. In contrast, here are a few other ways to journey through life, with a different mindset to serve you better:

Be grateful for both the people and things in your life, instead of obsessing over those who have more material things than you. As part of your daily routine, spend one minute every day writing yourself an email entitled, "I am grateful today for …" This practice is simple yet powerful. While you're at it, every day tell the people you love one thing that you appreciate about them. "Honey, I'm grateful you cooked dinner," or, "Sweetie, thanks for taking out the trash," are fine ways to start. We go into detail on this in Chapter Fourteen on Gratitude.

Recognize what money can and can't buy. As Bruce Springsteen wisely said in an interview long ago, "If you're makin' more than $500 a night, you're gonna have more than $500 problems." [8] The next time you are presented with the opportunity to make some sort of sacrifice of family time or friends time in order to make more money, ask yourself if this is getting you what you really want. We address this in Chapter Three on Work.

Learn from wonderful, inspiring role models and heroes. Celebrate Oprah Winfrey, Warren Buffett, Mother Teresa, Richard Branson, or whoever you choose. And apply their lessons to your life. But don't beat up on yourself if you have not yet achieved their levels of success. As far as I can tell, none of them is or was perfect, either!

Simply pay attention to how you feel when you're exposed to advertising — online, in print, on the radio and TV, on billboards, on product packaging, walking through the mall, etc. And realize that you can be perfectly at peace the way you already are, rather than having to strive for some "ideal," as envisioned by an ad agency. Madison Avenue has never made a lot of money by telling people, "You are fine."

We discuss the skill of paying attention in Chapter Twelve on Meditation.

If you incorporate these simple practices into your everyday life, you'll go a long way toward avoiding the Comparing Mind and living your unique life as only you can define it.

Writing Activity 19:

Compare who you were at the end of high school to who you are today. How have you changed?

Consider your development professionally, financially, socially, physically, emotionally, and spiritually/philosophically.

_____

_____

_____

_____

_____

_____

_____

_____

_____

_____

_____

_____

_____

_____

This writing activity is a nice excuse for you to reach out to high school friends. If you're still in regular contact with them, then they can easily compare the "you" that they know today to the "you" that they knew in high school. If you reach out to someone with whom you have not spoken for 20 years, you might be amazed at how they remember you. Sometimes we forget who we were then, and how far we've come.

My hope is that after doing this writing activity — comparing yourself only to your prior self — you will feel good about the progress you've made.

Hope That the Comparing Mind Lessens with Age

In late 2016 I attended my 20-year business school reunion. It was a tremendous experience, in part because I was honored to give a 15-minute TED-style talk to my classmates, entitled, "Live AS IF You Had Cancer."

At the reunion, I noticed a few major themes:

Conversations tended to focus a lot less on money, career,

and status, and a lot more on family, friends, and health as this group was heading for middle age. One classmate had been infected with a flesh-eating virus, contracted through oral surgery, which had almost killed him. Another seemed to be in great health — and nonetheless had had a severe stroke, which paralyzed half of his body for a year. And a third had had seven surgeries and 39 rounds of chemotherapy to fight colon cancer.

Several (including me) had gone through tough divorces — or were in the process of separating. Some had the courage to say they had faced severe depression. Others had realized that they were queer, and decided to leave their straight marriages.

People had gotten nicer. Or maybe I'd become less judgmental. At the reunion I had lots of wonderful, kind conversations with people I hardly knew before. It felt very comforting to be able to make completely new friends with people I'd known for 22 years, yet never really took the time to connect with.

Then there were the people I used to think of fairly negatively. In contrast to prior reunions, I did not try to avoid them. And in many cases, I had delightful, sincere conversations with them about personal issues. I can try to tell myself that these other people have changed for the better. But much more likely, I'm more self-loving and self-forgiving than before, which makes it a lot easier for me to accept and honor others. My perception of "the world" — it seems — is really just a mirror of who I am, right now.

Careers are unpredictable. I met up with people who had always been very low-key, but who were quietly able to start multiple companies that had been successfully acquired. I also recall the people who were flying high in their careers 10 years earlier, but were then wiped out in the Great Recession. Some who used to be quite arrogant had been humbled. (I liked them a lot more this way!)

Several classmates had completely changed their careers.

One went on to get a degree in psychiatry and now helps people in prisons in Massachusetts. One helped repeal the U.S. military's "Don't ask, don't tell" policy, had a successful career in finance, and now works as a psychologist in San Francisco. And one later studied theology at Harvard and now teaches mindfulness and improvisation.

Others had been successful entrepreneurs who are now using their wealth, time, and energy to work for nonprofits. Some were full-time homemakers.

Despite all that they had accomplished — or *not* accomplished — many members of the Stanford Graduate School of Business Class of 1996 were still trying to figure out what they'd write in the next chapters of their lives. I felt hopeful that whatever they wrote, it would be based on living up to their own true potential, rather than trying to outcompete their classmates.

Writing Activity 20:

Think about the people you work with right now, or the people from your latest work. Now imagine you're meeting them again, at a reunion, 20 years from now. What would you like to say about yourself?

What do you want to be true about the work you've done, between now and then? And why?

_____

_____

_____

_____

_____

_____

_____

_____

_____

_____

_____

_____

If you have a trusted friendship with any work colleagues, go ahead and ask them this question. You may find that they have a completely different set of career goals and life expectations than you do.

Chapter Nine:
Enjoy the Journey

The "I'll Be Happy Only When ..." Syndrome

I remember working very hard for a Silicon Valley start-up. One day I heard the founder/CEO say in exasperation, "I'll be happy only when we go public!" That was clearly the goal for everyone in the company — having an initial public offering, or IPO, would be a major achievement — and all of us early employees would stand to make millions of dollars.

There's nothing wrong with having goals and working hard to accomplish them. In fact, as we discuss in Chapter Three on Work, engaging with something that gives you purpose is a key element of happiness. But problems begin when we lead our lives under the never-ending assumption that "success," "happiness," or "peace" are states of being that can be reached only once we overcome all our current obstacles, after which life is suddenly perfect. Along the way, we act as if this state of contentment cannot be here and now, but rather sometime in the future.

You can call this the "I'll Be Happy Only When" Syndrome. Here's what it might look like at various stages in a person's career:

I'll be happy only when I get out of high school.

I'll be happy only when I get good grades on my college admissions exams.

I'll be happy only when I get into a top university.

I'll be happy only when I graduate from that top university.

I'll be happy only when I get a fantastic job after college.

I'll be happy only when I pay off my student loans.

I'll be happy only when I get promoted to manager at that great job.

I'll be happy only when I earn $100,000 per year.

I'll be happy only when I get promoted to director at that job.

I'll be happy only when I switch companies and leave that job I hate.

I'll be happy only when I earn $200,000 per year.

I'll be happy only when I save $1,000,000 for my retirement.

I'll be happy only when I retire.

I'll be happy only when I figure out what hobbies I should have in my retirement.

In parallel, this syndrome can take many forms in someone's personal life:

I'll be happy only when I have a boyfriend/girlfriend in high school.

I'll be happy only when I have a boyfriend/girlfriend in college.

I'll be happy only when I lose my virginity. (This could happen at many different stages in one's life ... but only once, as far as I can tell!)

I'll be happy only when I get engaged.

I'll be happy only when I get married.

I'll be happy only when we have our first child.

I'll be happy only when we have our second child.

I'll be happy only when our kids get into an outstanding kindergarten/ grade school/high school/college/graduate school/postdoctoral program in astrophysics at Princeton.

I'll be happy only when all of the kids are out of the house.

I'll be happy only when I get a divorce.
I'll be happy only when the child custody issue is resolved.
I'll be happy only when I get remarried.
I'll be happy only when I get a divorce again.
I'll be happy only when I undergo my gender transition.

Those are examples of major life events. But this syndrome can plague our daily lives as well:

I'll be happy only when tax season is over.
I'll be happy only when the Golden State Warriors win the NBA championship again.
I'll be happy only when this out-of-town visitor is gone.
I'll be happy only when we finalize plans for our upcoming vacation.
I'll be happy only when we get better marketing materials for our product.
I'll be happy only when that stupid colleague of mine switches departments.
I'll be happy only when the stock market goes up.
I'll be happy only when it stops raining.

You may be waiting a long time.

Impact Bias and Hedonic Adaptation

The "I'll Be Happy Only When" Syndrome means that you think your life will be way better once a certain desired event takes place. Psychologists Daniel Gilbert from Harvard and Tim Wilson from the University of Virginia call this phenomenon "impact bias." As described in *The New York Times*, the research means that "Yes, we will adapt to the BMW and the plasma TV, since we adapt to virtually everything. But Wilson and Gilbert and others have shown that we seem unable to predict that we will adapt. Thus, when we find the pleasure derived from a thing diminishing, we move on to the next thing or event and almost certainly make another error of prediction, and then another, ad infinitum."[1]

If you're like many people, it's normal that you study hard and work hard in your career, so that you can afford basic necessities and buy useful things. For your transportation, if using your feet, scooters, bikes, buses, trains, or ride-sharing isn't good enough for you, then you'll probably end up buying a car. At first, you're thrilled to have that new car. But over time, you get used to that car, your passion dissipates, and you take it for granted.

If you're a typical human being, then you will set your sights on some new object of desire. You work to be financially successful enough to buy your own home. But eventually that dream home will just become a place to live. I remember buying a beautiful new house in Cupertino, California, in 2001, never imagining that I could ever be unhappy living in that home. About seven years later, I was moving out of that home when I decided to end my marriage. That lovely house did not save my marriage, and it did not maintain my happiness, either. (It was, however, a source of great disagreement in the divorce proceedings!)

Scientists describe the phenomenon of getting used to nice things as "hedonic adaptation." Speaking to *The New York Times*, Carnegie Mellon University economist George Loewenstein characterizes this human tendency as follows: "Happiness is a signal that our brains use to motivate us to do certain things. And in the same way that our eye adapts to different levels of illumination, we're designed to kind of go back to the happiness set point. Our brains are not trying to be happy. Our brains are trying to regulate us."[2]

Psychology Professor Sonja Lyubomirsky writes in *The How*

of Happiness that hedonic adaptation occurs because of rising aspirations and social comparisons.[3] As we continue with material successes in life, we keep raising the bar to even higher success. And we tend to surround ourselves with people who are successful like us — with even more successful people closely within sight.

Long-term research confirms that this behavior does not bring happiness. University of Southern California economist Richard A. Easterlin asks us to "Consider, for example, Americans born in the 1940s. Between the years 1972 and 2000, as their average age increased from about 26 to 54 years, their average income per person — adjusted for the change in the price of goods and services — more than doubled, increasing by 116 percent. Yet, their reported happiness in the year 2000 was no different from that 28 years earlier. They had a lot more money and a considerably higher standard of living at the later date, but this did not make them feel any happier."[4]

Writing Activity 21:
Even if you got everything you desired in Writing Activity 14, how much happier do you think you would become? How long would that last?

This question forces you to imagine your dreams coming true. Visualizing that might be exciting. Or actually scary. Or both. Could you imagine one day adapting to the point where all your highest aspirations become reality — and you find it totally normal and boring?

Wouldn't that be sad, and pretty absurd? What can we do to prevent this from happening?

Instead, Enjoy Your Journey

How do you break the cycle of impact bias and hedonic adaptation? First, you need to recognize when it happens. You need to notice every time you say something like, "I'll be happy only when …" You need to stop and consider that it is possible to be quite content *even before* that certain special thing happens. One of my daily affirmations is, "All I need for a peaceful, fulfilling life is to have a peaceful, fulfilling now." It's simple, practical, and comforting.

Enjoying your journey should be one of your major life strategies. It's the Pleasure part of my Happiness Framework. (See Chapter Four.)

If this is not your focus, then you run a huge risk of never really learning how to savor this present moment — no matter how imperfect it may be, or how much better you think "things will be in the future."

For example, I have a friend whose father worked for many years running a successful family business in Boston. Although the family was quite affluent, the father kept putting off retirement. Finally, he sold the business and moved with his wife to Florida. Sadly, within just months of the move, he suffered a massive stroke, disabling half of his body. His devoted wife helped with his care, but he was never the same. He suffered more strokes, and died 10 years into his retirement.

I know that my friend's family found these events challenging — but they also grew in commitment and love for each other. Nevertheless, I could not help but observe the situation, and think, "Gosh! I wish the dad had quit working sooner, so he could have enjoyed his retirement more."

I want *you* to think about the choices you have, right now, to enjoy your journey — or else risk falling for the illusion that everything will be resolved ... some day.

If you need a more vivid example, I'll remind you that there is no guarantee that you'll have *any* future, let alone a perfect one. After all, how long can you be certain that your life will continue? I was wondering about this one day, and concluded that I could really only count on being alive for another five to 10 seconds. I live in California, so a deadly earthquake could happen at any moment.

What, you don't live in an earthquake zone? There are still tornadoes, floods, hurricanes, terrorist attacks, and random assault rifle shootings in public places throughout the United States of America. As I look outside the window right now, San Francisco is choking from a dense layer of smoke from wildfires. The most likely cause of death for most Americans, during most of their lives, is automobile accidents. (Some people have a "fear of flying," but it's more logical to have a "fear of riding.") As you get older, heart attacks and strokes can take your life very quickly.

I'm not trying to freak you out or render you paralyzed in fear. Instead, just as we discussed in the section on "Imagine Your Death Day" (Chapter One), I want you to appreciate that you're mortal — and that no one knows how much, or how little, time they have. But even if you live for another 90 years, I'd like you to *enjoy* those 90 years.

As the great French philosopher Albert Camus advised, "Real generosity towards the future lies in giving all to the present."[5]

What Is "Stress," Anyway?

What is the opposite of Camus's recommendation to "give all to the present"?

It's when you are hung up on what has already happened, or freaked out about what might happen. When you think this way, you feel stress.

Ah yes … our faithful companion, "stress." We could address this in the chapter on Relationships — because all sorts of relationships can be stressful, right? We can discuss stress in the Work chapter — because work is a huge source of stress for many of us. Indeed, Stanford Professor Jeffrey Pfeffer, who wrote the book *Dying for a Paycheck*, has said, "I look out at the workplace and I see stress, layoffs, longer hours, work-family conflict, enormous amounts of economic insecurity. I see a workplace that has become shockingly inhumane."[6]

It helps to think about stress with regard to how present we are … or *aren't*. Stress is driven by our relationship to events in the past, right now, and the future.

The past. This came before. It is finished. There is nothing you can do to change it if you wanted to. Nothing you can do to change what happened in 1998. Nothing you can do to change what happened 98 seconds ago, either. By definition, it has passed.

Even so, the past affects who you are today, and while you can't go back and change it, how you think about it is important. Here are some possibilities:

Recalling events positively: with pride, satisfaction, or gratitude for what happened. Maybe you overcame adversity, conquered a huge challenge, or received tremendous love from others. This is a productive way to think about the past, because it reinforces your self-image as the hero of your life journey. You can think to yourself, "Wow, I've had tough problems to solve before, and I overcame them. I can do it again. Nothing succeeds like success!"

Looking back longingly: with nostalgia. Wishing that you could go back to the "Good Old Days." This outlook is less constructive, because it refuses to accept that things in life do change. You may also be overestimating the "good stuff" from the past and forgetting that there was plenty of "bad stuff" going on as well. Be aware of this as you do the Writing Activities in this book.

What's more, you may be filling yourself with sadness, when instead you could think, "Well, at least I was lucky to experience that, if even just once in my life." There are times when I feel nostalgic for my days at Yahoo, around 1999. I got to work with smart, motivated, fun, funky, relaxed, creative people at the leading global company in a bleeding-edge, important industry. And I was getting paid a lot. On the one hand, I'm sorry that none of my other jobs since then has been able to compare. On the other hand, I'm grateful that I was able to have that remarkable experience — even once.

Seeing things regretfully: with sorrow for events that happened to you, many of which might have been totally out of your control. For what you *did* control, you may be disappointed about things you did or did *not* do. What's a helpful way to come to terms with these emotions?

If you have a regret about the past, and you can still act on that regret, then I suggest that it's better late than never. For example, let's say you wish you had started learning to play the guitar when you were eight years old. For whatever reason, it did not happen. So would you *still* like to learn to play the guitar? Regardless of your age right now, why don't you pursue this desire? For the things you do control — either make them happen or accept that you can't make them happen.

Regret does not have to be worthless. This emotion can be used for learning, growth, focus, and inspiration. You can look back at your setbacks and use them as motivation to get better. I have made many mistakes in my life, but each time I try to learn my lesson and apply it going forward. In this way, I never feel like my mistakes were a "waste of time."

Do you spend a lot of energy dwelling on the past? Many

people do. I encourage you to use the recommendations above to think about the past in a more constructive way, so that you can enjoy the present moment more.

Right now. You have a lot of control over this. It's not perfect control — if you walk outdoors and it's 103 degrees, you will sweat. Or, as another example, you are subject to the laws of any country you live in, more or less, sooner or later. But you actually have a lot of say regarding whether you get out of bed in the morning, eat or not, work or not, interact with others or not. You have a lot of freedom to do what you want … as long as you understand there will be consequences for what you do.

As for the old saying about the certainty of death and taxes, you actually don't even have to pay taxes! Just be aware that you will probably end up in jail if you refuse to pay. (Alas, death still remains certain.)

Living in the "right now" is a great place to be. Recall the study from the chapter on Pleasure, in which Harvard researcher Matt Killingsworth found that we are happiest when we stay in the present moment. [7]

You feel like admiring the passing clouds? Do it now.

You feel like enjoying a sip of tea? Do it now.

You feel like giving your partner a big, long hug, and saying "I love you, darling"? Do it now.

Many of the exercises and practices in this book are aimed at helping you savor right now.

The future. You might be the sort who obsesses over the future. But, in fact, it does not exist yet. The future *never* exists. It only reveals and manifests itself in the right now, one little moment at a time. There are fundamental ways to think about the future:

Optimistically: You can look forward to things. During the college football season, I anticipate the next time that Stanford or Nebraska play. You can get excited as you plan your next vacation — even get thrilled as you look online at restaurant options. This can feel wonderful. The Germans even have a saying, *"Vorfreude ist die schönste Freude"* (say that five times fast), which can be translated as "anticipation is the greatest joy." But if you spend all your attention on whatever's in the future, and don't know how to savor the present, then you're guilty of the "I'll Be Happy Only When" Syndrome, which we discussed earlier.

Pragmatically: The future may never really exist, but ignoring it will make right now more difficult. It's hard to pass tests in school if you never study. It's hard to work long term for anything if you're solely focused on whatever you feel like doing right now. My Happiness Framework is based in part on balancing the pleasure in the now versus working for something with purpose, even if you don't achieve that goal until far in the future.

Anxiously: This is when we envision negative outcomes.

For events that are *likely* to happen, you can fear the worst scenarios playing out. In those cases, you need to simply do the best you can to get the best results. Yes, you might have to declare bankruptcy and lose your home. I know people who had to go through that. It was very hard for them, but eventually they came out on the other side, stronger than ever.

For events that are *not likely* to happen, you may still worry about worst-case scenarios — no matter how unlikely. This becomes unreasonable, paranoid, or neurotic. Is it possible that the plane you're flying on is going to crash? Yes. Is it *probable*? Not at all. In fact, you're extraordinarily safer flying in that plane than driving in a car to the airport.[8]

To address any unnecessary anxiety you have, I refer you to this wisdom, often attributed to Mark Twain: "I am an old man and have known a great many troubles, but most of them never happened." [9]

I try to encapsulate my stress-reduction approach with this affirmation: "I learn from the past. I fully enjoy the present. I do the best that I can. And I let it be."

A Bucket List for Mindfulness

Do you have a "bucket list"? A lot of people maintain lists of things they want to do, be, or experience before they die. Many people have unwritten "bucket lists" in the back of their minds: "I'd like to start my own company." "I'd like to do a triathlon." "I'd like to see Venice someday." I'm lucky to have traveled the world, and have had a varied career, so I've enjoyed a lot of fun, fulfilling experiences, long before I heard the term "bucket list."

I have mixed feelings about these lists. On the one hand, I like the idea of setting goals for things that are important to you, and then figuring out how to accomplish those goals. A goal can be purposeful, such as volunteering for a political campaign to help someone you admire get elected. Or the goal can be for something pleasurable, such as swimming with dolphins in Mexico.

On the other hand, I detest when people do things so superficially that the activity hardly "counts" at all. For example, I once made great efforts to help someone see a European cathedral, just to have him walk out after two minutes because he only needed 120 seconds to "do" the cathedral.

My belief is that your life will be richer and more meaningful if you slow down enough to pay attention and savor your experience. (We mention this in Chapter Fourteen on Gratitude, when we discuss how to move events from short-term memory to long-term memory.) In fact, many of us are so busy multitasking and racing around experiencing things that we really shortchange ourselves of the beauty of the present moment.

For instance, have you ever hiked a long distance to get to the top of a mountain, and once you're at the top, you immediately start thinking about your ride back home? Or you're on vacation in Montreal, but you're already talking about your next trip to New Orleans? Or you're watching an expensive Broadway musical but worrying about the next day's trip to the Statue of Liberty?

These are problems that arise when we are not being "mindful" or aware of the present moment. (Chapter Twelve on Meditation offers excellent ways to develop your ability to be present.)

I'm reminded of the saying, "The purpose is not to fit more years into your life, but to fit more life into your years." At first glance, I can interpret this quote to mean, "Go ahead! Do more stuff! Don't just do the same thing! Live life intensely."

OK, that's a great approach. But then, you can imagine that, taken to an extreme, a person following this suggestion is just running around, striving to "do" their bucket list, while not really slowing down to enjoy any of it. The rise of social media has made this insanity even worse, as people experience life more as an efficient photo shoot than as ... well ... *life*!

As an alternative, you can interpret the quote to mean, "Stop racing and start living! No matter how long you live, you'll be a lot happier and more successful if you savor each hour of each day — whether you're visiting a city on your bucket list, sitting at home listening to music, or just reading a good book."

If you can't learn how to enjoy the simplest of daily pleasures, then extraordinary experiences probably won't have much positive impact on you either. Instead, why not create a bucket list of the day — "a bucket list *du jour*," if you will. A daily bucket list for mindfulness. That list might look like this:

- I notice many variations of smells and savor the ones I like.
- I smell and taste the food I eat while consciously putting words to the flavors and textures.
- I smell and taste the liquids that I drink, giving them the same attention I would if I were at a luxurious wine-tasting event.
- I recognize the beauty of colors, shapes, and patterns throughout the day — orange and turquoise, curved and straight, plaid and polka dot, leopard skin and lavender.
- I appreciate my sense of touch of things warm, cool, cold, hot, rough, smooth, soft, fuzzy, prickly, squishy, shallow, or deep.
- I notice all the varieties of sounds — espresso machines, barking dogs, rustling leaves, pounding drums, TV commercials, and the voices of people talking to me.
- I marvel at my bodily sensations and my ability to move and feel gravity.
- I notice the eye color of those who are speaking with me.
- I pay attention to whether someone I see looks happy, sad, or any other emotion. I attempt to put their emotion into words.
- I seek opportunities to be compassionate to others — by word, or action, or thought.
- I laugh.

Writing Activity 22:
What is your bucket list for mindfulness, just for today?

_____

_____

_____

_____

_____

_____

_____

_____

_____

_____

Go ahead and create your "racing all over the world" bucket list, if you insist. But make sure you practice your daily mindfulness bucket list as well — so that you can live each day. Rick Hanson, the Bay Area psychologist and author, likes to quote a Tibetan saying: "If you take care of the minutes, the years will take care of themselves."[10]

You Can Have It All — Just Not at the Same Time

Are you impatient? My mom will be the first to tell you that I'm quite impatient. My wife would concur. Impatience seems to be a key aspect of the "I'll Be Happy Only When" Syndrome. No matter how great our current situation is, and no matter how much better it is now than it was before, we tend to want to hurry up and get on to the newer, better situation. It's OK to want to improve, but if we can't even enjoy how good life is right now, then we'll simply rush to get to our new life — and not appreciate *that* once we get there, either.

Mahatma Gandhi is believed to have cautioned, "There is more to life than simply increasing its speed." To remedy this tendency to rush through life, the advice I like to give is, "You can have it all — just not at the same time."

Yes, you can work 90 hours per week to create a venture-capital-backed Silicon Valley start-up, which might even be successful and help a lot of customers.

And you can also have a superb diet, exercise a lot, run a half-marathon, get a lot of sleep, and take great care of your health.

You can be a wonderful, caring, giving, loving, highly involved parent.

You can have excellent relationships with your parents, siblings, and extended family, while also having a delightful circle of friends and an amazing social life.

You can lead a "book of the month" club, volunteer for political activist groups, help your university's alumni network, and mentor those less fortunate than you.

In fact, if you simply look at your social media accounts, you probably know various people who seem to be doing all of these things — and more! But in reality, I don't believe anybody can do *all* of these things at the *same* time.

It's not lazy or defeatist to simply recognize certain constraints of time and space. Don't beat yourself up for not being able to "do it all." Yes, there was a phase in my life when I worked extremely long hours — but at the expense of my relationships. Later I got married and had my first daughter, so I cut back dramatically on my work hours, and then was a stay-at-home dad for a year. I'm glad that I made this choice — even though it slowed my career advancement. After my divorce, I was working long hours again — but to the detriment of my physical and emotional well-being. These days, my priority is taking care of my health and having a successful marriage and family life. Those things are a higher priority than working as much as I can to earn as much as I can, as fast as I can.

You might think that others are smarter than you. Or harder working. Or more creative. Or more dedicated. Or simply better qualified. But as I discuss in the chapter on the "Comparing Mind," ultimately you just need to ask yourself if you're doing your best, according to your own unique gifts.

Women especially may benefit from this approach. *In Lean In: Women, Work, and the Will to Lead*, Facebook executive Sheryl Sandberg urges women to take a more proactive role in their careers. But even then, she writes, "Trying to do it all and expecting that it all can be done exactly right is a recipe for disappointment. Perfection is the enemy. Gloria Steinem said it best: 'You can't do it all. No one can have two full-time jobs, have perfect children and cook three meals and be multi-orgasmic 'til dawn ... Superwoman is the adversary of the women's movement.'"[11]

If you actually can "do it all," and you're happy while doing it, then I'm happy for you. Otherwise, you can make more conscious decisions about your priorities. Your approach can be that described by business author Stephen R. Covey and others in the book *First Things First:* "Doing more things faster is no substitute for doing the right things."[12]

Live today fully. Tomorrow, too. Who you were 10 years ago is different from who you are today, or who you will be 10 years from now. Show respect and compassion for the greatness that you are, each day.

Live each day.

When you do that, you can feel better about yourself, even if you're not a superhero. (Though you might play one on social media.)

Looking Backwards and Forwards

The challenges of life are never fully resolved. No doubt, you have met many challenges so far. And you will have to encounter, address, and struggle with many more — "successfully" or "unsuccessfully." The outcomes will be good, bad, or mixed. (For more on that, make sure to read the Chapter on Equanimity.) Sometimes you will solve one problem, which directly leads to another. Other times, you have challenges that are particular to your age and stage in life.

This writing activity helps you evaluate how certain challenges arrive at different seasons in your journey:

Writing Activity 23:
Thinking back upon your life, what challenges did you face when you were 15? When you were 20? 25? 30? (Keep going in five-year increments until you get to your current age.)

_____

_____

_____

_____

_____

_____

_____

_____

_____

_____

_____

_____

In my master classes, I love to ask this question. When I ask people to think back to when they were 15 years old, they might think back with nostalgia and fondness for that time. But if someone had asked you *back then* whether you were loving your high school years, most likely you would have said something like, "I'll be happy only when I graduate."

Age 20 is not exactly perfect either. Yes, you've survived high school. But if you're in college, your academic performance is way more important than it was in high school. If you're already working full time, then that is a huge adjustment. Either way, you may also be in your first serious romantic relationship — which usually ends for one reason or another. Once again, if I ask you today to think back to when you were age 20, you might be filled with longing for those years. But at the time, you were probably quite worried, and looking forward to the great life you were going to have "once I graduate and get a job."

Age 25 can be hard. And amazing, too. Same with 30. Same with 40.

If you notice this pattern, then it's easier to look at your current age — whatever it is — and see the beauty of your here and now.

Now let's try to look into the future.

Writing Activity 24:

What major challenges do you think you'll have in your life five years from now? Ten years from now? 20? 30? 50? 70? 90?

_____

_____

_____

_____

_____

_____

_____

_____

_____

_____

_____

_____

_____

_____

_____

_____

The purpose of this activity is to help you understand that you will certainly have challenges in the future.

I recall doing my Happiness Workshop for the Stanford Graduate School of Business Alumni Chapter in beautiful La Jolla, California. We were meeting in the offices of a respected law firm. The founder of the firm attended. He was 83 years old and considered to be hugely successful and influential. Let's call him Mr. Jones.

As I discussed the topic of life's constant challenges, I asked Mr. Jones, "Do you still have challenges in your life?"

"Hell, yes!" he said. Maybe he did not worry about money anymore. Or his career. Or where he was going to live. But he easily could have had health challenges. Or family concerns. Or something that no one would guess based on surface impressions. The problems of an 83-year-old are very different from the problems of a 25-year-old.

As you imagine your challenges in the future, you can anticipate that some are the same ones you have right now. And others you can easily predict, such as the loss of friends and family, or declining health. For example, I rejoice that I have excellent health and mobility, but if I live long enough, both will dissipate.

This is a wonderful question to share with your parents, aunts, uncles, or older friends. You can simply ask them, "What's the hardest thing about being 82?" The next time I talk to my mom, I'm going to ask her. Right now, I really don't know what she would answer. But I'd like to know.

You see, you will *always* have challenges in your life. No matter how hard you plan, there will be situations that cause you heartache. But with awareness, you can recognize and accept when they happen, and realize that difficulties are an unavoidable part of life. This is something that the Buddha came to understand through his own journey, and his teachings inform a great deal of mindfulness practice, even outside of Buddhism. The Buddha's First Noble Truth states that "suffering is characteristic of existence."[13] In other words, "To live is to suffer."

Unhappy Ending

We started this chapter with my account of the CEO who exclaimed that they would only be happy "once we go public." This executive sent the message to everyone in the company that happiness would not be experienced until the IPO. At the time of this writing, that company was still not public. I don't know whether the CEO has enjoyed the journey during the many years since, but I suspect the answer is "no."

Don't be that way. Enjoy your journey.

It may not seem so at first, but forgiveness is another way to cultivate enjoyment along the way.

Chapter Ten:
Forgive

The Two Prisoners

I like to tell a version of a story I first heard from the wonderful Jack Kornfield, an American Buddhist monk who had worked in the Peace Corps in Southeast Asia before getting his Ph.D. in clinical psychology.[1] In this tale, there are two prisoners of war, who survived their internment and met at a reunion 20 years later.[2]

The one turned to the other and asked, "Have you forgiven our captors?"

The other replied, "What? Forgiven our captors? After they tortured us? Starved us? Killed our friends? I will never forgive them! NEVER!"

"Well," said the first man sadly, "then I guess they still have you in prison, don't they?"

The second man was no longer physically in prison. But he was still psychologically in prison. He was still suffering every day from the tragic and no doubt horrible events that had taken place 20 years earlier.

What Forgiveness Is and Isn't

Do you find it hard to forgive? Although forgiveness is an important part of my Catholic upbringing, I find it very hard to forgive. But it's much easier to forgive with a proper understanding of what forgiveness is — and isn't.

Laurence Sterne, the Anglo-Irish novelist and clergyman, stated, "Only the brave know how to forgive ... A coward never forgave; it is not in his nature."[3]

Forgiveness is not something you give another. Forgiveness is something you lovingly give yourself, so you can reduce your own suffering.

Or, as one student noted in one of my happiness workshops, "My forgiving you does not mean that you're right and I'm wrong. It just means that I value our relationship more than I value my ego."

Forgiveness starts by accepting what already is. It's the Serenity Prayer's "accepting the things I cannot change." Or as many others have said, "Forgiveness means giving up all hope for a better past."

Forgiveness is for *your* sake, not for the sake of the person you're angry at. It's so you can be happy, right here and now. Because when you refuse to forgive and accept, who is it hurting? Is it hurting them or you? They might be enjoying fine dining at a fancy restaurant in Houston, while you're at home, still upset about an event that happened three weeks ago — or 30 years ago! All because you have not found a way to let go of your anger.

Let me be clear — *forgiveness does not mean you have to be friends with that person, see that person again, or condone their action.*

It does *not* mean "forgive and forget."

It's completely appropriate to seek justice for what happened and to make sure this injustice does not happen again to anybody.

It might make sense that you never meet this person again. Your healing may be a long, slow process that can take years. But eventually, forgiveness will get you to a place where you can be happier, here and now. So you're not suffering today for what happened in the past.

There are many inspirational examples of what I'm calling "forgiveness."

The Dalai Lama, for example, has been exiled from his native Tibet for decades because of political repression. Yet his message about forgiveness stays consistent. In an interview with Oprah Winfrey, the Dalai Lama noted, "Hatred, jealousy, and fear hinder peace of mind. When you're angry or unforgiving, for example, your mental suffering is constant. It is better to forgive than to spoil your peace of mind with ill feelings."[4]

Forgiveness also occurs in less sweeping yet still profound circumstances. The remarkable TED Talk, "Our Story of Rape and Reconciliation," tells of Tom Stranger, who, as an 18-year-old, raped his 16-year-old girlfriend, Thordis Elva. Nine years after the event, and on the verge of a nervous breakdown, Elva reached for her journal and began spontaneously writing a letter, addressed to Stranger. As she recounts in their TED Talk, "Along with an account of the violence that he subjected me to, the words, 'I want to find forgiveness' stared back at me, surprising nobody more than myself. But deep down I realized that this was my way out of my suffering, because regardless of whether or not he deserved my forgiveness, I deserved peace. My era of shame was over." [5] Over the course of years, the two began an email correspondence, eventually met face-to-face, reconciled what had happened, and co-authored the book, *South of Forgiveness: A True Story of Rape and Responsibility.*

Forgiveness can help you if you've survived horrible betrayal from someone you loved and trusted.

Forgiveness can help you if your country has been overrun and your culture systematically destroyed.

And forgiveness is essential for dealing with even the simplest of your daily challenges.

"Forgiveness is … making peace when you didn't get what you want," says Dr. Fred Luskin, founder and director of the Stanford University Forgiveness Projects, who has worked around the globe to help people heal from the effects of violence. He also offers this definition: "No matter what has happened in any of our lives, at this moment we can be at peace … Forgiveness is the experience of being at peace right now, no matter what story, no matter what drama, no matter what has occurred, five minutes ago or five years ago."[6]

Forgiveness at Work

Although I've been extremely lucky in my career, there have been many challenging times along the journey. In 1995, between my first and second years in business school, I had a summer internship at McKinsey and Company, in Germany. In many ways, landing this prestigious and well-paid summer job was the culmination of everything I'd been working for up to that point.

But I really did not like management consulting very much. I was not thrilled with the project. And I did not enjoy living again in Germany as much as I thought I would, after having spent the prior four years in gorgeous Northern California.

At the end of the internship, McKinsey did *not* give me an offer to work with them once I completed my MBA, which is part of the expectation for such an internship. This was bad. This was failure. This was going to be embarrassing to explain to all of my fellow Stanford MBA classmates, who were going to soon be asking me, "So, how was McKinsey in Germany? Are you going back? Did you get an offer?"

Never mind that I did not like the work. Or that I really didn't give 100 percent effort during the summer. Or that I was having an affair with the wife of one of the firm's partners. (The day I met her, she said she was in the process of divorcing him. I'm not sure he knew that, though.)

Never mind all that. In any case, I felt humiliated by McKinsey. For months thereafter, I was bitter and frustrated and blamed them. I ranted about them to anybody who would listen. Finally, my girlfriend (who by this time had moved from Germany to California) said, "Get over it, Jim! All you do is complain! You didn't work that hard last summer. You didn't really want the job anyway!"

She was right. I decided to start living more in the present. Soon afterwards, in December 1995, I went to a presentation at school where an internet start-up cofounder spoke softly about his rapidly growing company. His name was David Filo, and his company was Yahoo! Nineteen months later, I became employee #258.

So Jim lives happily ever after, right?

Well …

Many things were wonderful in the early days of Yahoo, but as the company grew exponentially, the pressure mounted. Yahoo was the hottest company in the world by 1999, but we were facing threats from eBay and others. I was the company's first international product manager dedicated to e-commerce, which meant I was the person at headquarters in California who was supposed to help our international offices launch online classified ads, auctions, and shopping.

Up until this point, the international Yahoos had had a lot of freedom to build their businesses as they wanted. Now, as my direct supervisor told me, my job was to "show them how we do it here in the U.S." I took his advice literally. I was working my butt off, but my heavy-handed and probably arrogant approach alienated our fellow Yahoos in Europe. I was not savvy about how to navigate the tricky politics of the situation. And I did not ask for help from the executive leadership, who could have provided "air cover" for me when dealing with delicate international fiefdoms.

By late June 1999, I was put on a 30-day performance improvement plan. This is the first and last step that many companies take when they are about to fire you. It did not matter that I had been working 60 to 80 hours per week for the previous two years. It did not matter that I had been taking on high-profile, risky projects while many of my colleagues chose to "vest in peace," as their stock options made them millionaires, little by little, month by month. Yes, I had also become a dot-com millionaire — but if I got fired, then that money train would come to a premature, screeching halt.

The day I was put on the performance improvement plan was one of the worst in my life. I immediately left the office and went for a swim at the nearby health club, just to try to clear the turmoil in my mind. It took a few days for the shock to turn into anger. My previous manager was very hands-off — other than telling me to force the Europeans to follow headquarters' orders. And my new, internationally focused manager felt like his job was to implement law and order amongst the fun, funky, groovy people who came to Yahoo in 1996 or 1997 because they loved the internet, not because they were obsessed with getting rich.

Somewhat miraculously, during my 30-day plan I got a wonderful new manager from Australia, who partnered with me and made sure I did not get fired. I was able to hang on at Yahoo until August 2001, by which time all of my initial four years of stock options had vested. I made a lot more money in that time, although the Yahoo stock had started crashing as part of the Dot-Com Meltdown.

So, did making all that money ease Jim's pain?

Not really.

I still felt horrible about almost being fired. I still felt angry about the managers who chose to make me their scapegoat. I still suffered from knowing that my career advancement at Yahoo ended on that day in June 1999. I carried this anger and self-doubt with me for years.

I wish I had known more about forgiveness at that time. If I had, I could have perhaps gotten over this heartbreak in a matter of months, not years. I could have taken ownership for my own mistakes, and learned my lessons sooner.

As Dr. Luskin explains, "We are the ones who created the lack of peace, so we're the only ones who can remedy the situation. Life happened, and then we objected to life. And ... our objecting to our own life causes emotional and physical and spiritual turmoil. Forgiveness is the resolution of our objection." [7] He cites research finding that forgiveness reduces anger, hurt, depression, and stress, and leads to greater feelings of optimism, hope, compassion, and self-confidence.[8]

The negative impact of *not* forgiving is huge. "When we think about a hurt, our body reacts as if it is in danger and activates what is known as the fight-or-flight response. The body releases chemicals ... known as stress chemicals," explains Dr. Luskin. "What is unfortunate is that your nervous system cannot tell whether the danger you are seeing is occurring now or ten years ago. Your nervous system responds the only way it knows how whether you have thought about a problem once or twelve hundred times."[9]

So how exactly do you "forgive"?

Forgiveness Practices

You cannot change your past. But you can change how you think about it, especially with respect to forgiveness, which can be a hard thing to achieve. Luskin suggests the following approaches to forgiving:

Take a hurt less personally. Realize that you're not the only one who goes through this sort of challenge. Understand that the world did not owe you anything different anyway.

Take responsibility for how you feel. Don't let that other person dictate how you're going to feel right now. Luskin notes, "There is great danger in giving people without your best interests in mind power over you."[10]

Become a hero rather than a victim in the story you tell. Your mantra can be, "Look how I courageously bounced back from such a tough situation! I'm more resilient and confident than ever!"[11]

Dr. Luskin also describes a way of reframing your hurt, which I've personally found extremely effective. He calls this the "HEAL" method. I'll give you an example from my Yahoo experiences.

H is for Hope. I hoped that I was going to do great in my role as international product manager for Yahoo, and I would have perfect working relationships with my supervisors and all of my international colleagues.

E is for Educate. I understand and accept the reality that I am not perfect, managers are not perfect, international rollouts can be extremely messy, organizations are not perfectly functional, and people do not always communicate perfectly. Even if I do a phenomenal job, I realize that my work may not be fairly recognized and rewarded.

A is for Affirm. I affirm to be the best product manager that I can be, and recognize that the most valuable learning often comes when things do not go the way I wanted them to.

L is for Long-Term Commitment. I make a long-term commitment to do my best at work, which includes respectful communication, excellent organization, and the wisdom to solicit support from management rather than fight political battles on my own. I realize there are always setbacks in any long journey.

You'll notice that this statement focuses on areas I control and skills where I can improve. So instead of obsessing over the injustice of being put on a 30-day plan, I take ownership for my role in the situation and use it to get better in my career.[12]

Here are some additional ways to forgive, recommended by the first motivational speaker who touched my life — the late Dr. Wayne Dyer:

Take responsibility for your part. It does not make sense that the other person is 100 percent to blame and you had zero percent role in the problem. You might even legitimately conclude, "This was 50 percent my fault, because I was too nice and did not set proper boundaries." As a good Nebraska boy, I was raised to think that "nice" works in every situation. But over time I've learned that I need to appropriately assert my interests, or else I'll be badly taken advantage of.

Be kind instead of right. Throughout my life, I've sought to know what is right, do what is right, and make sure others know what I think is right. But I'll have less conflict if I let others freely disagree with me. There are times that I argue with my wife on a point, and I know that I'm 100 percent factually correct. But in the long run, I don't need my wife to *think*, "Wow, my husband was 100 percent right on that point!" I need her to *feel*, "Wow, my husband is a wonderful man."

Send love. Dr. Dyer suggested this response: "I end on love, no matter what!" His approach encourages you to visualize yourself putting a peaceful end to the disagreement. For me, I find it helpful to *not* have the last word in an argument. It's amazing how an argument fizzles out once I stop talking.[13]

A formal forgiveness practice can help make forgiving second nature. In Chapter Twelve, we discuss the many physical and mental benefits of meditation. Here, we look at a forgiveness practice, courtesy of the wise teacher, Jack Kornfield.

He describes a "forgiveness meditation" in three directions, which I summarize as follows:

1. I have harmed others, for many reasons. I remember these times. I feel the sorrow that I still carry. "In this moment, I ask your forgiveness."

2. I have also hurt myself, in many ways. I remember these times. I feel the sorrow that I still carry. "In this moment, I offer myself forgiveness."

3. Others have harmed me. I remember this, and still feel these sorrows. "To the extent that I'm ready, I forgive you … I release you. I will not carry the pain of hating you in my heart."[14]

When I was doing a personal retreat at the remarkable Esalen Institute in 2018, I met someone who was attending a meditation class there. We started talking about forgiveness, as we watched the ocean waves crash upon the rugged California coastline. He suggested the following, which you can say repeatedly in your head: "I forgive myself. I forgive you. Please forgive me."

The ocean gradually wears down a rocky coast.

Forgiveness gradually softens a hardened heart.

Since I incorporated these phrases into my daily affirmations,

I've felt some pain and anger toward others wash away. It's an ongoing practice, but I feel good that I'm heading in the right direction. It's a lot more pleasurable than reinforcing the same pain over and over.

I asked my wife about forgiveness. On our first date, I was amazed at how positive and kind she was, despite the fact that she had undergone trauma, heartbreak, and loss throughout her life. Some of her advice was:

Realize that this other person taught me a lesson. It may not have been a fun lesson, but it was a worthwhile growth experience, from which I'm stronger and wiser. I now know myself better and understand others better as well.

Have compassion for the other person. My wife said, "Most people are not evil. They are just lost." She tries to understand what events might have formed this person in the first place.

And, at the risk of gloating ...

Living well is the best revenge. It's glorious to realize that this other person has failed to destroy me or my happiness, despite how much they may have tried.

Somewhat along these lines, we can quote the delightful Oscar Wilde, who quipped, "Always forgive your enemies — nothing annoys them so much."[15]

Reaching Out for Forgiveness

Doing any of the above forgiveness practices (or "attitude adjustments") might give you all the peace of mind that you want and need — without ever contacting the person you're angry at. But in certain circumstances, you might benefit from actually making contact.

I once ended my relationship with a very good woman, with whom I had lived for a few years. The breakup was hard for me, but it was devastating for her.

A couple of years later, after I had spent several months in psychological therapy, I realized that I needed to ask her to forgive me — whether I deserved it or not. I contacted her, and she agreed to meet me face-to-face in a café on Fillmore Street in San Francisco.

She was very gracious in accepting my apology. I was relieved to learn that she had already moved on in her life and was happily dating another man, whom she later married. In the weeks after this important meeting, I noticed that I was much more at peace with myself. As a result, I was in a far better emotional state to start dating again. I had learned to forgive myself for my hurtful actions, and I had learned to ask for forgiveness as well.

But what about if you're the one who's been wronged? Even if you logically understand that "holding a grudge is like drinking poison and expecting the other person to die," what can you do? What *should* you do?

Here's one approach: Forgiveness advocate and Holocaust survivor Eva Kor suggests that you write a letter exploring all of your feelings related to the event. "It might take you four months … or even a day. It depends on how quickly you can work through the pain you have been carrying around. No matter what, your letter is not finished until you can write 'I forgive you' at the end, and mean every word you say. You don't even have to send your letter to anyone — it is for you."[16]

In those situations where reaching out to the other person feels right to you, I encourage you to do so. Maybe you drop them a letter in the mail, send an email, have a phone call, or even suggest that you two meet for coffee.

As the Serenity Prayer reminds us, there are things we control, and things we don't. So regardless of what the other person says to you, you control your actions, you take responsibility for your feelings, and you can eventually forgive them — for *your own* sake.

Writing Activity 25:

A). What are three things from your personal life that still upset you, but which you can't change?

B). What three things from your work life?

_____

_____

_____

_____

_____

_____

_____

_____

_____

_____

_____

_____

_____

_____

_____

I remember asking this question in a happiness workshop in Washington, D.C. A father and daughter came to the event together and shared their answers during the one-on-one pairing. It turns out the daughter was still very angry at some decisions the father had made. Later, they told me that having that conversation was an important first step in their healing.

In leading my workshops, I've found that participants sometimes have trouble coming up with answers if I ask them, "What do you need to forgive?" But if I ask about what upsets them, they can quickly make a long list of people, events, or circumstances that make them angry. Some things they have direct control over, such as where they work or where they live. Other things they have no control over, such as the fact that terrorist attacks killed a lot of people on September 11, 2001. And other events they might have once had control over, but they don't anymore, such as where they attended college.

As you look over your list of people, events, or circumstances, how can you apply the forgiveness practices we've discussed in this chapter?

How can you use Dr. Luskin's approach to reframe your thinking and become the hero of your story? How can you use his "HEAL" method to get a healthier perspective?

How can you take Wayne Dyer's advice to be kind rather than right?

How can you use Jack Kornfield's forgiveness meditation to forgive yourself and others who have harmed you?

How can you use journaling as a therapeutic way to process your emotions, so that eventually you may write, "I forgive you"?

And finally, would it ever make sense to reach out to the other person directly?

Forgiveness is one of the hardest things we undertake as humans. It's also one of the most rewarding.

Forgive and Build Your Resilience

Forgiveness gives you the opportunity to reframe what has happened to you. It's an excellent way to break the cycle of playing the same sad soundtrack in your head, *ad nauseam*.

Instead of "That never should have happened," it's, "Well, of course bad stuff happens all the time. Why should I think that bad stuff would never happen to me? In fact, I've been lucky in my life overall." (For more on Gratitude, please see Chapter Fourteen.)

Instead of, "I've been undermined and weakened and harmed," it's, "I'm courageous, resilient, and will get better because of this. I always bounce back!"

Instead of, "I'm the victim in this story," it's, "I'm the hero in this story, because …"

Instead of, "They've ruined my life," it's, "My life right now is fine … no matter how much they've tried to ruin it."

These are essential roots in growing resilience — your ability to recover from difficulties. As the great French painter Georges Braque beautifully said, "Art is a wound turned to light." [17]

Think of resilience as an emotional muscle that you can strengthen through practice, no matter your age.

Dennis Charney is a researcher as well as the dean at the

Mount Sinai School of Medicine. He wrote *Resilience: The Science of Mastering Life's Greatest Challenges* with Dr. Steven Southwick of Yale Medical School. Dr. Charney had been studying resilience for 25 years when he himself experienced trauma and had to apply some of the lessons of his life's work to his own recovery. To build your resilience, Charney and Southwick recommend:

Practicing optimism. With effort, you can always see the glass as half full. It's helpful to hang out with other optimistic people.

Supporting others. Yes, it helps to have family, friends, and community who watch out for you. But consistent with the research we saw in the section on Longevity, you can boost your resilience by *giving* support, not just receiving it.

Taking stress breaks. You can increase your capacity to deal with challenges, but nobody benefits from non-stop stress. As such, it's important that you get relief by meditating, taking a walk, or spending quality time with a friend.

Going out of your comfort zone. Exposing yourself to new, challenging situations will help you get used to them.[18]

I'm not a very good singer. In fact, my wife would say I'm a *horrible* singer! But I love karaoke, because it forces me to get in front of a bar of drunken strangers and sing. So far, nothing terrible has happened to me while doing my best Mick Jagger or Amy Winehouse impersonations. I've had a lot of fun. And, as a result, I'm quite calm and confident when I need to deliver a TED Talk or lead a master class. In comparison to singing "Rehab," they're easy!

A Mindset for Resilience and Growth

Another researcher who has done pioneering work on resilience is Stanford University Psychology Professor Carol Dweck. In her groundbreaking book, *Mindset: The New Psychology of Success*, she defines a *fixed mindset* as "believing that your qualities are carved in stone." In contrast, a *growth mindset* "is based on the belief that our basic qualities are things you can cultivate through your efforts. Although people may differ in every which way ... everyone can change and grow through application and experience."[19]

She notes, "The passion for stretching yourself and sticking to it, even (or especially) when it's not going well, is the hallmark of the growth mindset. This is the mindset that allows people to thrive during some of the most challenging times in their lives."[20]

In other words, the growth mindset drives what we often call "resilience," "tenacity," or "grit."

How we think about our experiences is critically important. How do people develop the growth mindset? According to Dr. Dweck, people with the growth mindset believe that "Intelligence can be developed. [This] leads to a desire to learn and therefore a tendency to embrace challenges, persist in the face of setbacks, see effort as the path to mastery, learn from criticism, and find lessons and inspiration in the success of others. As a result, [growth mindset people] reach even higher levels of achievement."[21]

Having a growth mindset helps us respond skillfully to life's inevitable challenges. It means that we can embrace these challenges as an opportunity for growth. This conscious willingness to adapt can also help us take events as they come. The ability to know when to "go with the flow" can be called "equanimity." We explore that next.

Chapter Eleven:
Embrace Equanimity

In Chapter Seven we discussed the Serenity Prayer, in which a person asks for "the wisdom to know the difference" between what a person can and cannot change.

But how can you "know the difference" in the first place?

Sometimes it's hard to even know if you should be happy or sad about something. The best approach might be to know that you *can't know*. Here are two stories to illustrate my point:

On February 19, 2014, Facebook announced that they were buying the start-up WhatsApp for a total value of $19 billion dollars, making this an astonishingly large acquisition of a five-year-old company with only 55 employees.

What fascinates me is that both of the cofounders of WhatsApp — Jan Koum and Brian Acton — were earlier rejected when they applied for jobs at Facebook back in 2009. (Acton was also rejected when he applied to Twitter that same year.) I would imagine that both Koum and Acton were disappointed when Facebook did not hire them.

But this "bad news" for Koum and Acton led directly to something that turned out to be far better. If Koum or Acton had gotten hired by Facebook in 2009, it's hard to imagine that either one of them would have ever been able to do anything as impactful by working within the company. Five years later, they had delighted a couple hundred million consumers, and built a wildly successful business — WhatsApp.

The reality of Koum and Acton turning defeat into victory reminds me of "The Farmer's Luck" story. It's the tale of a farmer in China, long ago. One day the farmer's only horse runs away. All of the farmer's neighbors say, "Oh, what bad fortune!"

The farmer merely replies, "Perhaps. We'll see."

Then, the next day, the farmer's horse returns to the farm with a wild stallion. Now the farmer has two horses.

"Oh, what great fortune!" the neighbors say.

"Perhaps. We'll see," replies the farmer.

Then, the farmer's only son needs to tame the wild stallion. In the process, the son is thrown off the horse, and the young man breaks his leg.

"Oh, what bad fortune!" all the neighbors say.

"Perhaps. We'll see," replies the farmer once again.

A couple of weeks later, the army comes into town, to round up men to fight in the war. The farmer's son cannot join the army, because of his broken leg.

"Ah, what wonderful fortune that your son cannot go to fight in the war, because he broke his leg!"

"Perhaps ..." says the farmer, yet again.

As you can see, we can extend this story as long as we want. And even though we can view this story as funny, or silly, or absurd, I think it's a vivid illustration of how we think about our lives: we believe we fully understand what's going on and tend to immediately judge events as "good" or "bad." Perhaps we have a need to feel like we're in control of our lives. We feel more in charge when we have strong opinions on the impact of events on our health, careers, and communities.

But even our common wisdom seeks to offer comfort in the face of changing fortunes. So we have adages such as, "Every dark cloud has a silver lining," "It's a blessing in disguise," and, "The Lord works in mysterious ways."

Some people even say, "It all worked out for the better." I find this amusing, because it presumes that the result was "better" than what it would have been. But how would you know? How much time would need to pass before you "know" how well or how badly an event turned out?

It's good to strive for things you find meaningful — that's a core part of my Happiness Matrix. It's totally normal to have an opinion on events, especially when they seem to be true tragedies — be it a death in the family, the loss of employment, a mass shooting, a health crisis, financial ruin, or environmental destruction. But even in the most extreme cases, people can find a way to address the challenge and make meaning out of their suffering.

Perhaps the best word for this is "equanimity." I like this definition: "a state of psychological stability and composure which is undisturbed by experience of or exposure to emotions, pain, or other phenomena that may cause others to lose the balance of their mind. The virtue and value of equanimity is extolled and advocated by a number of major religions and ancient philosophies."[1]

Modern scientific research confirms the wisdom of equanimity. Harvard's Daniel Gilbert describes our "impact bias": "[People] expect positive events to make them much happier than those events actually do, and they expect negative events to make them unhappier than they actually do ... A recent study showed that very few experiences affect us for more than three months."[2]

I've tried to look back on events in my own life through the lens of equanimity. As I graduated from my Jesuit prep school in Omaha, I was accepted to Georgetown University with the promise of a full-ride scholarship. I was overjoyed to be admitted to that elite school. But in a last-minute bureaucratic reversal, the financial aid office withdrew the financial assistance. I was devastated to realize that I would not be studying political science in Washington, D.C.

After many hours of crying, I had no choice but to attend my backup school — the University of Iowa — where I ended up receiving a solid education and spending a year abroad in Vienna. That helped me win a Fulbright Scholarship to study political science in Tübingen, in what was then West Germany. Next I taught English in Frankfurt, which led me to getting a teaching job in Madrid.

But things in Madrid did not go as planned, either. The Spanish employment officials gave me the wrong kind of work visa. I remember crying on my 26th birthday, wondering how I could stay on in Spain. That anguish forced me to rethink what I was doing, and led directly to my working (illegally) as a business journalist in Madrid. Which led me to moving to the San Francisco Bay Area in 1991. Which led me to getting an MBA at Stanford. Which led me to Silicon Valley, just as the internet was taking off.

Would all of this have happened if I had gone to Georgetown? Impossible to say. Would I today be the United States Secretary of State if I had gone to Georgetown? Who knows? Would it have been "better" if I had gone to Georgetown instead of Iowa, and would any of these alternative realities have made me "happier"? That's right — impossible to say. Equanimity can give us an appreciation of what we have rather than agitation about what might have been.

Another example is my cancer diagnosis. I know that I would not be writing books, giving keynote speeches, or leading happiness workshops if I had not been forced to face my mortality.

When I originally published this story as a blog post in 2014, it looked like Facebook's acquisition of WhatsApp was something "really good" for the founders of WhatsApp. But by early 2018, in the wake of controversy surrounding Facebook's handling of private user data, WhatsApp cofounder Brian Acton was supporting a "Delete Facebook" campaign.[3]

So, was the sale ultimately a bad thing?

Perhaps. At least for now. Time will tell …

Writing Activity 26:
You're about to make two lists. Label one, "Really Good Things." Label the other, "Really Bad Things." Now, think back over the major events of your life, and list them under one heading or the other.

_____

_____

_____

_____

_____

_____

_____

_____

Below each heading, fill in with as much detail as you'd like. Feel free to think about your parents, your family, where you grew up, where you went to school. Consider who you've dated, married, or divorced. Think about the work and career choices you've made. How has your health been? How have people treated you? Make sure to include major events in the world, the environment, or your community — even things beyond your control.

Take your time filling this out. Then, compare the lists. How are they interrelated? You might find that the lists quickly become so intertwined that it's hard to really label anything as "good" or "bad" with confidence.

I strongly encourage you to sit down with a friend or significant other and do this exercise together. Even if you have an extremely long list of "Really Bad Things," you can probably see how there was only one scenario that could have brought you to that other person. If anything on the list had been different at all, you probably would never have met them, right?

With these insights, I hope that you're able to handle life's daily challenges with a sense of equanimity and balance, knowing that perhaps you *can't* know.

And that's OK.

In the next section, I will share with you science-based, surprisingly simple daily practices that will help you maintain your equanimity and create your happiness, so you can truly live each day.

PART FOUR

Practices

Stories can bring insight. Scientific research is vitally important. And I'm delighted that you're doing the writing activities to help you process and clarify your thinking and come up with specific action items.

But when you put down this book, I want to make sure you have specific, science-based activities that you can do, starting immediately, to help you create more happiness in your life.

Have you ever done meditation before?

How about affirmations?

They are two very different practices, but each can help you be happier.

Meditation is about being here now, being mindful, and accepting what is, without judgment — so you have the serenity to accept the things you cannot change.

Affirmations help you focus on how you want to be and what meaningful things you need to accomplish — so you have the courage to change the things you cannot accept.

Meditation and affirmations are science-based practices that allow you to *live* the Serenity Prayer, every day.

Chapter Twelve:
Meditation: How to Keep Calm and Be at Peace

Does this sound familiar?

Just clear your head …

Don't think about anything …

Think about nothing …

Focus so intensely you don't think about anything …

Purge any thoughts from your head …

Release any grasping or longing …

Let go of any attachment …

If you're anything like me, you probably end up with this:

No thinking

No thinking!

No thinking!!

No thinking!!!

NO thinking!!!

NO THINKING!!!

Oh my God — I'M THINKING!!!!!!

Unfortunately, for some people, their first interactions with meditation are not positive. They feel frustrated when they try, in vain, to "think about nothing." Actually, I'm not sure if it's even possible to "think about nothing." Or it's merely a semantic debate about what is "not thinking" versus "noticing without judgment."

The good news is that there are scores of different types of meditation. You might be encouraged by some of my experiences.

"You Will Be Doing Absolutely Nothing."

People often ask me how I started doing meditation.

In high school, I was an ambitious, high-strung overachiever. (I am still ambitious today, though I'm not so sure about the overachiever stuff.) When I started at the University of Iowa in 1982, I learned that I had to fulfill physical education requirements as part of my liberal arts degree. I figured that college would be even more stressful than high school, so I enrolled in a class called "Introduction to Relaxation Techniques."

The course was taught by a middle-aged woman from New Zealand. I can still hear her with her broad accent, saying, "In this class, you will be doing *absolutely nothing* ..." Really, they could have just as well called the class "Meditation 101," but I think the word "meditation" in a course title would have scared away too many potential students back in that place and time.

I learned various visualization techniques, such as picturing a flame or imagining my breath coming up to my lungs through my toes. I explored how to use my mind to scan my body, from head to foot, tightening and then relaxing muscles. A few times in class, I fell asleep. I did not start regularly practicing meditation at that time, but I immediately started focusing on my breath when I needed to go to sleep and found that very effective.

Later, in 1996, I was going through a very tough time around the holidays. I was working at the *San Jose Mercury News*, where a

Vietnamese colleague of mine gave me a series of cassettes from Jack Kornfield, the Buddhist monk.

I was raised strictly Catholic but had left the church in my early 20s. I had no intention to become part of any organized religion again. But as I listened to Jack Kornfield's gentle teachings during that rainy Northern California winter, I realized that you can benefit from meditation even if you are a complete agnostic or atheist.

And you can benefit from meditation if you are very spiritual or religious, as well.

I really liked that I didn't have to *believe* in anything. I just had to do the practice. Then I could judge for myself whether this was a good use of my time or not.

I also realized that every spiritual tradition that I'm familiar with — Christianity, Judaism, Islam, Hinduism, Buddhism — has meditation, prayer, chanting, quiet time, and contemplative practice as part of their rituals, going back thousands of years. It was easy for me to remember when I was a child in the 1970s, hearing the little old ladies at Christ the King Church in my hometown of Omaha quietly reciting their rosaries. I found the repetition hypnotic.

Meditation Gains Scientific Acceptance

What is "meditation" in the first place?

Some call it "present-focused awareness." The Mayo Clinic, one of the leading medical and research institutions in the United States, notes that there are many different ways to meditate, with common practices that include focused attention, relaxed breathing, a quiet setting, a comfortable position, and an open attitude (letting distractions come and go).[1]

I'm old enough to remember when people thought jogging

was weird — until scientific research confirmed the benefits of vigorous exercise. Then people thought yoga was weird — until millions gave this ancient Eastern practice a try and discovered how great they felt physically and mentally. In time, medical studies verified the benefits of yoga as well.[2]

Similarly, it's taken a while for "mindfulness meditation" to become widely accepted in the West. Since I first tried meditation in 1982, there has been a growing body of scientific research on its merits. Finally, meditation seemed to cross into the mainstream with *Time* magazine's cover story on February 3, 2014: "The Mindful Revolution [—] The science of finding focus in a stressed-out, multitasking culture."

That article explained, "Though meditation is considered an essential means to achieving mindfulness, the ultimate goal is simply to give your attention fully to what you're doing. One can work mindfully, parent mindfully and learn mindfully. One can exercise and even eat mindfully."[3]

Meditation can help you reduce your stress. Dr. Elizabeth Hoge is a professor of psychiatry at Georgetown University Medical Center. She led a rigorously designed study, sponsored by the National Institutes of Health, that "found objective physiological evidence that mindfulness meditation combats anxiety."[4]

A few years earlier, while still at Harvard Medical School, Dr. Hoge told the Harvard Health Letter that people can learn how to revise their approach to "'unproductive worries': You might think 'I'm late, I might lose my job if I don't get there on time, and it will be a disaster!' Mindfulness teaches you to recognize, 'Oh, there's that thought again. I've been here before. But it's just that — a thought, and not a part of my core self.'"[5]

Among other benefits: University of Washington scientists found that meditation "can boost memory and improve brain connections in people with mild cognitive impairment (MCI) and early stage dementia," such as Alzheimer's Disease.[6]

Even more broadly, the Mayo Clinic notes that "the emotional benefits of meditation can include:

- Gaining a new perspective on stressful situations
- Building skills to manage your stress
- Increasing self-awareness
- Focusing on the present
- Reducing negative emotions
- Increasing imagination and creativity
- Increasing patience and tolerance."[7]

Other research at the University of California, San Diego found mindfulness practices helped both Olympic athletes and Navy Seals boost their confidence and achieve peak performance.[8]

Massachusetts General Hospital examined the brain scans of participants in an eight-week mindfulness meditation course. As ABC News' Dan Harris and Erin Brady have reported, at the end of the training, the study found that "parts of the participants' brains associated with compassion and self-awareness grew, and parts associated with stress shrank."[9]

If you happen to be a stress junkie who thinks chronic intense pressure is wonderful for you, consider this conclusion from Harvard psychologist Daniel Gilbert: "I know of no data showing that anxious, fearful employees are more creative or productive."[10]

I don't know of a single businessperson in Silicon Valley — or the world — who would not love to have reduced anxiety, less depression, greater calm, improved focus, better imagination, or more creativity. In fact, at business school, we could call this a definite "competitive advantage" over your rivals.

But wait! Meditation has *physical* benefits as well.

A National Institutes of Health study found that mindfulness meditation reduced serum cortisol, the main hormone involved in stress and the "fight-or-flight" response. The researchers concluded that meditation can "lower stress and may decrease the risk of diseases that arise from stress such as psychiatric disorder, peptic ulcer and migraine."[11]

Scientists have also found that meditation can boost one's immune system.[12] In one exercise, workers at a technology company meditated just a few minutes per day, over the course of several weeks. Neuroscientist Richard Davidson, the University of Wisconsin researcher who conducted the study, told NPR that "Just two months' practice among rank amateurs led to a systematic change in both the brain as well as the immune system in more positive directions." For example, the meditation group had developed more flu antibodies than the non-meditation group.[13]

According to the Mayo Clinic, "research suggests that meditation may help people manage symptoms of conditions such as:

- Anxiety
- Asthma
- Cancer
- Chronic pain
- Depression
- Heart disease
- High blood pressure
- Irritable bowel syndrome
- Sleep problems
- Tension headaches."[14]

I'm pretty sure that if people could take just one pill to get all these benefits, then people would be taking a lot of these pills. Best of all, mindfulness does not cost anything to practice. You don't need health care insurance. You don't need a prescription.

Many of the top performers in our society — those facing some of the greatest physical and mental challenges — have embraced meditation. Famous executives who meditate regularly include Oprah Winfrey, Jerry Seinfeld, Salesforce CEO Marc Benioff, LinkedIn CEO Jeff Weiner, Bridgewater Associates founder Ray Dalio, former Monsanto CEO Bob Shapiro, and Ariana Huffington.[15]

Michael Jordan, Kobe Bryant, LeBron James, and Derek Jeter are all star athletes who meditate. The NBA's Golden State Warriors, who won championships in 2015, 2017, and 2018 and set records for most wins in a season and most wins over a four-year period, have attributed their success to "four core values: joy, mindfulness, compassion, and competition."[16]

Closer to home, I have a dear friend who labored for months under an incompetent manager in a dysfunctional work environment. Let's call him Chris. Chris recently showed up at work, but could hardly breathe. He called his health care provider, who urged Chris to go to an emergency room immediately. Upon arrival, Chris was diagnosed with shortness of breath and heart palpitations. After additional tests, the doctors concluded that his symptoms were the result of ongoing stress.

What did they suggest that Chris do to get better? Mindfulness meditation! Interestingly, they never called it "meditation." Instead, they called it "breathing exercises" — probably for the same reason that my first meditation class was called "Relaxation Techniques." I'm happy to report that Chris has started implementing a variety of meditation techniques into his life, which have helped him reduce his anxiety, improve his outlook, and get more sleep. They also helped him reconsider whether he needed to stay in that job, or move on to something potentially better.

An Easy Meditation Practice

Earlier we talked about the "extremely hard/maybe kind of impossible" way of trying to meditate by clearing your mind entirely for many minutes. Now, I'd like you to practice a much easier, more effective way to meditate — in a way that *you cannot fail.*

One of the simplest instructions I know is from Thich Nhat Hanh, a Vietnamese Buddhist monk. A passage on his website describes the breath as "a faithful friend," and suggests that we recite:

"Breathing in I know that I am breathing in.
Breathing out I know that I am breathing out."[17]

Adding to this, I warmly invite you to:

Sit or lie down however is comfortable to you.
Notice your breath.
Notice any physical sensations you experience, without judgment
or pressure to make anything different.

If you notice your mind drifting off, you simply acknowledge this fact, and let go of it, without trying to make anything different. Return to your next breath.

Next is an example of the longer "invitation" that I use in my master classes. As you read, you can imagine you are following this guided meditation:

Sit or lie down however is comfortable to you.

Give yourself the gift of being here, now.

Allow your eyes to shut, if you'd like.

It's very normal that your mind is bouncing all over the place for a while. That's OK. Welcome this, accept it, and just notice what your mind is doing.

Let yourself notice your breath. Notice the sensation of inhaling. Maybe it's the cool air touching your nostrils. The sensation of the air passing down your windpipe. The movement as your breath fills your abdomen.

Then simply notice how you exhale. How does the breath leave your body? What movement do you feel? What sounds do you hear?

Simply continue, noticing how your breath breathes itself.

Feel how your body responds with each additional breath. Just this breath, breathing in. Just this breath, breathing out. Each breath is new. Each breath is unique. Each has its own time, its own sensation.

After a while, you're welcome to simply notice any physical sensations you may have. Can you smell anything? Can you taste anything? If your eyes are closed, do you notice any color or images at all? If your eyes are open, what do you see?

What sounds do you hear? How might they be changing? What is your sense of touch? Your feet on the floor? Your seat on the chair, or your body on cushions or on the floor? Can you sense your clothes touching your skin?

Do you notice the movement of your shoulders? Are you twitching or shifting? Does something itch?

You have no need to judge or suppress anything. You have no need to choose anything.

It's OK to notice, without judgment or thought. However you are doing it is fine.

You have no need to change anything either. Simply accept what is, right here and now. There is no need to have an opinion.

*You don't need to think about the past, or the future. Just notice this
next breath. And this next one.*

*When your mind wanders, just kindly notice that, and bring your
attention back to this next breath. Let go of whatever you were thinking
about. Let that be. Then let this moment be here, too.*

You're welcome to gently end your meditation whenever you
want. You can slowly stretch, yawn, or do whatever else feels
natural.

How was that experience? What did you feel?

While you were sitting there, your blood pressure went down
a little bit. Your heart rate slowed a little bit. Your stomach secreted
slightly less acid. In a small but powerful way, you experienced
the physical and mental benefits described earlier.

Many people in my master classes look very calm and relaxed
at the end of our initial five-minute meditation. Some say they're
surprised that the time went by so fast. Others are glad that I
"guided" the meditation, to bring their minds back to the next
breath, as their attention had wandered.

I remind participants that it's OK if their mind was racing the
whole time. That's actually quite normal. There are days when I
lie down and meditate, and my mind is all over the place. But I
don't panic — I simply notice, "Wow, I have a lot going on in my
mind today," and return to that next breath.

Jack Kornfield, the meditation teacher, likes to remind us that
this is called a mindfulness *practice*. If you play the violin, for
example, you were probably lousy the first time you tried to play.
But you kept on playing — and practicing — until you got better.

Meditation is similar. You will probably suck at meditation
the first time. And subsequent times. But as long as you continue

your practice, you *will* get better at it. More important, the process itself helps you build useful physical and mental skills.

How does that work? Physically, meditation is often the only time of the day when you allow yourself to notice sensations in your body. Most of us are so busy running around, stressed out, that we hardly notice that our left knee hurts, or we're feeling run-down, or we feel weak and hungry. But through meditation, suddenly you have a chance to directly experience your anatomy, and simply pay attention to what *is*. Your body will talk to you, if you're willing to listen.

Lots of times, people will say that they feel very sleepy during meditation. (I get these comments regardless of whether I lead the meditation at 10:00 in the morning, 3:00 in the afternoon, or 8:45 at night.) I reply by saying, "Yes, that makes complete sense. And that's your body telling you … that you need more sleep. Or more coffee. Or healthier food. Or more exercise. Or you need to work less. Or you need a vacation. Or *all of these things.*"

Mentally, meditation allows you to notice the chaos that is your awareness most of the time. One meditation teacher said to me that often during the first 10 minutes of meditation, "your mind is just clearing its desk." You think about things you need to shop for today. You remember that email from your friend, which upset you two weeks ago. You think about your next vacation, and related decisions you need to make. You think about your kids.

But eventually, your mind settles down a little. You're able to keep your attention on your breath a bit more. You start developing the mental skill of letting go of what happened before, and ignoring what might happen in the future, and just opening to the possibility of this moment, right here.

Meditation's Immediate Benefits

Do these meditation benefits sound lovely, but a bit abstract? Actually, they're very practical.

Imagine you're at work, and you've just gotten off of a very frustrating phone call. You glance at your watch and see that you're late for your next meeting, which is with the team that you lead.

You could simply storm down the hallway, walk into the conference room where your team is waiting, and turn your frustration on them — even though your anger is at the person on the phone, not at the people you manage.

Clearly, this is not a good way for you to earn your team's respect.

Now, imagine this alternate scenario, but with the benefit of a mindfulness practice: You are still frustrated as you get off the phone. As you walk down the hallway, you notice how upset you are. You feel the heat from your face, and the tension in your neck and jaw. Your stomach is tight. Your breath is short. Your mind is filled with hateful words toward the person on the phone. You might even be getting angrier as every second passes.

But instead of rushing into the next meeting with your group, you step aside in the hallway, stop, and breathe deeply.

Inhale. Exhale.
Inhale. Exhale.
Yet again: *Inhale. Exhale.*
Last time: *Inhale. Exhale.*

How long did that take? Go ahead, try it out right now — about 15 or 20 seconds? That's all the time you would need in order to let go of the unpleasantness of the phone call, so that you can be present, mindful, and relaxed. By developing this response, you'll be able to understand that when you're stressed, your team gets stressed. And you'll see that when you're relaxed and creative, your people are as well.

Later you might have to return to the issues from the phone call — but right now you can't undo what has already taken place. You can instead be your best — right here and now — so as to not make a difficult situation even worse for those around you.

For me, meditation is an essential tool that I use when I'm dealing with my highest-stress situations, such as delivering important speeches, preparing for media interviews, representing myself in a court hearing, having to fire somebody on my team, undergoing dental work, or dealing with awkward, uncomfortable biopsies. It's easy to think that meditation is a luxury — until you really, *really* need to be calm. Then, it becomes a necessity — and when these moments arrive it's good to have some experience cultivating this response.

Once you find yourself resorting to meditation to handle high-stress situations, you'll easily realize that it helps with more frequent medium-stress challenges as well. If you have a daily meditation practice, it will help you enjoy grocery shopping, give you the patience to listen to your children, and allow you to savor the sunset.

Let's explore some more options!

Pick a Practice — Any Practice!

Other than breathing exercises, aren't there other ways to meditate?

Yes, absolutely. Research indicates that different sorts of meditations will have different effects on your brain.[18]

Here are just a few examples that I encourage you to play

with:

Visualization: Choose to focus on an object in front of you and keep your attention on it. Ideally, you're looking at ocean waves, falling leaves, or passing clouds. But you can look at anything else, in a nonjudgmental way. Or you can close your eyes and imagine a beautiful, calming, or hypnotic image, such as a flame. Focusing on *some* thing prevents the mind from thinking about *any* thing.

Mantra in a foreign language: Slowly, deliberately repeat a word or phrase (sometimes called a "mantra") from a language you don't speak. For example, you could chant, "Om shanti shanti shanti," which in Sanskrit means, "Om (the sound of God or the Universe) peace peace peace." A mantra helps you unite sound, body, and mind in one practice.[19]

Mantra in your native language: Slowly repeat a word or phrase in a language you do speak, such as "Love" or "I am blessed" for English speakers.

Walking meditation: Very slowly walk and notice the sensations of touch, gravity, balance, movement, and temperature. If you can do this barefoot, even better. Walking on the beach in Malibu is amazing, but you can do this in your backyard in suburban Milwaukee, too.

Hearing meditation: Notice any sounds you hear, without having an opinion on whether they're "good" or "bad." That includes birds chirping outside your window, cars honking, tires rolling in the street, garbage trucks roaring, refrigerators humming, TVs blaring in the next room, and air whistling through your nostrils.

Eating meditation: As you eat, mindfully notice the smell, taste, touch, texture, temperature, sounds, and movement of the food. What spices can you discern? Is the food crunchy, chewy, or mushy? Just as wine lovers savor a fine Cabernet Sauvignon, so can you, too, focus on fully experiencing every mouthful of your food.

Label-the-emotion meditation: This is simple yet quite powerful. For example, if I start my meditation and I'm upset about something, I just name the emotion — and keep labelling it and re-labelling it as it develops. By doing this, I better understand what I really feel. Over time, the emotion almost always changes. For example, the progression might be:

Angry ... angry ... angry ... angry ...
Frustrated ... frustrated ... irritated ... irritated ...
Confused ... confused ... confused ...
Baffled ... baffled ... baffled ...
Wondering ... wondering ... wondering ...
Reassessing ... reassessing ... reassessing ...
Concerned ... worried ... questioning ...
Remorseful ... remorseful ... remorseful ...
Resolved ... resolved ... resolved ...
Forgiving ... forgiving ... forgiving ...

In this instance, I noticed that I was angry at another person, but pretty quickly realized my own responsibility for the disagreement. From that, I was able to take ownership of my actions, identify what I needed to do differently going forward, and seek forgiveness from the other person. Jack Kornfield describes a version of this process in his book, *The Wise Heart*.[20]

Naming-whatever-you-notice meditation: Andy Puddicombe is the cofounder of Headspace, a company that produces a popular smartphone app. He has given advice on how to meditate by simply noticing whatever you happen to notice.[21]

Based on this approach, here is my instruction to you:

I notice that I'm breathing in … breathing out …
Feeling an itch on my right index finger … still feeling that itch …
Still feeling that itch … that itch has gone away now …
Noticing my heels on the floor … feeling the weight of my body on the carpet …
Noticing how soft the carpet feels … suddenly hearing a siren outside the window …
Noticing that the siren is getting closer … now it's passing …
Now the siren is fading in the distance … and I hear birds chirping …
Noticing the sound of my breath as I inhale …
Remembering that I'm naming whatever comes to my attention right now …

This might sound like a lazy person's way to meditate. But you don't have to judge it that way! I've found that it's an excellent practice in paying attention to what is here, now, rather than ruminating on the past or worrying about the future.

Lovingkindness meditation: This is one of the most basic meditations, though it's more about "intention" than mindfulness. We discuss intention a lot more in the next section on Affirmations, but I'd like you to see how this meditation fits with the other practices listed above. Dr. Kornfield gives a wonderful, simple instruction, noting that "without loving yourself it is almost impossible to love others." These are the phrases that you can repeat to yourself while meditating:

May I be filled with lovingkindness.
May I be safe from inner and outer dangers.
May I be well in body and mind.
May I be at ease and happy.

Over time, you can expand your practice by picturing a person you love easily, thinking:

May you be filled with lovingkindness.
May you be safe from inner and outer dangers.
May you be well in body and mind.
May you be at ease and happy.

Dr. Kornfield notes, "Finally, include the difficult people in your life, even your enemies, wishing that they too may be filled with lovingkindness and peace. This will take practice. But as your heart opens, first to loved ones and friends, you will find that in the end you won't want to close it anymore."[22]

You Might Be Wondering ...

How long should I meditate? The good news here is "as long as you want." You've probably heard stories of people who meditate several hours per day. No matter how busy Mahatma Gandhi was with seeking Indian independence, he took one full day per week to meditate. Some religious orders, such as the Jesuits, take multi-day and week-long silent retreats every year. [23] If you ask around, you probably know people who meditate 30 or 40 minutes per day.

But you can start your meditation practice with much smaller increments of time.

If you can't do five minutes, then do one minute.

If you can't do one minute, then do 30 seconds — which I've also found very helpful.

Set the bar ridiculously low, and then just do it. Check off that box and say, "I did it today!" This will boost your confidence and help establish the habit. From there, increase your minutes, if you want. (We discuss how to create and maintain good routines in Chapter Sixteen on Habits.)

I usually do only 10 minutes of meditation per day, though to that I add 10 minutes of affirmations. I'm sure I'd "get deeper" and derive more benefit if I did 20 minutes rather than 10, but I figure that 10 minutes is better than five ... or zero.

When should I meditate? Experiment to see what feels best for you. In the chapter on Habits, we discuss that it's easiest to establish a new habit if you're able to piggyback on an existing habit. So maybe after you brush your teeth each morning, you sit down and meditate for five minutes.

Some people meditate as they're slowly waking up and lying in bed. I like to do my practice after my initial 10 minutes of yoga and stretching in the morning, or after I've gone for a swim. (A lifeguard once approached me while I was meditating, because he was afraid I was having a stroke!) I sometimes have meditated in my car, right after my commute but before walking into the office. Some people carve out 10 minutes during their lunch hour to just be quiet in an empty conference room. Others will sit on an outdoor bench or in a park, and mindfully notice everything that transpires around them. No need for judgment. No need to have an opinion.

After your commute back from work, meditate for a few minutes before you walk into your home. This is an excellent way to unwind from the stress of the day and be at your best for time with your loved ones. Many people meditate right before going to sleep. I've found that focusing on my breath is an excellent way to get back to sleep if I've woken up in the middle of the night.

Do I have to meditate alone? I enjoy meditating by myself, but many people like to meditate with others. If you're trying to establish a new meditation habit, it's great to have a buddy who is equally committed. Some people love the feeling of group meditation, often found in a community such as a Buddhist *sangha*. You may find group meditations in your local Buddhist or Hindu communities, and there are also contemplative practice groups for other spiritual traditions. Many meditation groups have no religious affiliation at all. If you do choose to seek out a community, I encourage you to keep exploring until you find a group that feels right for you.

What kind of posture should I have when I meditate? Given the diversity of meditation practices, there is also a diversity of opinions of what posture you should have. Many teachers suggest that you sit upright, with a sense of dignity. I like to be lying down, flat on my back, with my hands at my sides. Other teachers have told me that you can sit, stand, lie down, curl up, or lounge about however you want when you meditate.

Do I need silence in order to meditate? No, you don't. Listening meditations ask that you simply notice whatever sounds you are hearing — so you can do this just fine at a basketball game, or in an airport terminal. I tend to like silence when I'm doing a mindfulness meditation, but my wife strongly prefers to hear atmospheric, New Age-y background music when she meditates. (As a music snob, I get very judgmental whenever I hear *any* music, so that can interfere with my attempts to notice without judgment.)

Is meditation just about "mindfulness"? No. There are various forms of meditation, and they can address various issues. For example, an internet search will yield "meditation for anxiety and panic attacks," "meditation for stress relief," "meditation for depression," and "meditation for loss of a loved one," not to mention "meditation for losing weight" — which I address in the next chapter on Affirmations. If you're having trouble getting to sleep or staying asleep, then go ahead and try out meditations for insomnia. Zzzzzzzzzzzzzzzzzzz …

How can I get access to additional guided meditations?
Even though I've been meditating for decades, I really enjoy
being "guided" by an instructor who speaks every minute or two
and helps me return to the here and now when my mind starts
wandering. Technology makes it easier than ever to have access
to expert meditation teachers, no matter where you are:

- **YouTube** — has thousands of different types of meditations.
  Try out different ones and see which you like.
- **Spotify** — I like the meditations by Mark Williams, emeritus
  professor of clinical psychology at the University of Oxford.[24]
- **iTunes** — lots here, too.
- **Smartphone apps** — Headspace or Calm. (These kinds of
  apps tend to have a "freemium" hybrid free/paid model.)
  Andy Puddicombe's Headspace has become extremely
  popular. As a business guy, I'm delighted to see the success
  of anybody bringing meditation to the masses!
- **Internet sites, CDs, podcasts, and streaming** — these
  options offer a variety of instruction and guided
  meditation from well-known teachers such as Pema
  Chödrön, Thich Nhat Hanh, Ram Dass, Marianne
  Williamson, Jack Kornfield, Eckhart Tolle, and Deepak
  Chopra.

Is meditation all I need to get through life? Probably not.
Meditation is a powerful practice that offers substantial benefits
and possibly a different outlook on life. But it is not a cure-all.
Even if we do meditate regularly, most of us still need to run a
household or earn an income. Most of us need to be proactive,
define goals, and work to achieve them. Most of us need to have
the courage to change the things we cannot accept. To do all of

these things as well as we can, we need not only meditation, but also affirmations.

Chapter Thirteen:
Affirmations: How to Train
Your Brain for Success

The desire to quiet the mind, or at least observe its workings, arises, in part, out of an understanding that we are always thinking …

There! I caught you thinking right now!

Now, how many of your thoughts do you suppose are negative, on average?

According to Stanford University's Dr. Luskin, "Most of us don't realize how much negativity we generate. And there is some research that shows that left to [their] own devices, most people's minds generate negativity 75% to 80% of the time."[1]

For simplicity's sake, let's just call it 80 percent. So that's your mind, thinking: "Bad. Bad. Bad. Bad. Good. Bad. Bad. Bad. Bad. Good. Bad. Bad. Bad. Bad. Good …" all day long.

(It's worse, of course, for pessimists!)

Your "Negativity Bias"

There are good biological reasons why we have this "negativity bias."

Many many years ago, our early human ancestors were more

vulnerable than we are now to the many predators — lions, snakes, hyenas — who lived among them. They had to always be on guard for the next threat from their immediate environment.[2]

Humans who failed to maintain sufficient alertness would become some other animal's dinner. Those people would not live long enough to grow older, procreate, and propagate their genes. Over time, those ill-prepared humans got eaten a lot.

At the same time there were humans who tended to be more paranoid and cautious. They were downright scared when they ventured across the savanna. They were more likely to remember that animals tended to attack from behind those boulders. They developed weapons to defend themselves. They steered clear of the rocks, avoided being eaten, and lived for another day. Perhaps best of all, they survived long enough to procreate and extend their genes to future generations — eventually to you and me.

Charles Darwin called this "natural selection" — "a process by which species of animals and plants that are best adapted to their environment survive and reproduce, while those that are less well adapted die out."[3]

Writing in *Slate*, Rob Dunn notes, "Many traits that influenced our ability to spot predators or flee from them have been under strong natural selection for much of the past 40 million years of primate evolution and even before then. (We have been prey essentially since the beginning.)" [4]

Over time, the negative humans who remembered bad things tended to survive. The positive humans who forgot bad things tended to get killed. There was a big evolutionary advantage to being a pessimist.

Researchers call this our "negativity bias." In his excellent book *Just One Thing*, neuropsychologist Rick Hanson writes, "The brain is like Velcro for negative experiences, but Teflon for positive ones."[5] This is why you remember the person at Starbucks who was a jerk this morning more than the person who was really nice this morning. This is why you remember traumatic experiences with amazing clarity, while wonderful experiences tend to fade in your memory.

Until about 40,000 years ago, most humans died before they reached age 30.[6] Stone Age humans did not live long enough to suffer from stress-related diseases.

But today, we're living much longer. The threat is not from cave bears. The threat is from a huge range of stress-related illnesses: heart disease, asthma, obesity, diabetes, depression, anxiety, gastrointestinal problems, and Alzheimer's disease, to name a few.[7]

So being negative in the 21st century is not good for your health. It's not good for other aspects of your life, either. If you think negatively 80 percent of the time, you probably are not the best employee, manager, or leader you could be. It's hard to imagine being a visionary entrepreneur if you expect bad results four out of five tries. And your negativity bias will not help you be the most loving, kind person you can be.

Do you really want to think negative thoughts 80 percent of the time?

How Do You Overcome Your Negativity Bias?

With affirmations!

Affirmations are specific, positive statements in the first person present tense of what you currently love about yourself, or what you want to love about yourself. It's a way for you to visualize and focus on your aspirations and goals (such as your "Purpose" from PART ONE) and then repeatedly think about or speak that desire.

Some examples:

"I have killed the tiny little cancer cells in my body."

"I choose a positive attitude in every moment."

"I have the serenity to accept the things I cannot change, the courage to change the things I can, and the wisdom to know the difference." (The Serenity Prayer)

"I deserve to do work that is meaningful and helps others."

"I forgive Mom, I accept Mom, I like Mom, I love Mom."

If you're old enough, you may be rolling your eyes, thinking of the hilarious 1990s *Saturday Night Live* skit, "Daily Affirmations with Stuart Smalley," which satirized self-help programs. The character, played by Al Franken, was famous for his affirmation, "I'm good enough, I'm smart enough, and doggone it, people like me!"[8]

Ironically, at the same time I was laughing at Stuart Smalley, I was hearing about "self-talk" and how important it was for salespeople to develop and maintain a positive attitude. I was selling phone systems door-to-door to businesses in the San Francisco East Bay. I was facing a ton of rejection every day. I was frustrated. And because I was initially lousy at sales, I was making very little money.

One day, a seasoned colleague said to me, "Jim, you've really got to listen to these sales training cassettes. They'll help you develop a positive focus." I was initially very skeptical, and thought this stuff was hokey. Cheesy. Corny. But soon I began to devour cassettes from Wayne Dyer, Zig Ziglar, Tom Hopkins, and Brian Tracy as I drove my Buick from office park to office park, knocking on doors and wearing my navy blue suit in 100-degree weather.

I started saying affirmations such as "I'm a great salesman," "I'm closing this sale today," and "I'm excellent at understanding and solving my customers' needs." It took a while, but over time I started feeling more confident, relaxed, and successful. I heard the phrase "Fake it 'til you make it," which was exactly what I was doing. I used these new positive thinking skills to get much better at sales, which led to a better sales job at AT&T.

I used affirmations to tell myself that I could somehow get into Stanford for business school. On the top of my clunky Dell desktop computer, I pasted a picture of Stanford's gorgeous campus. I looked at it throughout the day, imagining myself among the eucalyptus and palm trees, and proclaimed, "I'm a student at Stanford!"

My affirmations worked! Yes, I had had a lifetime of caring parents, privilege, good luck, studies, career choices, GMAT tests, and essays, all of which led to my admission to one of the top MBA programs in the world. But on top of all that, *I had to believe* that I could get admitted, or else I never would have tried. My affirmations helped me believe. My affirmations helped me overcome my well-evolved negativity bias.

Enduring Insights Meet the Latest Neuroscience

Now, you can say, "I don't buy into any of this California New Age-y hippie BS." I understand. And that could have been a legitimate objection to affirmations back in the early 1990s, when so many people were laughing at Stuart Smalley. But common wisdom, dating back millennia, has recognized the power of positive thinking.

Some 2,400 years ago, the Buddha said, "We are what we think. Your worst enemy cannot harm you as much as your own thoughts, unguarded. But once mastered, no one can help you as much, not even your father or your mother."[9]

Paradise Lost author John Milton (1608 – 1674) wrote, "The mind is its own place, and in itself can make a heaven of hell, a hell of heaven."[10]

In 1905, American poet Walter D. Wintle wrote, in *Thinking*:

If you think you are beaten, you are;
If you think you dare not, you don't …
Life's battles don't always go
To the stronger or faster man;
But soon or late the man who wins
Is the one who thinks he can.[11]

In the years since these statements were made, the field of neuroscience has given us proof that affirmations really do work.

How, you may ask?

Different parts of the brain have different functions, including processing emotions.

Thanks to advancements in imaging and computing power, these days we have a fairly well-developed map of where emotions and responses to stimuli are processed. One study used 3D imaging to examine 20 unique regions of the brain. It found, among other things, that the medial prefrontal cortex dealt with emotional processing; the amygdala addressed fear; sadness was found in the subcallosal cingulate; while the occipital cortex and the amygdala handled visual stimuli.[12]

Another example, described in *The New York Times:* "The frontal insula is where people sense love and hate, gratitude and resentment, self-confidence and embarrassment, trust and distrust, empathy and contempt, approval and disdain, pride and humiliation, truthfulness and deception, atonement and guilt." [13]

It's remarkable that modern science has been able to discover these various functions in the human brain. It's even more remarkable to understand the degree of control you have over your own brain — and your own mind.

Dr. Norman Doidge is a psychiatrist and researcher at

Columbia University in New York City. In his acclaimed book, *The Brain that Changes Itself: Stories of Personal Triumph from the Frontiers of Brain Science,* he explains that for hundreds of years, scientists had believed that once you passed childhood, your brain anatomy could only change for the worse, as you got older and your mental faculties declined. But by the early 1970s, neuroscientists had discovered that "the brain changed its very structure with each different activity it performed, perfecting its circuits so it was better suited to the task at hand. If certain 'parts' failed, then other parts could sometimes take over ... They began to call this fundamental brain property 'neuroplasticity.'"[14]

Columbia University Professor Eric Kandel is a pioneer in the study of neuroplasticity, and his early work while at New York University garnered the 2000 Nobel Prize in medicine. As Doidge explains, "Kandel was the first to show that as we learn, our individual neurons alter their structure and strengthen the synaptic connections between them. He was also the first to demonstrate that when we form long-term memories, neurons change their anatomical shape and increase the number of synaptic connections they have to other neurons."[15]

What's more, Kandel's research found that learning could "trigger" the transcription function that expresses a gene. As Doidge notes, "Most people assume that our genes shape us — our behavior and our brain anatomy. Kandel's work shows that when we learn our minds also affect which genes in our neurons are transcribed. Thus we can shape our genes, which in turn shape our brain's microscopic anatomy."[16]

In other words, as Rick Hanson writes in *Just One Thing,* "as your brain changes, your mind changes; and as your mind changes, your brain changes ... what you pay attention to, what you think and feel and want, and how you work with your reactions to things all sculpt your brain in multiple ways ...

Neurons that fire together, wire together."[17]

Should you care which of the neurons in your brain are firing and wiring, and which ones are not?

Yes!

"The *brain* takes the shape the mind rests upon," writes Dr. Hanson. "For instance, you regularly rest your mind upon worries, self-criticism, and anger, then your brain will gradually take the shape — will develop neural structures and dynamics — of anxiety, low sense of worth, and prickly reactivity to others. On the other hand, if you regularly rest your mind upon, for example, *noticing you're all right right now, seeing the good in yourself,* and *letting go* ... then your brain will gradually take the shape of calm strength, self-confidence, and inner peace."[18]

Indeed, as Professors Geoffrey L. Cohen of Stanford and David K. Sherman of the University of California, Santa Barbara, found in an exhaustive review of the benefits of "self-affirmations," "Timely affirmations have been shown to improve education, health, and relationship outcomes, with benefits that sometimes persist for months and years. Like other interventions and experiences, self-affirmations can have lasting benefits when they touch off a cycle of adaptive potential, a positive feedback loop between the self-system and the social system that propagates adaptive outcomes over time."[19]

You can use affirmations as a "brain hack," thanks to the neuroplasticity that we all have. Affirmations are a direct, practical way to rewire your brain for happiness and success. In my keynotes, I often start by saying that "Happiness is a skill that you can develop!"

This is great news — as long as you focus on thinking positively. As Dr. Hanson says, *"How you use your mind changes your brain* — for better or worse."[20]

So, if you wake up every morning and say to yourself, "I'm ugly.

I'm always sick. I'm stupid. People don't like me. My colleagues hate me. My boss is a jerk. I hate this bus system. This city sucks. The system is rigged …," then, as a result of neuroplasticity, your brain circuits will connect, strengthen, and speed up to reinforce these messages. Your brain will physically transform over time in response to those thoughts. You will become a very negative person. (Do you know any people like this? Are you one of them?)

On the other hand, if you wake up every morning and say to yourself, "I'm beautiful. I'm healthy. I'm brilliant. I get along great with people. I have fun with my colleagues. I do quality work for my boss. I appreciate living here. I see the beauty in the simplest things in life. I do the best I can in this society. In fact, I'm happy I'm alive …," then other specific neurons in your brain will fire and reinforce those messages, too. (If you know people like this, I suggest you spend more time with them! And if you don't know people like this, then you need to be the beacon of positivity in your surroundings.)

Who would you rather be?

How would you rather be?

Which approach will help you overcome your negativity bias, so you're not thinking negative thoughts 80 percent of the time?

Which approach will help you achieve your dreams and goals?

I once conducted a workshop in Oakland, California. One participant asked skeptically if I had ever taught affirmations to low-income people. I said that I had, and that the audience reaction had been really positive. She then suggested that maybe lower-income people simply did not have the time to do affirmations, and that it was just a luxury that higher-income people could pursue because they had more time to spare. I noted that, given how much time people spend watching TV, playing video games, or hanging out on social media, everybody — regardless of socioeconomic status — could make time to do affirmations and train their brains for success. Waiting for a bus, for example, is an ideal time to do affirmations. I noted that lower-income people probably need affirmations the most, to overcome all of the systematic challenges and disadvantages that they face.

Suffering from Anxiety? Do Affirmations

You might choose to ignore the power of affirmations, until life forces you to reconsider. I have a close friend who prided herself on her toughness and strength. But over a period of years, she became engulfed in conflict with her manager at work. My friend showed up to the office one morning, noticing that she could barely breathe. She wisely called her health care provider, Kaiser Permanente, who suggested she get immediate treatment.

Her diagnosis? Heart irregularities and shortness of breath due to workplace stress. Fortunately, she was *not* having a heart attack, stroke, or pulmonary embolism. But she was experiencing what some would call a "panic attack." Or even a "nervous breakdown." She was also suffering from depression.

The physicians recommended a holistic treatment approach for my friend, encouraging her to meditate, exercise regularly, get more sleep, and remove herself from a toxic work environment. But Kaiser Permanente, which happens to be one of the largest American health care plans, also recommended cognitive behavioral therapy, or CBT.

Psychology Today describes CBT as "a form of psychotherapy that treats problems and boosts happiness by modifying dysfunctional emotions, behaviors, and thoughts. Unlike traditional Freudian psychoanalysis, which probes childhood wounds to get at the root causes of conflict, CBT focuses on solutions, encouraging patients to challenge distorted cognitions and change destructive patterns of behavior." [21] Another source says CBT's goal is to "change patterns of thinking or behavior that are behind people's difficulties, and so change the way they feel."[22]

Does cognitive behavioral therapy work? Dr. Ben Martin in *PsychCentral* writes, "CBT can substantially reduce the symptoms of many emotional disorders — clinical trials have shown this. In the short term, it's just as good as drug therapies at treating depression and anxiety disorders. And the benefits may last longer."[23]

When I asked my friend about CBT, she said the concept was simple:

How you *think* affects how you *feel.*

And how you *feel* affects how you *behave.*

Of course, how you behave goes on to affect how you think, then how you feel, so the cycle continues.

Reviewing Kaiser Permanente's course handouts, I found a full page of "Negative Thoughts" and their corresponding, reframed "Positive Thoughts." Examples included:

- "I am powerless" vs. "I have choices"
- "I did something wrong" vs. "I learned from this"
- "I deserve only bad things" vs. "I deserve good things"
- "I am a disappointment" vs. "I have things to be proud of"
- "I should have done something" vs. "I did the best I could"[14]

Our thought process can be a virtuous cycle or a vicious cycle. People who suffer from anxiety and panic attacks tend to think negative thoughts — repeatedly, obsessively, uselessly, unconstructively — whereas people who are more mentally healthy think more positive thoughts — which help them feel and behave better. After a few weeks of CBT, my friend started to recognize her negative thought patterns, was able to halt the downward cycle, and started thinking more optimistically.

When I suggest that you do affirmations, I'm not asking you to become a narcissistic egomaniac. (There are enough of them in our society already!) Instead, I'm encouraging you to have a humble confidence — or a confident humility — which gives you permission to overcome your negativity bias and helps you focus on your best self.

I love this quote, often mistakenly attributed to Nelson Mandela, but actually from spiritual teacher Marianne Williamson: "Our deepest fear is not that we are inadequate. Our deepest fear is that we are powerful beyond measure ... We ask ourselves, 'Who am I to be brilliant, gorgeous, talented, and fabulous?' Actually, who are you not to be? ... Your playing small does not serve the world ... as we let our own light shine, we unconsciously give others permission to do the same."[25]

So how can *you* let your light shine?

How can *you* give to the world your genius, creativity, beauty, intelligence, love, joy, and compassion — filled with both pleasure and purpose?

What Do You Want to Affirm?

To do affirmations, first you have to be able to define what you love about yourself. What you aspire to. How far you want to stretch. The wording is very important if you want your brain's neuroplasticity to work in your favor.

For example, you could say:

"I can be promoted this year."

But it's better to say:

"I am the new manager,"

... because you're stating this as a fact, rather than something that "can" happen.

You could say:

> *"I want to be a better sister."*

But it's stronger if you say:

> *"I am a compassionate sister."*

You could also say

> *"I call my siblings every month,"*

… which is excellent, because it's easy to put a monthly recurring reminder in your calendar to do this. (We discuss this in Chapter Sixteen on Habits.) It might be hard to know if you're a compassionate sister or not. But if you call your siblings monthly, you probably will become a better sister.

You could say:

> *"I will lose 15 pounds."*

But "will" is more a promise or hope and less a statement of fact. It might be better to write:

> *"I make healthy choices,"*

… since you can act upon that at any moment of the day, and you're less likely to get frustrated if you have not yet dropped those 15 pounds.

Your affirmation can be:

> *"I would like to be happy."*

But "I would like" is not a strong statement of fact.

> *"I deserve to be happy"* is a better alternative, opening a whole

world of affirmations for good things you deserve.

Remember that you should not have a negative in an affirmation, or else you'll just be reinforcing the thing you don't want to be true. (Go ahead, try saying, "I don't think about pink zebras" and see where this gets you.) So instead of affirming:

> *"I am not angry about the past,"*

… how about:

> *"I'm grateful for all the experiences in my life"*?

(We will go through the importance of a gratitude practice in the next chapter.)

Are You Bad at Names?

Many people love to say, "I'm bad at names," anticipating that they're not going to learn the name of the person they've just been introduced to. But just as Rick Hanson says, "How you use your mind changes your brain — for better or worse," [26] you need to make sure you're not reinforcing something about yourself that you don't want to be true. In general, you should be very careful to ever say anything about yourself you wouldn't love to see as reality.

Now, I'm not suggesting that you should be delusional, or live in denial. But at least you can refocus your energy, intention, and behavior. After all, why would you want to be bad with names? Do you like being bad at names? Does this serve you well? Is this a part of your identity that you embrace?

Better to focus on how you want to be. So your affirmation can be, "I'm getting better with names." Or, "I'm in the process of improving with names." Or, "I used to be horrible at names, but now I'm pretty good!"

And then you can keep faking it until you make it. If you start saying to yourself, "I'm good with names," then the next time you're at a cocktail party or important business meeting, you'll introduce yourself, look the other person in the eye as you say their name, say it again, smile and nod, ask them how they spell it, make a funny joke so you can remember it, remind yourself of someone else you know who has that name, picture this person with a famous person with this name, and say their name again, as soon as you can, while talking to this person. Then maybe you introduce them — by name –– to somebody else.

I understand — some readers might be thinking, "Every time

I meet a person like this, I realize they've done some sort of sales training, and this is just a little circus trick they perform to learn people's names."

On the other hand, other readers might be thinking, "Wow, regardless of the motives, this person has bothered to learn my name. This takes some effort and skill. This probably serves them well. It's impressive."

I'm great with names — and I tell myself this fact all the time. This affirmation and subsequent reality have helped me enormously throughout my life.

You can categorize your affirmations according to major themes. Here are just a few of an infinite number of examples:

Health
- All of the cells in my body are vibrant with health
- I run a half marathon in less than three hours
- My shoulder and knee are getting stronger
- I have killed the tiny cancer cells in my body
- I eat and drink healthfully and in moderation

Family/Friends/Community
- Today I'm the best parent I can be for my kids
- I always find time to reach out to my friends
- I answer the phone when my brother calls
- I do mentorship calls when other alumni reach out for help
- I make eye contact when I talk with other people

Play/Fun/Travel
- I am getting better at salsa dancing
- We are going on a family vacation to Spain this fall
- We go out on a date night every week to a nice restaurant
- I deserve to be happy and enjoy the life I have right now

- I am an excellent surfer

Intellectual/Creative/Artistic
- I read at least two interesting books per month
- I'm getting better at using iMovie to make videos
- I'm open-minded about listening to other points of view
- I'm great at making organic smoothies for breakfast
- I am confident when choosing wine in a restaurant

Spiritual/Contemplative
- I meditate for at least five minutes per day
- I'm loving and kind to myself and others
- I forgive others, I accept others, I like others, I love others
- All I need for a peaceful, fulfilling life is to have a peaceful, fulfilling now
- I observe the practices of my religion, because I value being part of this community

Financial
- I have a net worth of $400,000
- I earn $100,000 per year
- I am calm and patient during volatility in the stock market
- I am frugal and live within my means, while being generous with others
- I do the necessary research before I make important investments

Work
- I'm the best user experience designer in Silicon Valley
- I'm doing the best I can in leading this master class today
- I recognize challenges as opportunities to grow at work
- I am a patient, mature, and supportive colleague

- My team is the best team in our company

Now it's your turn to write out your affirmations! Just the mere process of thinking about what to write is very powerful.

Writing Activity 27:
Write out at least 10 affirmations for yourself (specific, positive statements in the first person present tense, which are true, or you want to be true).

_____

_____

_____

_____

_____

_____

_____

_____

_____

_____

I encourage you to take multiple passes at writing your affirmations. It's fine to have a fairly general affirmation, such as, "I'm in great health." Or you might like to craft a very specific, lengthy affirmation, such as, "I am a phenomenal leader, because I set up my group for success by listening well, delegating, and raising the skill level of my team members."

Would you like to get to know someone better?

Then do this writing activity with that other person — be it your spouse, child, sibling, friend, or colleague. It might feel a little silly or embarrassing at first, but pretty quickly you can get comfortable and encourage each other.

One of the many beautiful parts of my workshops is when I ask people to write out 10 affirmations, and then to pair up with another person and read the affirmations out loud. I can see that participants are sometimes nervous, but others feel proud, glad, or inspired. Some are in tears, due to the intense, joyous liberation of their hopes and dreams.

It's extremely powerful to think about what you love about yourself, write down those thoughts, and verbalize them to another.

Frequent Questions

How aspirational should you be?

Only you can answer that. It's great to have a mix of "things I already love about myself that are true" affirmations, and some big goals and hopes you have, which are not true for you ... *yet*!

In my interactive keynote talks, sometimes participants feel like they're being arrogant if their goals are especially lofty. They may think they have to proceed more meekly through life, hoping that really great things will just end up happening to them. But I ask them, "How are you ever going to achieve this goal, if you can't even see it? If you can't even say it out loud?"

True, there might be some guy whose definition of success was to just play drums in a garage band, and he ended up being in the world's biggest rock 'n' roll group. But for most of us, we have to believe in ourselves and visualize that we can make our successes happen. I used to live just a few blocks from the childhood home of Steve Jobs, in Mountain View, California. His vision for Apple Computer was, quite simply, insane. But Jobs did not pay attention to the doubters. In fact, his ability to think big is what made him "visionary." He thought he could "put a dent in the universe."[27] And he did.

Indeed, technology is driven by people who dream big. I've worked in Silicon Valley for more than two decades. One thing I love about working here is the spirit of innovation. The belief that there are few constraints. Or that we're all figuring out new industries, new revenue models, new ways of doing business that have never been done before.

Yes, you can worry all the time about "how things are done here." And you can become paralyzed by all sorts of self-limiting beliefs.

For example:

- You have to be a technologist or engineer to start a company
- You have to have a degree from an elite school to get hired at a great company
- You have to have a college degree if you want anybody to hire you at all
- You need to be really well networked and know the right people
- You have to have an MBA or be a successful entrepreneur if

you want to work as a venture capitalist
- You have to be the "first mover" in a new industry
- You have to show customer traction before anybody will fund you
- You have to physically be in the San Francisco Bay Area if you want to create a successful internet company
- You have to be a straight, white male if you want to have an awesome career in tech.

There are people — sometimes lots of people — who believe any one of these statements. But regardless of whether they're never true, sometimes true, or *always true up until now*, it helps you most if you ignore whatever the "rules" are supposed to be. (Please note that I'm not encouraging you to *break the law*. I'm encouraging you to challenge the unwritten norms in a particular situation.)

Ignore what the past might have been for others.

And have unshakeable faith that you can be different. You can break through. You can be the exceptional person who accomplishes what no one else has. Well-crafted affirmations are a key part of training your brain for innovation and success.

Just as Lord Voldemort from the *Harry Potter* stories is known as "He-Who-Must-Not-Be-Named," you probably have a Voldemort Goal: "That-Desire-Which-I-Am-Too-Scared-To-Affirm."

Go ahead ... say it. Think it. Write it. Dream it. Affirm it! Then work with tenacity and love to make it happen.

After you write your affirmations, what exactly do you do with them?

Because "neurons that fire together, wire together," you need to give those neurons some proper practice.

You can say affirmations out loud. You can whisper them to

yourself, like a quiet chant or prayer. You can simply hear them in your head — as long as you are able to maintain that focus.

I usually say an affirmation three times:

The first time is to just remember what I want to say.

The second is to get my attention and bring my mind back to here.

The third time is to drive home the point.

I tend to say about 10 minutes of affirmations at home every morning, after I meditate. But for years, I did affirmations while I swam. Or while I was driving to work on Highway 101 in the Bay Area. Or while shaving. I find that the more important the thing is I'm trying to accomplish, the more time I need for affirmations. When I drive to an important meeting or speech, I have no problem uttering a variety of affirmations for 45 minutes. It is, without doubt, a lot more uplifting than listening to news on the radio.

How many affirmations should you have?

As many as you want. I tend to have 40 to 50 — many of which are variations on themes such as, "I deserve to be happy … I deserve to do work that I love … I deserve to …" You can keep them the same over the years, or you can have a one-day-only theme, such as, "I'm closing this important sale with Ms. X today."

Some Affirmations That I've Created for Myself

Here are my affirmations, which I say every day. I always mention the person's name ("Stacy" rather than "my wife"), but I've made the following section generic. I also go through various people (such as both of my brothers, all of my step-kids, etc.), mentioning each one by name. There are endless variations.

Good morning!

It's a nice day, it's a beautiful day, it's a lovely day.

I'm happy that I woke up.

I'm happy to be alive.

I'm happy that I'm alive for a few more moments, at least.

I'm grateful for all of the experiences in my life, and I'm thankful for the life I have now.

I'm grateful for my daughters being alive and healthy.

I'm grateful for becoming a father.

I'm grateful for trying to be the best father that I can be.

I'm grateful for moving to Mountain View.

I'm grateful for moving to San Francisco.

I'm grateful for meeting my wife — who's beautiful, kind, sweet, silly, smart, tough, courageous, sexy, compassionate, adventuresome, and really fun. I'm grateful that she's a great cook, loves wine, and loves travel.

I'm grateful for my step-kids.

I'm grateful that Mom and Dad are still alive and mostly healthy.

I'm grateful for my brothers and sister, and for their spouses.

I'm grateful that I'm healthy.

I'm grateful for my financial situation, and for being able to do the work that I do.

I'm grateful for the investments I've made.

I'm grateful that I get to do work that touches people's lives in a positive way.

I'm grateful that I live in a beautiful home in San Francisco.

I'm physically, emotionally, and spiritually healthy.

I'm physically healthy from doing my stretching, doing my yoga, doing my meditation, doing my affirmations, icing my arms,

and doing challenging swims.
I'm physically healthy from doing long walks, the elliptical
machine, rowing, push-ups, and the arm bike.
I'm physically healthy from eating healthy and in moderation,
drinking healthy and in moderation, working in moderation, and
having a healthy, balanced life.

I'm physically healthy from having enough rest time, having
enough downtime, having enough vacation time, getting enough
sleep, not drinking and driving, taking my vitamins, taking my
supplements, using my CPAP machine, and taking glucosamine
for my joints.

And when I do my PSA tests and biopsies I find that I have killed
the tiny cancer cells in my body.
All the cells in my body are vibrant with health.

I'm emotionally healthy *because I choose an optimistic attitude*
in every moment.
I have an unbreakable spirit.
I have the serenity to accept the things I cannot change, the
courage to change the things I can, and the wisdom to know the
difference.

I'm spiritually healthy *because today I'm the best dad I can be*
for my daughters.
I'm very kind with my daughters, very patient with my daughters,
and very firm with my daughters.

Today I'm the best husband I can be for my wife.
Today I'm the best parent I can be for my step-kids.
Today I'm the best son I can be for Mom and Dad.

Today I'm the best brother I can be for my brothers and sister.

I deserve to be happy and dance to the life I have.
I deserve to do work that is meaningful and helps others.
I'm loving and kind to myself and others.
I'm brilliantly creative and efficient.

All I need for a peaceful, fulfilling life is to have a peaceful, fulfilling now.
I'm at peace because I forgive myself, I accept myself, I like myself, I love myself.

I'm a forgiving person.
I'm at peace because I forgive others, I accept others, I like others, I love others.

I forgive my daughters, I accept my daughters, I like my daughters, I love my daughters.
I forgive my ex-wife, I accept my ex-wife, and I let it be if she's angry with me, so I can be happy right now.

I forgive my current wife, I accept my wife, I like my wife, I love my wife.
I forgive my step-kids, I accept my step-kids, I like my step-kids, I love my step-kids.

I forgive Mom, I accept Mom, I like Mom, I love Mom.
I forgive myself. I forgive you, Mom. Please forgive me.

I forgive Dad, I accept Dad, I like Dad, I love Dad.
I forgive myself. I forgive you, Dad. Please forgive me.

*I forgive my brothers, I accept my brothers, I like my brothers, I
love my brothers.*
I forgive my sister, I accept my sister, I like my sister, I love my sister.

*I forgive my in-laws, I accept my in-laws, I like my in-laws, I love
my in-laws."*

Action Plan: Do your affirmations every day, starting now.

Figure out a way to incorporate affirmations into your life
— when you brush your teeth, take a shower, wait for a train,
wash the dishes, walk down the street, ride your bike, commute
to work, go for a jog, wake up, or get ready to sleep. Just pick one
time and start doing it. You can spend the next 30 seconds saying
one of your affirmations, if you'd like. See Chapter Sixteen on
Habits for some very simple, practical ways to incorporate this
practice into your day.

My affirmations, which I do in the morning, remind me of
how I would like to behave throughout the upcoming day. One
of my affirmations is, "Today I'm the best husband I can be for
my wife."

On occasion, my wife texts me from work and asks that I buy
some groceries around the corner. I actually might *not* want to
stop my work and buy the groceries. But then into my mind pops
my affirmation, "Today I'm the best husband I can be for my
wife." It's how I want to be. I affirm this every day. My neurons
fire and wire on this message, every day. And suddenly I realize,
"Yeah, honey, sure, I'll go get those groceries for you." Simple,
but true.

Go ahead and write out your affirmations, say them daily, and
see how you're using neuroplasticity to boost your confidence
and train your brain for success.

Meditation, Affirmations, or Both?

You may have noted that the line between meditation and affirmations can get blurry. And that's OK.

To harken back to the Serenity Prayer, remember that many forms of meditation help you have the serenity to accept what you cannot change. And affirmations help you have the courage to change what you cannot accept.

I remember doing a master class for a small tech start-up in San Francisco. In our group discussion, the CEO and founder of the company, who is a brilliant and very successful entrepreneur, said, "Wow, meditation has always been really hard for me because my mind is always racing. But doing the affirmations, saying the same positive thought to myself over and over, was really easy. I can definitely do affirmations!"

Your experience may be the same. In general, I believe that most people today are not extremely mindful and living in the present moment. But lots of people dwell on repetitive, unproductive, and negative thoughts.

The University of Wisconsin's Dr. Richard Davidson is one pioneering neuroscientist who understands the benefits of neuroplasticity, mindfulness, and affirmations. He has collaborated with the Dalai Lama and other monks to do research on the impact of meditation on the brain.

Speaking to NPR, he made the point that "You can sculpt your brain just as you'd sculpt your muscles if you went to the gym. Our brains are continuously being sculpted, whether you like it or not, wittingly or unwittingly."[28]

And in a talk presented at the Greater Good Science Center's Mindfulness & Well-Being at Work conference, he identified four essential skills for well-being, noting, "Each of these four is rooted in neural circuits, and each of these neural circuits exhibits plasticity — so we know that if we exercise these circuits, they will strengthen."

1. Resilience. He cites his team's research confirming that resilience-specific brain circuits "can be altered by regular practice in simple mindfulness meditation."[29]

2. Outlook. This refers to the ability to see the positive in others and in the world. Dr. Davidson states, "Simple practices of lovingkindness and compassion meditation may alter this circuitry quite quickly, after a very, very modest dose of practice."[30]

3. Attention. We're happy when we're living in the moment. This is true, according to not only Dr. Davidson, but also Harvard's Matt Killingsworth, whose research we discussed in Chapter Four on the Happiness Framework. Mindfulness meditation is an ideal way to develop the skill of paying attention.[31]

4. Generosity. Dr. Davidson cites "a plethora of data showing that when individuals engage in generous and altruistic behavior, they actually activate circuits in the brain that are key to fostering well-being. These circuits get activated in a way that is more enduring than the way we respond to other positive incentives, such as winning a game or earning a prize."[32]

In addition to volunteering for a local charity, you could repeat an affirmation such as, "I am generous," "I am giving," or even, "I give a dollar to the first homeless person I see today."

In your daily practices, are you meditating? Are you affirming something noble? Are you savoring something beautiful? Are you sending love? As long as you're firing your neurons to sculpt your brain for the better, it does not matter what label you put on these activities. Happiness is a skill you can develop, and these are some of the surprisingly simple ways you can do it.

But there is one more wonderful practice I'd like to share with you.

Chapter Fourteen:
Gratitude: How to Appreciate
What Already Is

A lot of people ask me, "What makes a person happy?"

Sometimes I say, "Finding the right balance between pleasure and purpose."

Sometimes I say, "Living like you have cancer."

But often I simply say, "Being grateful."

I think gratitude and happiness are almost synonymous. Think about the most grateful people you know. Are they happy? How about the least grateful, most entitled people that you know. Are they unhappy? In any situation, you can focus on who you're not, or what you *don't* have in your life. Or, you can focus on who you are, how you can be, and what you *do* have in your life.

But to do this, you first have to *recognize* all the things to be grateful for.

Benefits of a Gratitude Practice

We humans have evolved to get used to nice things. This is the "hedonic adaptation" we discussed in Chapter Nine — it diminishes your appreciation for what you have.

But a gratitude practice can help you savor and appreciate

your possessions and your surroundings. If you take the bus to work, you can be grateful that there is public transportation. If you live in a dark, dingy studio, you can be grateful that you're not homeless. If all you can afford to eat is instant ramen, you can be grateful that you're not one of the roughly 815 million fellow humans who go to sleep hungry every night.[1]

You will be happier when you're thankful for the "stuff" in your life. But it's even more important to be grateful for the people in your life. A gratitude practice will strengthen your bonds with family, friends, and community. It will also increase your humility — because no matter how brilliant, talented, hardworking, and wonderful you are, there is a huge number of people throughout your life who have directly contributed to your success today. In fact, one of the many things I admire about Asian cultures is the deep respect paid to elders and prior generations for their sacrifices.

Gratitude does not mean you should feel guilty or indebted for the gifts that life provides to you. If you're going to eat the chocolate mousse, then savor it! It doesn't help anybody to eat it and not enjoy it. Similarly, it does *not* make sense to have a fine vacation in Cancun, but feel bad about the poverty in Mexico. Either don't go to that lovely country at all, or go there, spend your money in their economy, tip generously, be kind, smile, learn some *español,* and give to a local charity if you want.

Gratitude is the recognition and open acceptance that good things come your way, all the time. To that, it's worth saying, "Thank you!"

Gratitude's Timeless Wisdom Validated by Modern Science

Gratitude is a virtue that has been taught for millennia.

The Buddha stated, "Happiness will never come to those who fail to appreciate what they already have."

The French have this proverb: "Gratitude is the heart's memory."

Helen Keller, the first blind-deaf person to earn a bachelor's degree in the United States — from Radcliffe, no less — said, "If much has been denied me, much, very much, has been given me."[2]

And in a very wry, mindful way, the legendarily hard-living Rolling Stones guitarist Keith Richards cracked to a concert audience, "It's good to see you all, you know. It's good to see *anybody*."[3]

Modern research has confirmed the benefits of not only meditation and affirmations, but also of gratitude.

Harvard Health Publishing, associated with Harvard Medical School, states quite simply, "In positive psychology research, gratitude is strongly and consistently associated with greater happiness. Gratitude helps people feel more positive emotions, relish good experiences, improve their health, deal with adversity, and build strong relationships."[4]

In *The How of Happiness*, Psychology Professor Sonja Lyubomirsky writes that "The happiest participants in our studies … are comfortable expressing gratitude for all they have."[5]

In *Just One Thing*, neuropsychologist Rick Hanson cites research showing that "Gratitude is associated with greater well-being, better coping, and even better sleep."[6]

Stanford's Dr. Luskin says, "Your nervous system responds to 'thank you' in the exact opposite way it responds to tension … The whole purpose of our nervous system is to find out, 'Are you safe?' When you answer, 'Yes,' all the sentries that are standing guard all the time stand down for a little bit, and that resets your nervous system."[7]

Just think about that! According to Luskin, you *cannot* be grateful and stressed at the same time. It's neurologically impossible. So to reduce your stress, be grateful. The next time you're feeling anxious, one of the best things you can do is simply start counting your blessings. I've done this many times when I've been upset, and it's remarkable how quickly my tension subsides.

Being grateful means recognizing that things are "good," or at least not as "bad" as they could be. Or, as a 70-year-old Jamaican taxi driver in London once said to me, "Don't worry. Things could always be worse!"

To Be Grateful, Do This

The good news is that there is a wide variety of ways to practice gratitude. Here are a few:

Write a gratitude journal. This is very popular. Simply keep a notepad next to your bed, and every night before you go to sleep, write down three things you are grateful for. This practice is helpful in its own right, but the added benefit is that your brain continues to savor this goodness, even as you sleep. Or you could start your day this way, perhaps by writing this out in an email that you send to yourself, as you sit down to your computer.

Express gratitude to your loved ones. I'm convinced that more relationships would succeed if both partners shared their gratitude for each other. Every night before I go to sleep, I make a point of telling my wife that I'm grateful for something she did that day. It's (almost) always easy to find something. I know she appreciates hearing it, and I feel better, too.

Give thanks before meals. In the United States, we have the beloved national holiday of "Thanksgiving," which is essentially a big gratitude meal. During the six years that I lived in Austria, Germany, and Spain, Thanksgiving was the holiday that I missed the most — the only one that really made me homesick. It's easy to take issue with many aspects of the holiday, but if you look at the true spirit of sharing and being grateful, it's simply wonderful. For many Americans, Thanksgiving is a reminder of the importance of family, friends, and community.

I was raised to "say grace" before meals, which is related to the Spanish word "*gracias*," or "thanks." ("*Grazie*" in Italian.) It's a delightful practice to stop, look at, and smell your food, to be thankful that you have anything at all to eat, and then to savor and enjoy what you have. This meal-related practice can then expand to appreciating other aspects of your life.

In one of my workshops, a participant explained that she and her husband made sure to identify three good things that happened that day, as they started their dinner. "You can't believe how much more positive our dinner conversations have become!" she exclaimed.

Savor positive experiences. Think about the happiest times in your life. Bask in the good emotions from those times. The ability to savor good experiences is important, because of how your brain works. Your short-term memory can only hold around seven items for 20 to 30 seconds at a time. If you don't capture the memory immediately, it will be gone forever.[8]

But if you actively *savor* a positive event as intensely as you can, using all of your senses — sight, smell, touch, taste, and hearing — then you will move that episode from short-term memory to long-term memory. As a result, you develop a database of happy memories, which you can draw upon at any time. Rutgers University psychology researcher Megan Speer and others found that "recalling positive autobiographical memories is intrinsically valuable, which may be adaptive for regulating positive emotion and promoting better well-being."[9]

I remember crossing a bridge in Paris called the Pont Neuf in the summer of 1985. The golden sun was setting over the River Seine. My camera had just run out of film. When I noticed that I could no longer take a photo to preserve this image, I was frustrated. But I decided to simply look at the gorgeous sunset anyway. I've never forgotten that moment.

Live as if you're moving away a month from now. This is a fun practice. Many of us act like we're going to live where we live forever. But things change: people move, people die. Either way, you won't be there forever.

So you might appreciate your surroundings more if you get around to doing "the things tourists always do when they come here." (Some places don't ever have any tourists — which you can view as either really bad, or really good!) For example, if you live in New York City, then make it a point to actually go to the Statue of Liberty, or the top of the Empire State Building. In San Francisco, walk all the way across the Golden Gate Bridge (bring warm clothes!), or do a trip to Alcatraz Island. Living in London? Check out the British Museum, or see a show in the West End.

These are the sorts of things you might want to do if you knew you were moving away a month from now. Don't wait until you have to pack your bags to enjoy these activities. It's all part of being grateful for where you live now.

Volunteer. We addressed the benefits of volunteering already, in Chapter Two's section on "Volunteer Work as a Compassion Practice." In addition to helping you realize all that you have to be grateful for, volunteering will probably teach you a lot about courage, resilience, and love.

Writing Activity 28:
Related to your work, make a long list of people, things, and events for which you are grateful.

_____

_____

_____

_____

_____

_____

_____

_____

_____

_____

_____

_____

_____

Was that hard for you to write? If so, then here are some ideas which might resonate with you:

If you have a formal employer ...

You get paid for the work you do.

You might get paid really well.

You might get paid even more than you think you should.

You learn and develop your skills as you advance your career. You get to be creative, analytical, and efficient.

You learn to communicate better.

You get to meet clients and colleagues, some of whom might become your friends. Some of them will be friends for the rest of your life, regardless of where you work.

You might fall in love with someone you meet through work. You might get married and have children someday. All of this is a result of you "taking a job" somewhere.

You get to have an impact in the work you do. Maybe you build, repair, or manufacture things. Maybe you do analysis or give advice that helps others. Maybe you teach, train, or instruct people, and share lessons that can help others for decades into the future. Maybe you feed or entertain others, or take care of them. Maybe you help others make important buying decisions regarding products or services. Maybe you're part of a political movement to ensure more justice and opportunity. Maybe you make things beautiful.

If you commute to work ...

Your commute gives you a chance to listen to music, talk radio, or podcasts. You can read, see lots of other people, get outdoors, sleep, do affirmations, pray, or think about life.

You get to work in an office that might have better views, better design, better food, a better health club, better heating, or better air conditioning than your own home.

If you work from home …
You don't have to deal with a god-awful commute! It's less likely that you'll die in a car crash on the freeway. You save money on gasoline, car costs, and insurance. And you have less of a carbon footprint.

You have a lot more flexibility regarding when you work, how you work, how you look, and what you wear.

You can eat better at home, save on food costs, and not waste money on overpriced, addictive caffeine drinks.

You might have a lot more freedom to fit your schedule to the schedules of your partner or children.

If you are unemployed, underemployed, or in transition …
You might actually be able to enjoy a lot more free time than you would normally have, and take care of your diet, health, and relationships.

You have an opportunity to re-evaluate what sort of work you find truly rewarding and right for you.

And once you find good employment, you'll be more grateful for having that job.

If you are a stay-at-home mom or dad …
You do probably the most important work in our society — loving and caring for our youngest. This is often a very thankless job. It's always a good time to give thanks to the moms and dads, grandmas and grandpas, aunts, uncles, cousins, neighbors, and friends who keep our children safe and happy.

Simultaneously …

You get to be around and see your children as they grow.

You have the joy of hearing their first words, seeing their first steps, and experiencing so many other "firsts."

You put in the extremely hard work, but also experience the enormous joy that comes from raising children.

And some day — maybe — you'll hear your children say, "Thanks for everything you did!"

Is it naive or silly to be grateful for so many things, big and small?

Some grouchy, cranky, cynical people would say, "yes."

But I say otherwise. Gratitude does not mean closing our eyes to the challenges and injustices in our world. Rather, it allows us to be happy in the present moment — focused, energized, appreciative, and ready to fight for what's right.

Writing Activity 29: Action Plan
Express your gratitude to three people from your work list.

Go back to the list of people, things, or events for which you're grateful. Circle the names of at least three people who are still alive. In the next 72 hours, reach out to express your gratitude to them in as high-touch a way as possible: over lunch, having coffee, face-to-face, video conferencing, or by phone. At a minimum, you text them or send an email.

When you do this, I'm confident that you'll feel great about yourself. The other person will probably be surprised, delighted, and maybe even cry. (That's OK, too.) Ideally, you tell them *what* they did for you, *why* that was important, and *how* their actions made you feel. (Don't be surprised if they come back with a long list of things that they want to thank *you* for!) If you really want, you can put a recurring calendar reminder to reach out to three new people — say, every month.

Writing Activity 30:

Related to your personal life, make a long list of people, things, and events you are grateful for.

_____

_____

_____

_____

_____

_____

_____

_____

_____

_____

_____

_____

_____

Writing Activity 31: Action Plan
Express your gratitude to three people from your personal list.

I've conducted this gratitude writing activity for many diverse groups of people over the years. One of the most unsettling things I ever see is when a person can only come up with four or five things they're grateful for — either in their work lives or personal lives. Honestly, it's hard for me to imagine.

How can they not be grateful for their parents, or whoever raised them? How can they not be grateful for at least some teachers, coaches, or counsellors in grade school, high school, or college? How can they not be grateful for having a bed to sleep in, a roof over their head, and enough food to eat?

When I see people really struggling to write out their gratitude list, I like to give them little prompts to help them see things through the lens of gratitude:

Managers, colleagues, employees, IT support staff
Neighbors, security officers, sanitation workers
Firefighters, police officers, electric utility emergency workers
Restaurants, bars, lounges, wineries
College basketball teams, professional soccer teams, golf courses
Cities, countries, languages, civilizations
Mountains, rivers, trees
Pizza, cocktails, sushi
Artists, writers, musicians
Shoe designers, TV shows, magazines
Smartphone apps, social media sites, the internet
Beethoven, Van Gogh ... and the Grateful Dead

I could easily create a list of 50 rock 'n' roll bands I am grateful for. Just starting this list reminds me of the book, *14,000 Things to Be Happy About* by Barbara Ann Kipfer. Clearly she had a tremendous ability to give thanks.

Gratitude helps you enjoy the life you already have. We've also explored the practices of forgiveness to let be, meditation to keep calm, and affirmations to boost your focus and confidence. Reading, thinking, and writing can all be very powerful. But how can we actually practice all of this, and live each day more fully?

One way is what I call "the Magical 1 Percent."

Chapter Fifteen:
The Magical 1 Percent

Quick — tell me what percentage of your daily waking hours are 10 minutes?

I had no idea until I did the math:

Let's assume you sleep 8 hours per night.

24 hours in a day – 8 hours sleeping = 16 waking hours per day.

16 hours x 60 minutes per hour = 960 waking minutes.

Thus, 10 minutes / 960 minutes = 1.04 percent.

So 10 minutes make up almost exactly 1 percent of your hours awake, every day.

(If you get only 6 hours of sleep per night, then 10 minutes make up even less of your waking hours — just 0.93 percent.)

Why should you care? Because I want to show you that just 10 minutes per day of meditation, forgiveness, affirmations, or gratitude practice can make the rest of your day better. Probably a *lot* better. Which is why I call that time "the Magical 1 Percent." It's the 1 percent of your day that makes the other 99 percent of your waking hours better.

I need to point out that it's not really "magic" at all.

As you've already seen by reading this book, there is a

mountain of scientific evidence for the benefits of forgiveness, meditation, affirmations, and gratitude.

It's not mysterious. It's not supernatural.

The benefits of forgiveness, meditation, affirmations, and gratitude almost seem too good to be true. But they are real. They are surprisingly simple. And they're for you to enjoy.

Of course, if you want to spend 2 percent or 4 percent of your waking hours in forgiveness, meditation, affirmations, or gratitude, then I think that's wonderful. But I want to set the bar quite low, so that you can begin with this easy practice and then build from there, only as you wish.

The Magical 1 Percent is your way to incorporate all of the benefits we've discussed in this book:

THE MAGICAL 1%

**If you meditate for
10 minutes per day, that requires just
1% of your waking hours in meditation.**

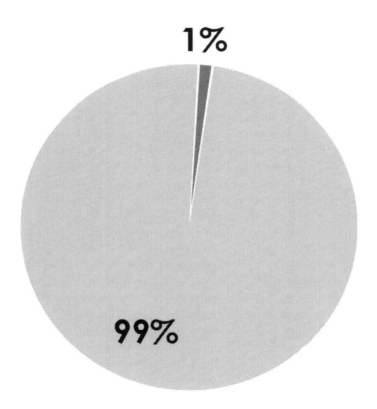

**99% of your waking hours
not in meditation.**

There are many ways to practice the Magical 1 Percent. I encourage you to do whatever feels right for you. Here is one way:

- Meditate for a few minutes.
- Contemplate forgiveness for a few minutes.
- Recite your affirmations for a few minutes.
- Think about gratitude for a few minutes.

That's a lovely way to end your Magical 1 Percent on a high note.

As for me, every morning, after doing about seven minutes of yoga and stretching, I set the timer on my iPhone and lie down on the floor. I meditate for 10 minutes. Immediately after that, I do my gratitude practice — naming softly all the people, experiences, and things for which I'm thankful. Then, I say my affirmations to myself. Finally, I think about how I desire to forgive myself and others. I quietly, under my breath, ask for forgiveness from those I've harmed.

What is the result? I feel calm and mentally focused to create a wonderful day for myself. I feel present, knowing that what's done is done. I'm hopeful for what I can affect going forward. I feel encouraged and confident that I have the discipline and process to execute on important, practical daily activities. (More on this in the next chapter on Habits.) I feel happy and thankful that there are so many spectacular aspects to my life.

In my keynotes and master classes, I like to summarize and synthesize by practicing the Magical 1 Percent with the group. It might go something like this:

OK, come back to your breath. Simply notice yourself breathing in, and breathing out …

You can let your eyes close, if you want …

You can sit or position yourself however you want …
Notice any physical sensations you may have …
You don't need to have an opinion on anything …
You don't need to judge or change anything …
When your mind wanders, just notice where it wanders to, and then gently, kindly, lovingly, bring your attention back to just this breath, here and now …

Next, I move on to forgiveness:

Think about actions you've taken, on purpose or unintentionally, that have hurt you. Recall the love you still feel for yourself. Hold yourself in compassion …

Remember how you've harmed others. Everyone does this. Extend forgiveness to yourself, for being human …

Recall how others have harmed you. Feel the weight of carrying this story, this pain in your heart. Consider the freedom that comes from letting be what has already passed. Sense the goodness of right now …

Eventually, I transition to the affirmations …

Now, I'd like you to think of just one of the affirmations you wrote earlier …

Say that affirmation, over and over again, in your head …

OK, now think of another affirmation you wrote. Go ahead and say that affirmation over and over again, in your head, as well. This is reinforcing the affirmation. Neurons that fire together, wire together. Imagine the reality of this affirmation as vividly and intensely as you can, using as many senses as you can …

Finally, I transition to the gratitude part:

So now, I'd like you to think of someone you deeply, deeply love, and who loves you in return. Maybe it's your son or daughter. Or your spouse or partner. Or your mom or dad. Or a close friend …

Think of how they've helped you. Think of how they've loved and supported and cared for you. How they've listened to you and given you advice. Think of how they were there when you needed them …

Picture them. Hear their voice. Feel their touch. Note their smell. Visualize them in as much detail as you can …

Notice how you feel right now, as you think of your love for them …

Now, think of another person you love deeply. See them. Hear them. Think of how they've helped you, loved you …

This whole process can be as short as three minutes. Afterwards, participants say they feel very calm, refreshed, and happy. If you spend a full 10 minutes doing it, that will be the Magical 1 Percent of your day.

You might be saying to yourself, "Hey, Jim, this sounds great. But as much as I'd like to practice the Magical 1 Percent, I can never find the time. I always want to do it, but other stuff comes up, so it doesn't happen!"

I get it. Finding time and developing new routines and practices can be extremely hard to do without the right instruction. So the next section will show you simple, scientifically proven ways to establish new habits.

To get the most out of this book, please keep reading!

Chapter Sixteen:
Create Good Habits

I really want you to be as happy as possible. I'm confident that if you actually incorporate all of these practices into your daily routine, you will feel better and create more pleasure and purpose in your life. You will be happier.

But many people aren't quite sure how to take that next step. They don't know how to put down this book and start doing the practices. So this chapter is a way to show you how to develop positive habits, such as the Magical 1 Percent.

You Are the Sum of Your Habits

I am fond of this maxim, which became popular in the 19th century:

We sow a thought and reap an act;
We sow an act and reap a habit;
We sow a habit and reap a character;
We sow a character and reap a destiny.

What percentage of your daily decisions are habits? According to Pulitzer Prize–winning writer Charles Duhigg, author of *The Power of Habit: Why We Do What We Do in Life and Business*, about 40–45 percent of our daily decisions are not really decisions at all, but habits that are done without a lot of contemplation. This might sound bad, but you can also make this fact work for you.[1]

Duhigg describes "the Habit Loop" as:

- the Cue — the reminder of what you want to do
- the Routine — the activity itself
- the Reward — a pleasurable thing you genuinely enjoy

Duhigg notes that people focus on the routine, but it's really the cue and the reward that influence how habits function. In order to change a habit, you need to premediate the cues and rewards — deciding ahead of time what you will do when you see that trigger, and then what your specific reward will be.[2]

In his example, instead of going to the café and eating a cookie at 3:15 p.m. every afternoon, he decides in advance that at 3:15 p.m. every day, he will walk over to a colleague and gossip for 20 minutes — which for Duhigg is pleasurable enough to constitute his reward. This is how he replaced a "bad habit" with a "good one" (and lost a lot of weight in the process).[3]

BJ Fogg, who directs the Behavior Design Lab at Stanford University, advocates that we develop what he calls "Tiny Habits."

When WRVO Public Media's Take Care program interviewed Dr. Fogg, he explained, "Habits are a lot like plants. You can start them small. Start them in the right place. And keep them nurtured and they will grow naturally to their predestined size … It's much easier and it's much more reliable to start habits that are small, and get them firmly rooted in the ground and you do that by feeling successful — that's what roots the habits in the brain

— and over time you allow it to grow and become a full habit."[4]

Dr. Fogg advises that you follow this template to create a new "Tiny Habit":

After I
[existing habit],
I will
[tiny new behavior].[5]

You make the decision *ahead of time*, so you don't have to ruminate over whether you're going to do something or not. You've already decided.

In the WRVO interview, Fogg went on to say, "When it comes to … lasting change it's really more of a design challenge than a motivation challenge, and that's a big shift in traditional thinking. There's a systematic way to match yourself with the right behavior that will lead to less stress or losing weight or so on."[6]

For example, do you floss your teeth every day? You know you should. So here is one of Fogg's examples of how you can develop the tiny new habit of flossing: "After I brush my teeth at night, I will floss one tooth."[7]

There! You've already decided it. You don't stop to think about the last time you flossed. You don't have to consider whether it's really good to floss or not. You don't have to recall what stuff might have gotten stuck in between your teeth since your last flossing! As Nike has been telling us for decades, "Just do it."

Leveraging what Duhigg and Fogg have told us about cues, simply put your floss right next to your toothbrush and toothpaste, so you can't help but see the floss right there. And then, after you brush at night, you see the floss and recall your prior decision: "After I brush my teeth at night, I will floss." Notice that you're building off of an existing habit (brushing your teeth), which is already a solid part of your routine.

All of this sounds simple, right? Good — that's the idea. This is not about you building superhero willpower. In fact, it's the opposite of that. Dr. Fogg encourages you to set the bar *so low* on your new habit that it's laughably easy to do. For example, if you find it too hard to floss all 32 of your teeth, then just floss one! The next day, floss two! Pretty soon, you'll probably say, "I can do better than this! I'll floss all of my teeth right now!"[8]

The Power of Tiny Habits

Even before I heard about this research, I experienced the power of the Tiny Habits method. My girlfriend at the time (now my wife) said, "Jim, you should build your upper body strength." (This is never what a man wants to hear from his girlfriend. In fact, I think she's wrong! But anyway …)

So I said, "OK, I'll start by doing daily push-ups. I'll start with five in the morning, and the next day I'll do six, and I'll add one per day. I'll do it right after I do my morning stretching and yoga."

She said, "That's ridiculous! You can do a lot more than five! Why don't you start with 20 or 30?"

"Nope," I said, "I'll start with five." Within a week I was up to 12. And in a matter of time, I was up to three sets of 25 per day. I started easy. I ramped up steadily. And I kept with it — establishing a solid habit that I've kept for the last five years.

Notice that I built off an existing habit — my morning stretching and yoga. *That* is a habit that I started more than 30 years ago, when I said to myself, "After I roll out of bed in the morning, I will do some stretching." Later, it was easy to add some yoga. And meditation. And affirmations. And writing my daily goals in a short email to myself.

If you had asked me in the late 1980s, "Hey Jim, how about

you do this every day for the next 30 years?" I would have said,
"That's almost impossible! I don't have that sort of willpower
or discipline!" But if you had said, "How about you simply do
this today? And then again tomorrow? And you keep at it?" That
would have been much easier to accept. Ultimately, that's how
I've thought about it.

This positive habit has built my self-confidence. I now know
that I can add all sorts of good stuff to my morning routine, since
one cue leads to the next. Here are other examples of habits you
might want to incorporate into your life:

- After I get into bed, I thank my partner for doing something
  nice during the day.
- After I make my morning protein smoothie, I take my daily
  vitamins and supplements.
- When I see my tennis shoes and gym bag next to my bed, I
  know that I'll do my workout.
- When I see the recurring reminder on my online calendar, I
  write out my weekly goals.
- After I dry my face, I put skin lotion on it.
- When I go to the grocery store, I only shop around the
  perimeter of the store, so I buy fruits and produce and real
  foods, and avoid the unhealthy, packaged foods in the center
  aisles.
- When I drive, I do not drink alcohol.

Dr. Fogg advises that to get the most out of the Reward part
of "the Habit Loop," you need to celebrate victory immediately
with a "tiny thrill." For example, you could pump your fists and
yell, "Yay! I'm awesome!" jump up and say, "Bingo!" or do a little
happy dance and sing, "I feel good!" à la James Brown.[9]

Does this sound silly? You bet!

Does it work? Absolutely, according to Fogg.

Why? In doing these movements and saying these words, you're sending a powerful, immediate message to your brain, letting it know that this habit is rewarding. In an interview with *Success* magazine, Fogg explained, "Our brains are very bad at distinguishing between 'I did this huge thing and I'm feeling awesome about it' and 'I did this tiny thing and I'm still feeling awesome about it,'" Fogg says. "Somehow in our heads we exaggerate, which is a good thing. That's part of the hack — building success momentum, allowing yourself to feel successful, allowing that success to be larger than it rationally should be, then growing and leveraging that attitude into bigger things."[10]

Do you need this to be any easier? I'm a big fan of "easy." This next step should help.

Block Out Your Calendar

In the previous section, we discussed the importance of a cue or trigger for the routine you already decided to do. As BJ Fogg suggests, you can sequence events so that one easily flows to another, such as flossing after you brush your teeth. That works great for ingrained habits. But I've found that blocking out my online calendar is the perfect reminder of what I premeditate to do, when I want to do it, how often, and for how long.

Here's what your "blocked out calendar" might look like:

BLOCK OUT YOUR CALENDAR

	SUN	MON	TUE	WED	THU	FRI	SAT
12pm		Write Daily Goals	Write Daily Goals	Write Daily Goals	Write Daily Goals	Write Daily Goals	
		Work Out		Work Out		Work Out	
1pm							
2pm							
3pm	Family Time						Time with Kids
4pm							
5pm							
6pm							
		Leave Office	Leave Office	Leave Office	Leave Office	Leave Office	
7pm	Call Mom and Dad		Call a Friend				
					Date Night		
8pm						Write Out Monthly Goals	
	Write Out Weekly Goals						

In this example, you could put in your calendar "Family Time" for every Sunday afternoon, and "Time with Kids" for Saturdays. Sure, you might need to change plans if something comes up, but otherwise you have decided in advance that these are important ways to spend your weekends.

Your calendar can remind you to call your parents, check in with a friend, or have a date night with your partner every week. You will need a lot less willpower to exercise, if you already have "Work Out" baked into your itinerary. Others will find it harder to schedule you for a meeting at 7:00 p.m., if you've already committed in your calendar to leave the office at 6:30 every evening.

My calendar gives me the cues to write out my daily, weekly, and monthly goals. "Write Daily Goals" might take up 30 minutes of space in my online calendar, but in reality I usually only need three minutes to do this. In general, I've found that one hour in planning saves me 10 hours in execution.

Importantly, I encourage you to schedule your Magical 1 Percent. I like doing mine early in the day, but you might find that lunchtime is the best time for you to invest 10 minutes in your physical, mental, and spiritual health.

By the way, you might have heard that it takes repeating a behavior 21 consecutive days before it becomes habit. I looked into this, and evidently there is no solid research on that number. Instead, studies indicate that some habits will take hold very quickly, and others could take months. The good news is that you can miss a few days, and then get back to practicing your behavior.[11]

In any case, if you're the kind to rely on a calendar, automated reminders can help you a lot. No, it's not sexy. It doesn't feel creative. There is no burst of genius. There is no *zest, flair,* or *panache* to this. It's just plain, simple, easy, achievable, mechanical implementation — of all the important stuff you want to make happen in your life. This is how many successful people succeed.

I get a great feeling of accomplishment and discipline knowing that I can use Tiny Habits to change my behavior long term. Andy Grove, the legendary former chairman and CEO of Intel, encouraged managers to create routine in their schedules in order to reduce stress. His sound logic was that you have enough unpredictable things happening in your life anyway, so it's better to operationalize whatever you can anticipate.[12]

"What gets measured, gets done," is a common quote from the business world. "What gets scheduled, gets done," is equally wise. As such, I encourage you to take a baby step by creating a recurring event for *just one thing* you want to do. (Go to the spa once per month? Call a high school friend every quarter? Exercise twice per week?) Just start there — and see how good it feels when you envision, schedule, and accomplish your goal.

Yay! You're awesome!

What's Next for You

I'd like to leave you with these parting thoughts:

Cancer has taught me a lot about happiness. I'm grateful that I received my diagnosis, because it has forced me to face my own mortality, practice mindfulness, and live each day.

I hope that this book will help you make similar gains and discoveries.

If you've invested the time to do the writing activities and you've shared your answers with someone you love, you will have a treasure trove of surprisingly simple ways to:

Live each day — by investing in your relationships and community, so you leave a legacy of love and impact that you are proud of.

Live each day — by doing work that you find meaningful, challenging, and fun, so you can look back and have no regrets.

Live each day — by striking your ideal balance between pleasure and purpose, comparing yourself only to your best self, and enjoying your journey.

Live each day — by practicing your Magical 1 Percent.

Live each day — and *create your happiness*.

So, from the bottom of my heart, I wish you abundant joy and success in your journey ahead.

Thank you!
Jim

Acknowledgments

First of all, thank *you* for reading this book. If you find it useful, then I'd like to encourage you to give a copy to someone you love. Also, leaving a review of *Live Each Day* on Amazon, Goodreads, or wherever else you find appropriate not only helps me, but other readers, too.

Writing this book is the culmination of a lifetime of loving support from my parents, siblings, teachers, professors, coaches, managers, colleagues, employees, romantic partners, and random strangers ... as well as others who belong to "family, friends, and community." My gratitude goes out to all those who have supported me along the journey.

Next, I'd like to thank the people who played an essential role in creating this book. Each of them has been a unique delight to work with:

Jessika Bella Mura, who did the editorial review and line editing. She was gentle yet tough, demanding yet kind in helping me make the final product much better. I thank her for her dedication, expertise, and encouragement.

Angela Howes, who was fast yet thorough in her copy editing.

Cathy McMahen, who was meticulous in creating the endnotes and doing the final proofread.

Mirko Pohle, who designed both the exterior and interior of *Live Each Day*. If you find this book beautiful, then you can thank him for that. Every time I thought we had done enough iterations of an idea, he would come up with some more — which were even better.

Jacquie Pirnie, who was my marketing and social media maven. Jacquie's ongoing efforts took a lot off of my plate, so I could put my head down and actually write this book.

Chad Dudley, who does an excellent job — working quickly and with quality — to manage my website.

In addition, there's my "Reading Team" — people who have given me feedback on my writing. They are, by first name in alphabetical order: Charlie Fields, Dan McCarthy, Dang Huynh, Dean Neese, Ed McCarthy, Gerald Wluka, Glenn Kurtz, Guille Castellanos, Jacquie Pirnie, Jan Biermeyer, Jason Fang, John Rodriguez, Kathy Chamberlain, Kerrie Carden, Kori Wees, Lauren Mai, Lindsey Harju, Mark Hayward, Martha Madero, Mary Huffman, Michael Bergdahl, Michael McCarthy, Mike Orsak, Nick Flores, Rahul Bhandari, Ranah Edelin, Ray Bamford, Reed Maltzman, Robbie Kellman Baxter, Roth Herrlinger, Stacy McCarthy, Stephen Small, Steven Chew, Ted Huffman, Thi Thumasathit, Tony Chen, and Tony Tang. Their ideas have been priceless.

I'd also like to thank all of the committed, caring, brilliant, kind teachers that I've had throughout my life. I learned from them at Christ the King Grade School and Creighton Preparatory School in Omaha, at the University of Iowa, at the Institute of European Studies (IES) in Vienna, at the Eberhard Karls University of Tübingen in Germany, and at Stanford's Graduate School of Business.

In addition to all the dear friends who are part of my "Reading Team," there is a group of incredible teachers and mentors, managers and friends which has had a lasting impact in my life:

Father Nick Pope, S.J., Professor David Schoenbaum, Romayne Wheeler, the Fulbright Program, Bill McAndrews, Professor María

Dolores González Portal, Marina Specht, Richard Friss, Justin O'Brien, John Haywood, Tony Surtees, Jennifer Dulski, Brandon Huff, Dave Zinman, Ricki Frankel, Kiana Sharifi, Jim Scheinman, Craig Stevenson, and Diane Hunt.

I've been lucky to work with smart, talented, fun, and very cool people all over the world, with all different sorts of backgrounds. They have taught me much.

Thanks to all the scientists, researchers, writers, and thinkers whom I cite and quote in this book. I am grateful for the universities, publishers, magazines, and newspapers who curate and distribute valuable information to benefit humankind. Scientific inquiry and free speech are essential for a democracy to function.

My gratitude to the American Cancer Society for their mission to eliminate this disease, and love to the health care providers who have attended to me with expertise and compassion.

Thanks to all of the people and organizations — start-ups, alumni organizations, nonprofits, and Fortune 500 companies — that have given me the opportunity to conduct my workshops and keynotes. Without them, I would never have been able to learn, grow, or touch people's lives in a positive way. Similarly, thanks to all the folks who've attended my talks: they showed up, gave me a chance, opened up, thought hard, shared their ideas and emotions, cried, laughed, went outside their comfort zones, wrote their action plans, and made their public commitments. They encouraged me and gave me insightful feedback so I could improve.

Thanks to the amazing Christopher Ategeka for asking me to do my first TEDx Talk in Oakland, California, in November 2018. It was entitled, "What Cancer Taught Me About Happiness."

Closer to home, I'd like to thank my brother Michael and his wife JoAnn McCarthy, my sister Kathy Chamberlain and her husband Duane, and my brother Dan and his wife Nilufar Umaralieva. I'm lucky to call you family. I'm also fortunate to call family David and Judy Lam, Amy Lam, Mr. and Mrs. Lam (my parents-in-law), and the extended Lam family.

Unique gratitude to my daughters, Coco and Daisy, and to my stepchildren, Matt, Andrew, and Kei — you continue to teach me about life and love, pleasure and purpose.

I do not have the words to express my eternal thanks to my mom, Joan McCarthy, and my dad, Edward J. McCarthy. They are very different people … and I feel like I've gotten the best from each of them! They have always loved and encouraged me, even when they did not always understand what I was doing, or why.

And finally, praise to my wonderful wife, Stacy. Every day, when I do my gratitude practice, I am thankful that she is beautiful, kind, sexy, funny, tough, courageous, smart, scrappy, creative, loyal, adventuresome, fun, forgiving, and compassionate.

She has taught me more about happiness than anyone.

Notes

Introduction

1. Wikiquote contributors, "Apology (Plato)," *Wikiquote*, December 21, 2016, https://en.wikiquote.org/w/index.php?title=Apology_ (Plato)&oldid=2205038.

2. Rick Hanson, *Just One Thing: Developing a Buddha Brain One Simple Practice at a Time* (Oakland, CA: New Harbinger Publications, 2011), 8-9.

3. Tara Parker-Pope, "Writing Your Way to Happiness," *Well* (blog), *New York Times*, January 19, 2015, https://well.blogs.nytimes.com/2015/01/19/writing-your-way-to-happiness/.

Chapter One

1. "Prostate Cancer - Statistics," *Cancer.Net*, June 11, 2018, https://docplayer. net/62942406-Stress-in-america-the-state-of-our-nation.html.

2. "Study Focuses on Strategies for Achieving Goals, Resolutions," Dominican University of California, accessed December 31, 2018, https://www. dominican.edu/dominicannews/study-highlights-strategies-for-achieving-goals.

Chapter Two

1. American Psychological Association, "Stress in America: The State of Our Nation: Stress in America TM Survey," 2017, https://www.apa.org/news/ press/releases/2017/11/lowest-point.

2. Dan Gilbert, "What is Happiness?" *Big Think*, video, 4:00, November 14, 2007, https://bigthink.com/videos/what-is-happiness.

3. Marjorie Korn, "5 Ways to Practice Compassion—and Get Better at It,"

Yoga Journal, October 7, 2015, https://www.yogajournal.com/yoga-101/importance-compassion-finding-happiness.

4. "Compassion Definition | What Is Compassion," *Greater Good,* Greater Good Science Center at UC Berkeley, accessed December 31, 2018, https://greatergood.berkeley.edu/topic/compassion/definition.

5. David M. Buss, "Mate Preferences in 37 Cultures," in *Psychology and Culture,* eds. Walter J. Lonner and Roy Malpass (Boston: Allyn & Bacon, 1994), 198, http://eyewitness.utep.edu/3331/Lonner&Malpass1994%20Chap%2028.pdf.

6. Martin E. P. Seligman, Flourish: *A Visionary New Understanding of Happiness and Well-being* (New York: Atria, 2011), chap. 1, location 427, Kindle.

7. "Compassion Definition | Why Practice It," *Greater Good,* Greater Good Science Center at UC Berkeley, accessed December 31, 2018, https://greatergood.berkeley.edu/topic/compassion/definition#why-practice.

8. Ibid.

9. Dacher Keltner, "The Compassionate Species," *Greater Good,* Greater Good Science Center at UC Berkeley, July 31, 2012, https://greatergood.berkeley.edu/article/item/the_compassionate_species.

10. Korn, "5 Ways to practice Compassion."

11. Kare Anderson, Adam Rifkin, and Panda Whale, "Pay It Forward With the Five-Minute Favor," *Forbes,* July 17, 2013, https://www.forbes.com/sites/kareanderson/2013/07/17/pay-it-forward-with-the-five-minute-favor/.

12. Albert Schweitzer, "Albert Schweitzer Quotes," *Goodreads,* accessed January 6, 2019, https://www.goodreads.com/author/quotes/47146.

13. James Baraz and Shoshana Alexander, "The Helper's High," *Greater Good,* Greater Good Science Center at UC Berkeley, February 1, 2010, https://greatergood.berkeley.edu/article/item/the_helpers_high.

14. Lara Aknin, Elizabeth Dunn, and Michael I. Norton, "Happiness Runs in a Circular Motion: Evidence for a Positive Feedback Loop Between Prosocial Spending and Happiness," *Journal of Happiness Studies* 13, no. 2 (April 2011), DOI: 10.1007/s10902-011-9267-5.

15. Adam Grant, *Give and Take: Why Helping Others Drives Our Success* (New York: Penguin Books, 2013), chap. 6, location 2868, Kindle.

16. "Doing Good Is Good for You: 2013 Health and Volunteering Study," United Health Group, accessed January 1, 2019, https://www.unitedhealthgroup.com/content/dam/UHG/PDF/2013/UNH-Health-

Volunteering-Study.pdf.

17. Baraz and Alexander, "Helper's High."

18. Stephen G. Post, "Altruism, Happiness, and Health: It's Good to Be Good," *International Journal of Behavioral Medicine* 12, no. 2 (2005): 69-70, https://greatergood.berkeley.edu/images/uploads/Post-AltruismHappinessHealth.pdf.

19. Grant, *Give and Take,* chap. 6, location 2905.

20. Mitchell Leslie, "The Vexing Legacy of Lewis Terman," *Stanford Magazine,* June 2, 2011, https://www.webcitation.org/5z8BMMDUy

21. Howard S. Friedman and Leslie R. Martin, *The Longevity Project: Surprising Discoveries for Health and Long Life from the Landmark Eight-Decade Study* (New York: Penguin, 2012), chap. 12, location 2622, Kindle.

22. Ibid., chap. 11, location 2494.

23. Ibid., chap. 11, location 2519.

24. Arthur A. Stone, Joseph E. Schwartz, Joan E. Broderick, and Angus Deaton, "A Snapshot of the Age Distribution of Psychological Well-being in the United States," Proceedings of the National Academy of Sciences 107, no. 22 (June 1, 2010):9985-90, DOI: 10.1073/pnas.1003744107.

25. David B. Blanchflower and Andrew J. Oswald, "Is Well-being U-shaped Over the Life Cycle?" *Social Science and Medicine* 66 (2008): 1733-49, https://www.dartmouth.edu/~blnchflr/papers/welbbeingssm.pdf.

26. Laura Carstensen, interview by Guy Raz, "Why Should We Look Forward to Getting Older," *TED Radio Hour,* on NPR, June 19, 2015, https://www.npr.org/templates/transcript/transcript.php?storyId=414999589.

27. Ibid.

28. Jessica Pappas and Vanessa Sink, "Connections with Community and Family—Not Money—Most Important for Seniors' Quality of Life," National Council on Aging, June 5, 2018, https://www.ncoa.org/news/press-releases/connections-with-community/.

29. Tom Wolfe, interview by Morley Safer, on *60 Minutes,* YouTube video, 11:30, aired November 22, 1998, https://www.youtube.com/watch?v=8tW9RNE0gyQ.

30. "Buddha Quotes," *BrainyQuote.com,* BrainyMedia, accessed January 1, 2019, https://www.brainyquote.com/quotes/buddha_164946.

31. *2018 Cigna U.S. Loneliness Report*, Cigna Intellectual Property, Inc, 3. https://www.multivu.com/players/English/8294451-cigna-us-loneliness-survey/docs/IndexReport_1524069371598-173525450.pdf.

32. Ibid., 3.

33. Ibid., 6.

34. Jean M. Twenge, Thomas E. Joiner, Megan L. Rogers, and Gabrielle N. Martin, "Increases in Depressive Symptoms, Suicide-Related Outcomes, and Suicide Rates Among U.S. Adolescents After 2010 and Links to Increased New Media Screen Time," *Clinical Psychological Science 6*, no. 1 (November 14, 2017): 3-17, https://doi.org/10.1177/2167702617723376.

35. "Guys, We Have A Problem: How American Masculinity Creates Lonely Men," hosted by Shankar Vedantam, *Hidden Brain*, on NPR, March 19, 2018, https://www.npr.org/2018/03/19/594719471/guys-we-have-a-problem-how-american-masculinity-creates-lonely-men.

36. Ibid.

37. Augustine J. Kposowa, "Marital Status and Suicide in the National Longitudinal Mortality Study," *Journal of Epidemiology and Community Health* 54, no. 4 (2000): 254, https://www.ncbi.nlm.nih.gov/pmc/articles/PMC1731658/pdf/v054p00254.pdf.

38. Martin Pinquart, "Loneliness in Married, Widowed, Divorced, and Never-Married Older Adults," *Journal of Social and Personal Relationships* 20, no. 1 (February 1, 2003): 31-53, http://journals.sagepub.com/doi/abs/10.1177/02654075030201002.

39. Kenneth Cramer and Kimberley A. Neyedley, "Sex Differences in Loneliness: The Role of Masculinity and Femininity," *Sex Roles* 38, no. 7-8 (April 1998): 2, https://link.springer.com/article/10.1023%2FA%3A1018850711372#page.

40. Kira Asatryan, "3 Surprising Truths About Gender and Loneliness," *Psychology Today*, January 4, 2016, https://www.psychologytoday.com/us/blog/the-art-closeness/201601/3-surprising-truths-about-gender-and-loneliness.

41. Rhitu Chatterjee, "Americans Are A Lonely Lot, And Young People Bear The Heaviest Burden," *Shots* (blog), NPR, May 1, 2018, https://www.npr.org/sections/health-shots/2018/05/01/606588504/americans-are-a-lonely-lot-and-young-people-bear-the-heaviest-burden.

42. Julianne Holt Lunstad, Timothy B. Smith, and J. Bradley Layton,

"Social Relationships and Mortality Risk: A Meta-analytic Review," *PLOS Medicine* 7, no. 7 (July 27, 2010), http://journals.plos.org/plosmedicine/article?id=10.1371/journal.pmed.1000316.

43. Twenge, Joiner, Rogers, and Martin, "Increases in Depressive Symptoms ."

44. "Guys, We Have A Problem," *Hidden Brain.*

45. Cigna U.S. Loneliness Index, 21.

46. Jill Suttie, "Compassion Across Cubicles," *Greater Good,* Greater Good Science Center at UC Berkeley, March 1, 2006, https://greatergood.berkeley.edu/article/item/compassion_across_cubicles/.

47. Melinda Sacks, "Chief Kindness Officers," *Stanford Magazine*, December 15, 2017, https://stanfordmag.org/contents/chief-kindness-officers.

48. Ibid.

Chapter Three

1. Bronnie Ware, *The Top 5 Regrets of the Dying: A Life Transformed by the Dearly Departing* (Carlsbad, CA: Hay House, 2012), Contents.

2. Oliver Wendell Holmes, *The Voiceless*, Bartelby.com: Great Books Online, https://www.bartleby.com/100/456.16.html.

3. Emily Esfahani Smith and Jennifer L. Aaker, "Millenial Searchers," *New York Times*, Sunday Review, November 30, 2013, https://www.nytimes.com/2013/12/01/opinion/sunday/millennial-searchers.html.

4. Sonja Lyubomirsky, *The How of Happiness: A New Approach to Getting the Life You Want* (New York: Penguin Group, 2007), 23.

5. Adam Grant, "Wharton's Adam Grant on the Key to Professional Success," interview by Rik Kirkland, McKinsey & Company, June 2014, https://www.mckinsey.com/business-functions/organization/our-insights/whartons-adam-grant-on-the-key-to-professional-success.

6. Laszlo Bock, *Work Rules! Insights from Inside Google That Will Transform How You Live and Lead* (New York: Hatchett Book Group, 2015), chap. 2, location 737, Kindle.

7. Laszo Bock, "Google's Using Workplace Data to Build a Better Employee," interview by Stephanie Ruhle, Bloomberg, video, 1:30, November 11, 2015, https://www.bloomberg.com/news/videos/2015-11-11/google-s-using-workplace-data-to-build-a-better-employee.

8. Amy Wrzesniewski, "Working for a Living: Scholar Explores Difference Between 'Callings' and 'Jobs'," interview by Tabitha Wilde, Yale Bulletin and Calendar, October 26, 2007, http://archives.news.yale.edu/v36.n8/story4.html.

9. Ibid.

10. Shawn Achor, *The Happiness Advantage: The Seven Principles that Fuel Success and Performance at Work* (New York: Virgin Books, 2011), 79.

11. Viktor E. Frankl, *Man's Search for Meaning*, rev. ed. (New York: Washington Square Press, 1984), 101.

12. Lucy Dawidowicz, *The War Against the Jews: 1933-1945* (New York: Bantam Books, 1986), 403.

13. Frankl, *Man's Search for Meaning*, 95.

14. Ibid., 100-101.

15. Ibid., 86.

16. Alexander W. Astin, Robert J. Panos, and John A. Creager, *National Norms for Entering College Freshman: Fall 1966* (American Council on Education, 1967), 21, https://www.heri.ucla.edu/PDFs/pubs/TFS/Norms/Monographs/NationalNormsForEnteringCollegeFreshmen1966.pdf.

17. Ibid., 47.

18. Kathleen Elkins, "The Age When 17 Self-Made Billionaires Earned Their First Million," *Inc.*, February 11, 2016, https://www.inc.com/business-insider/when-billionaires-made-their-first-million.html.

19. Robert Waldinger, "The Good Life," TEDx Talks, YouTube video, 0:45, published November 30, 2015, https://www.youtube.com/watch?v=q-7zAkwAOYg.

20. David G. Myers and C. Nathan Dewall, *Psychology*, 11th ed. (New York: Worth Publishers, 2015), 482-83.

21. Daniel Kahneman and Angus Deaton, "High Income Improves Evaluation of Life but not Emotional Well-being," *Proceedings of the National Academy of Sciences of the United States 107*, no. 38 (September 21, 2010): 16489-93, http://www.pnas.org/content/107/38/16489.

22. Ibid.

23. Ethan Wolff-Mann, "What the New Nobel Prize Winner Has to Say About Money and Happiness," *Money*, October 13, 2015, http://time.com/

money/4070041/angus-deaton-nobel-winner-money-happiness.

24. Carey Goldberg, "Too Much of a Good Thing," *Boston Globe,* February 6, 2006, http://archive.boston.com/yourlife/health/mental/articles/2006/02/06/too_much_of_a_good_thing/.

25. Nattavudh Powdthavee, "Putting a Price Tag on Friends, Relatives, and Neighbours: Using Surveys of Life Satisfaction to Value Social Relationships,"*The Journal of Socio-Economics* 37, no. 4 (August 2008): 1459-80, https://www.sciencedirect.com/science/article/abs/pii/S1053535707001205.

26. Eilene Zimmerman, "Research: All Money is Not Created Equal," Insights, Stanford Graduate School of Business, January 6, 2014, http://www.gsb.stanford.edu/news/headlines/research-all-money-not-created-equal.

27. Eilene Zimmerman, "Who Will Listen to a Billionaire's Troubles?" *New York Times,* February 19, 2017, https://www.nytimes.com/2017/02/19/your-money/who-will-listen-to-a-billionaires-troubles.html.

28. Elizabeth Dunn and Michael Norton, *Happy Money: The Science of Happier Spending* (New York: Simon & Schuster, 2013), chap. 1, location 133, Kindle.

29. Ibid., chap. 2, location 437.

30. Ibid., chap. 3, location 796.

31. Ibid., chap. 4, location 1155.

32. Ibid., chap. 5, location 1497.

33. Johann Wolfgang von Goethe, "Quotes," *Goodreads,* accessed January 2, 2019, https://www.goodreads.com/quotes/111306-at-the-moment-of-commitment-the-entire-universe-conspires-to.

34. "Class Notes," *Stanford Business,* Summer 2018, 114.

35. Charles R. Swindoll, "Charles R. Swindoll Quotes," *Goodreads,* accessed January 2, 2019, https://www.goodreads.com/author/quotes/5139.Charles_R_Swindoll.

36. H. Irving Grousbeck, "H. Irving Grousbeck Speech - President's Distinguished Speaker Series," University of New Hampshire, September 13, 2012, https://www.unh.edu/president/Grousbeck-Speech.

37. H. Irving Grousbeck, "Irv Grousbeck: Finding One's Way on the Entrepreneurial Path," interview by Michael Freedman, Insights, Stanford Graduate School of Business, October 7, 2013, https://www.gsb.stanford.edu/insights/irv-grousbeck-finding-ones-way-entrepreneurial-path.

38. Fran Hawthorne, "The Biggest Regret of All," Kellogg Insight, February 2, 2012, https://insight.kellogg.northwestern.edu/article/the_biggest_regret_of_all.

39. Wilco W. van Dijk, Lotte F. van Dillen, Mark Rotteveel and Elise C. Seip, "Looking into the Crystal Ball of Our Emotional Lives: Emotion Regulation and the Overestimation of Future Guilt and Shame," *Cognition and Emotion* 31, no. 3 (2017): 616-24, DOI: 10.1080/02699931.2015.1129313.

Chapter Four

1. Stanford University Roundtable, "Are You Happy Now?" moderated by Katie Couric, October 18, 2013, https://www.youtube.com/watch?v=Oheja4D6wDk.

2. Clifton B. Parker, "Stanford Research: The Meaningful Life is a Road Worth Traveling," *Stanford News*, January 1, 2014, https://news.stanford.edu/news/2014/january/meaningful-happy-life-010114.html.

3. Ibid.

4. Ibid.

5. "One Boy's Heroism in the Face of AIDS," *All Things Considered*, NPR, December 1, 2004, https://www.npr.org/templates/story/story.php?storyId=4195336?storyId=4195336.

6. "Ten Times Al Gore Inspired Us to Act on Climate," *The Climate Reality Project* (blog), November 23, 2015, https://www.climaterealityproject.org/blog/ten-times-al-gore-inspired-us-act-climate.

7. Smith and Aaker, "Millennial Searchers" (see chap. 3, n. 3).

8. Wikipedia contributors, "Protestant Work Ethic," *Wikipedia, The Free Encyclopedia,* accessed January 2, 2019, https://en.wikipedia.org/w/index.php?title=Protestant_work_ethic.

9. Daniel Gilbert and Annie McKee, *Happiness: HBR Emotional Intelligence Series* (Boston: Harvard Business School Publishing, 2017), 51.

10. B. J. Miller, "What Really Matters at the End of Life," TED2015, YouTube video,13:08, March 2015, https://www.ted.com/talks/bj_miller_what_really_matters_at_the_end_of_life.

11. Emily Esfahani Smith, "Meaning Is Healthier than Happiness," *The Atlantic,* August 1, 2013, https://www.theatlantic.com/health/archive/2013/08/meaning-is-healthier-than-happiness/278250/.

12. Joseph Sniezek, Matthew M. Zack, Richard E. Lucas, and Adam Burns, "Well Being Assessment: An Evaluation of Well Being Scales for Public Health and Population Estimates of Well Being among US Adults," *Applied Psychology: Health and Well-Being* 2, no. 3 (2010): 281, https://onlinelibrary. wiley.com/doi/epdf/10.1111/j.1758-0854.2010.01035.x?referrer_access_to ken=UrTMlSfL59rH50Fo7OBkv4ta6bR2k8jH0KrdpFOxC67W0HU0qrN gjiZn5tOhsa9-68-ZbOoADRGRSNc-kS0u5pJY2AIBa2aGItQ-yhq6T66_ uQdLbUBmgn2uVjji1NZWTur98KeZBJnlopt7u46vjw%3D%3D.

13. Smith, "Meaning is Healthier."

14. F.B Ahmad, L.M. Rossen, M. R. Spencer, M. Warner, and P. Sutton, "Provisional Drug Overdose Death Counts," National Center for Health Statistics, last updated December 12, 2018, https://www.cdc.gov/nchs/nvss/ vsrr/drug-overdose-data.htm.

15. D.M. Stone, T. R. Simon, K. A. Fowler and Scott R. Kegler, et al. "Vital Signs: Trends in State Suicide Rates — United States, 1999–2016 and Circumstances Contributing to Suicide — 27 States," *Morbidity and Mortality Weekly Report* 67, no. 22 (June 8, 2018): 617–24, DOI: http://dx.doi.org/10.15585/mmwr. mm6722a1.

16. "Excessive Sleepiness," National Sleep Foundation, accessed January 2, 2019, https://www.sleepfoundation.org/excessivesleepiness/content/the- complex-relationship-between-sleep-depression-anxiety.

17. Anthony Bourdain, "Anthony Bourdain on the Haiti episode of 'No Reservations'" *Television Academy Foundation Interviews*, YouTube video, 1:00, published January 7, 2016, https://www.youtube.com/ watch?v=SBTVDhIHiiA.

18. Anderson Cooper, "Anthony Bourdain Dies At The Age Of 61," CNN, transcript of broadcast airing June 8, 2018, http://transcripts.cnn.com/ TRANSCRIPTS/1806/08/acd.01.html.

Chapter Five

1. Charlayne Hunter-Gault, review of *The Prison Letters of Nelson Mandela*, ed. Sahm Venter, *New York Times*, July 10, 2018, https://www.nytimes. com/2018/07/10/books/review/nelson-mandela-prison-letters-sahm-venter. html.

2. "State of Homelessness," National Alliance to End Homelessness, accessed January 2, 2019, https://endhomelessness.org/homelessness-in-america/

homelessness-statistics / state-of-homelessness-report /.

3. Matthew Walker, "Why We Sleep," YouTube video, published August 14, 2015, https:// www.youtube.com / watch?v=_d583swchPA .

4. Honoré de Balzac, Old Goriot, in *The Harvard Classics Shelf of Fiction,* ed. Charles W. Eliot (New York: P.F. Collier & Son, 1917), para. 702.

5. Judith Rubin, ed., *Theme Index: Museum Index 2017,* (Themed Entertainment Association, 2017), 10, http:// www.teaconnect.org / images / files / TEA_268_653730_180517.pdf.

6. "Improving Heart Health Is Also Good for Your Brain," *Harvard Health (blog) Harvard Health Publishing,* November 2014, https:// www.health.harvard.edu / heart-health / improving-heart-health-is-also-good-for-your-brain-

7. Powdthavee, "Putting a Price Tag" (see chap. 3, n. 25).

8. Dacher Keltner, "Why Do We Feel Awe?" *Greater Good,* Greater Good Science Center at UC Berkeley, May 10, 2016, https:// greatergood.berkeley.edu / article / item / why_do_we_feel_awe.

9. Ibid.

10. Mihaly Csikszentmihalyi, *Flow: The Psychology of Optimal Experience* (New York: Harper Collins e-books, 2009), intro., location 211, Kindle.

11. Ibid., chap. 3, location 1205.

12. Ibid., chap. 3, location 1255.

13. Ibid., chap. 2, location 958.

14. Ibid., chap. 3, location 1196.

15. Contributor to Fight Mediocrity, animated book review of *Flow: The Psychology of Optimal Experience* by Mihaly Csikszentmihalyi, YouTube video, published June 19, 2015, https:// www.youtube.com / watch?v=8h6IMYRoCZw.

16. Csikszentmihalyi, *Flow,* intro., location 201.

17. James Clear, "The Goldilocks Rule: How to Stay Motivated in Life and Business," *JamesClear.com,* accessed January 2, 2019, https:// jamesclear.com / goldilocks-rule.

18. Veronique Greenwood, "The Longevity Project: Decades of Data Reveal Paths to Long Life," *The Atlantic,* March 10, 2011, https:// www.theatlantic. com / health / archive / 2011 / 03 / the-longevity-project-decades-of-data-reveal-paths-to-long-life / 72290 /.

Chapter Six

1. Lyubomirsky, *The How of Happiness,* 20-21 (see chap. 3, n. 4).

2. Jon Gertner, "The Futile Pursuit of Happiness," *New York Times Magazine,* September 7, 2003, https://www.nytimes.com/2003/09/07/magazine/the-futile-pursuit-of-happiness.html.

3. Lyubomirsky, *The How of Happiness,* 21 (see chap. 3, n. 4).

4. Ibid., 6.

Chapter Seven

1. Wikiquote contributors, "Reinhold Niebuhr," *Wikiquote,* accessed January 3, 2019, https://en.wikiquote.org/w/index.php?title=Reinhold_Niebuhr&oldid=2419736.

2. Fred R. Shapiro, "Who Wrote the Serenity Prayer?" The Chronicle of Higher Education, April 28, 2014, https://www.chronicle.com/article/Who-Wrote-the-Serenity-Prayer-/146159/.

3. Wikiquote, "Niebuhr."

Chapter Eight

1. "Unambitious Loser With Happy, Fulfilling Life Still Lives in Hometown," *The Onion,* July 23, 2013, http://www.theonion.com/articles/unambitious-loser-with-happy-fulfilling-life-still,33233/.

2. Robert A. Emmons and Michael E. McCullough, "Counting Blessings Versus Burdens: An Experimental Investigation of Gratitude and Subjective Well-Being in Daily Life," *Journal of Personality and Social Psychology* 84, no. 2 (2003): 387.

3. Stanford University Roundtable, "Are You Happy Now?" (see chap. 4, n.1).

4. Royal Society for Public Health, *Status of Mind: Social Media and Young People's Mental Health and Well-Being,* accessed January 3, 2019, https://www.rsph.org.uk/uploads/assets/uploaded/62be270a-a55f-4719-ad668c2ec7a74c2a.pdf.

5. Richard A. Easterlin, "The Economics of Happiness," *Daedalus* 133, no. 2 (Spring 2004): 26-33, https://doi.org/10.1162/001152604323049361.

6. Julie Bort, "Mark Zuckerberg: 'Bill Gates Was My Hero,'" *Business Insider,* September 11, 2013, http://www.businessinsider.com/mark-zuckerberg-bill-gates-was-my-hero-2013-9.

7. Louise Story, "Anywhere the Eye Can See, It's Likely to See an Ad," *New York Times*, January 15, 2007, https://www.nytimes.com/2007/01/15/business/media/15everywhere.html.

8. Bruce Springsteen, quoted in "30 Second Career Counselor," University of St. Thomas Career Development Center, YouTube video, 0:28, December 4, 2012, https://www.youtube.com/watch?v=5zEQb9BhiBI.

Chapter Nine

1. Gertner, "The Futile Pursuit" (see chap. 6, n. 2).

2. Ibid.

3. Lyubomirsky, *The How of Happiness*, 50 (see chap. 3, n. 4).

4. Easterlin, *"The Economics of Happiness."*

5. Albert Camus, *The Rebel: An Essay on Man in Revolt* (New York: Vintage Books, 1956), 304.

6. Dylan Walsh, "The Workplace Is Killing People and Nobody Cares," Insights, Stanford Graduate School of Business, March 15, 2018, https://www.gsb.stanford.edu/insights/workplace-killing-people-nobody-cares.

7. Matt Killingsworth, "Does Mind-Wandering Make You Unhappy?" *Greater Good*, Greater Good Science Center at UC Berkeley, July 16, 2013, https://greatergood.berkeley.edu/article/item/does_mind_wandering_make_you_unhappy.

8. "What Are the Odds of Dying From…" National Safety Council, accessed January 3, 2019, https://www.nsc.org/work-safety/tools-resources/injury-facts/chart.

9. Fred Shapiro, "Quotes Uncovered: Twain or Not Twain," *Freakonomics* (blog), April 25, 2011, http://freakonomics.com/2011/04/25/quotes-uncovered-twain-or-not-twain/.

10. Rick Hanson, "Find Your Own Way," *Life* (blog) *Huffington Post*, updated November 3, 2013, https://www.huffingtonpost.com/rick-hanson-phd/find-your-own-way_b_3823676.html.

11. Sheryl Sandberg, *Lean In: Women, Work and the Will to Lead* (New York: Alfred A. Knopf, 2013), 123.

12. Stephen R. Covey, A. Roger Merrill and Rebecca R. Merrill, *First Things First*

(New York: Fireside, 1995), 73.

13. Donald S. Lopez, *Encyclopaedia Britannica*, s.v. "Four Noble Truths," accessed January 3, 2019, https://www.britannica.com/topic/Four-Noble-Truths.

Chapter Ten

1. "About Jack Kornfield," *JackKornfield.com*, accessed January 3, 2019, https://jackkornfield.com/bio/.

2. "The Practice of Forgiveness," *JackKornfield.com*, accessed January 3, 2019, https://jackkornfield.com/the-practice-of-forgiveness/.

3. Wikiquote contributors, "Laurence Sterne," *Wikiquote*, accessed January 3, 2019, https://en.wikiquote.org/w/index.php?title=Laurence_Sterne&oldid=2359467.

4. Dalai Lama, interview by Oprah Winfrey, "Oprah Talks to The Dalai Lama," *Oprah*, August 2001, https://www.oprah.com/omagazine/oprah-interviews-the-dalai-lama/all.

5. Thordis Elva and Tom Stranger, "Our Story of Rape and Reconciliation," TEDWomen 2016, YouTube video, October 2016, https://www.ted.com/talks/thordis_elva_tom_stranger_our_story_of_rape_and_reconciliation/transcript#t-470392.

6. Fred Luskin, "What Is Forgiveness?" Institute of Noetic Sciences, YouTube video, 0:18, September 15, 2009, https://www.youtube.com/watch?v=66Yxs1C_iQo&list=PLoKHsax6QwNY5uqxP1RKOwiohr4WMy0pp.

7. Ibid., 0:55.

8. Fred Luskin, *Forgive for Good: A Proven Prescription for Health and Happiness* (New York: HarperCollins, 2002), 78.

9. Ibid., 26-28.

10. Ibid., 30.

11. Ibid., 110.

12. Ibid., 175-76.

13. Wayne W. Dyer, "How To Forgive Someone Who Has Hurt You: In 15 Steps," *Wayne's Blog* (blog) *Dr. Wayne W. Dyer*, accessed January 3, 2019, https://www.drwaynedyer.com/blog/how-to-forgive-someone-in-15-steps/.

14. Jack Kornfield, "Forgiveness Meditation," *Greater Good*, Greater Good

Science Center at UC Berkeley, video, August 2011, https://greatergood.berkeley.edu/video/item/forgiveness_meditation.

15. Oscar Wilde, "Quotes," *Goodreads,* accessed January 3, 2019, https://www.goodreads.com/quotes/4583-always-forgive-your-enemies-nothing-annoys-them-so-much.

16. Eva Kor, "What Is the First Step Toward Forgiveness, and How Do I Convince Myself to Do That?" *Quora,* December 10, 2014, https://www.quora.com/What-is-the-first-step-toward-forgiveness-and-how-do-I-convince-myself-to-do-that/answer/Eva-Kor?srid=SFj&share=1.

17. David H. Cropley, Arthur J. Cropley, James C. Kaufman, and Mark A. Runco, eds., *The Dark Side of Creativity* (New York: Cambridge University Press, 2010), 279.

18. Tara Parker-Pope, "How to Build Resilience in Midlife," *New York Times,* July 25, 2017, https://www.nytimes.com/2017/07/25/well/mind/how-to-boost-resilience-in-midlife.html.

19. Carol S. Dweck, *Mindset: The New Psychology of Success* (New York: Ballantine Books, 2006), 6-7.

20. Ibid., 7.

21. Ibid., 245.

Chapter Eleven

1. Wikipedia contributors, "Equanimity," *Wikipedia, The Free Encyclopedia,* accessed November 24, 2018, https://en.wikipedia.org/w/index.php?title=Equanimity&oldid=876463605.

2. Daniel Gilbert, interview by Gardiner Morse, "The Science Behind the Smile," *Harvard Business Review,* January-February 2012, https://hbr.org/2012/01/the-science-behind-the-smile.

3. Olivia Solon, "WhatsApp Co-founder Joins Call to #DeleteFacebook as Fallout Intensifies," *The Guardian,* March 20, 2018, https://www.theguardian.com/technology/2018/mar/20/facebook-cambridge-analytica-whatsapp-delete.

Chapter Twelve

1. Mayo Clinic Staff, "Meditation: A Simple Fast Way to Reduce Stress," Mayo Clinic, October 17, 2017, https://www.mayoclinic.org/tests-procedures/

meditation/in-depth/meditation/art-20045858.

2. Rachael Link, "13 Benefits of Yoga that Are Supported by Science," *Healthline,* August 30, 2017, https://www.healthline.com/nutrition/13-benefits-of-yoga#section1.

3. Kate Pickert, "The Mindful Revolution," *Time,* January 23, 2014, http://time.com/1556/the-mindful-revolution/.

4. "Mindfulness Meditation Training Lowers Biomarkers of Stress Response in Anxiety Disorder," Georgetown University Medical Center, January 24, 2017, https://gumc.georgetown.edu/news/mindfulness-meditation-training-lowers-biomarkers-of-stress-response-in-anxiety-disorder.

5. Julie Corliss, "Mindfulness Meditation May Ease Anxiety, Mental Stress," *Harvard Health* (blog) *Harvard Health Publishing,* updated October 3, 2017, https://www.health.harvard.edu/blog/mindfulness-meditation-may-ease-anxiety-mental-stress-201401086967.

6. Genevieve Wanucha, "Mindfulness as Medicine," UW Medicine Memory and Brain Wellness Center, February 19, 2016, http://depts.washington.edu/mbwc/news/article/mindfulness-as-medicine.

7. Mayo Clinic Staff, "Meditation."

8. Christina Johnson, "Mindfulness Training Program May Help Olympic Athletes Reach Peak Performance," UC San Diego News Center, June 5, 2014, https://ucsdnews.ucsd.edu/feature/mindfulness_training_program_may_help_olympic_athletes_reach_peak.

9. Dan Harris and Erin Brady, "Re-Wiring Your Brain for Happiness: Research Shows How Meditation Can Physically Change the Brain," *ABC News,* July 28, 2011, https://abcnews.go.com/US/meditation-wiring-brain-happiness/story?id=14180253.

10. Gilbert, "Science Behind the Smile."

11. W. Turakitwanakan, C. Mekseepralard, and P. Busarakumtragul, "Effects of Mindfulness Meditation on Serum Cortisol of Medical Students," *Journal of the Medical Association of Thailand* 96, no. 1 (January 2013): S90-5, https://www.ncbi.nlm.nih.gov/pubmed/23724462.

12. UHN Staff, "3 Surprising Immune System Boosters: Meditation, Mindfulness, and Yoga," *University Health News Daily,* June 1, 2018, https://universityhealthnews.com/daily/stress-anxiety/3-surprising-immune-system-boosters-meditation-mindfulness-and-yoga/.

13. Barbara Bradley Hagerty, "Prayer May Reshape Your Brain … And Your Reality," NPR, May 20, 2009, https://www.npr.org/templates/story/story.php?storyId=104310443.

14. Mayo Clinic Staff, "Meditation."

15. James Paine, "11 Wildly Successful Entrepreneurs Who Swear by Daily Meditation," *Inc.*, September 16, 2016, https://www.inc.com/james-paine/11-famous-entrepreneurs-who-meditate-daily.html.

16. Jason Marsh, "Three Greater Good Lessons from the Golden State Warriors," Greater Good, Greater Good Science Center at UC Berkeley, June 14, 2017, https://greatergood.berkeley.edu/article/item/three_greater_good_lessons_from_the_golden_state_warriors.

17. "Breathing," PlumVillage.org, accessed January 3, 2019, https://plumvillage.org/mindfulness-practice/breathing/.

18. Kira M. Newman, "How to Choose a Type of Mindfulness Meditation," *Greater Good,* Greater Good Science Center at UC Berkeley, October 11, 2016, https://greatergood.berkeley.edu/article/item/how_to_choose_a_type_of_mindfulness_meditation.

19. Yelena Moroz Alpert, "13 Major Yoga Mantras to Memorize," *Yoga Journal*, February 25, 2016, https://www.yogajournal.com/yoga-101/13-major-mantras-memorize.

20. Jack Kornfield, "Practice: Recognizing Our Mental States," *JackKornfield.com*, accessed January 3, 2019, https://jackkornfield.com/practice-recognizing-our-mental-states/.

21. Andy Puddicombe, "How to Meditate in 10 Easy Steps," *The Guardian*, January 22, 2011, https://www.theguardian.com/lifeandstyle/gallery/2011/jan/22/how-to-meditate-ten-steps-headspace.

22. Jack Kornfield, "Meditation on Lovingkindness," *JackKornfield.com*, accessed January 3, 2019, https://jackkornfield.com/meditation-on-lovingkindness/.

23. "Ignatian Silent Retreats," Seattle U, accessed January 4, 2019, https://www.seattleu.edu/campus-ministry/retreats/ignatian-silent-retreats/.

24. Mark Williams, "Mindfulness Meditation with Mark Williams," *Spotify*, accessed January 4, 2019, https://open.spotify.com/album/67uxFWx39wI8frDJuF2InX.

Chapter Thirteen

1. Fred Luskin, "Forgiveness, Stress Management, and Happiness," Inflection, Inflection Speaker Series, YouTube video, 2:00, published August 30, 2012, https://www.youtube.com/watch?v=hSGfMVRVWZw.

2. Rob Dunn, "What Are You So Scared of? Saber-Toothed Cats, Snakes, and Carnivorous Kangaroos," *Slate*, October 15, 2012, http://www.slate.com/articles/health_and_science/human_evolution/2012/10/evolution_of_anxiety_humans_were_prey_for_predators_such_as_hyenas_snakes.html.

3. *Collins Dictionary,* s.v. "natural selection," accessed January 4, 2019. https://www.collinsdictionary.com/us/dictionary/english/natural-selection.

4. Dunn, "What Are You So Scared of?"

5. Hanson, *Just One Thing*, 18 (see intro., n. 2).

6. Maggie Koerth-Baker, "Who Lives Longest?" *New York Times Magazine,* March 24, 2013, https://www.nytimes.com/2013/03/24/magazine/who-lives-longest.html.

7. R. Morgan Griffin, "10 Health Problems Related to Stress That You Can Fix," WebMD, reviewed on April 1, 2014, https://www.webmd.com/balance/stress-management/features/10-fixable-stress-related-health-problems#1.

8. "Daily Affirmation: Michael Jordan," YouTube Video from a performance of *Saturday Night Live* with Michael Jordan and Al Franken, aired September 28, 1991, https://www.youtube.com/watch?v=xNx_gU57gQ4.

9. Jack Kornfield, *The Teachings of Buddha,* (Boulder, CO: Shambhala, 1993).

10. Wikiquote contributors, "John Milton," *Wikiquote,* accessed January 4, 2019, https://en.wikiquote.org/w/index.php?title=John_Milton&oldid=2501221.

11. Wikiquote contributors, "Optimism," *Wikiquote,* accessed January 4, 2019, https://en.wikiquote.org/w/index.php?title=Optimism&oldid=2431185.

12. K. Luan Phan, Tor Wager, Stephan F. Taylor, and Israel Liberzon, "Functional Neuroanatomy of Emotion: A Meta-Analysis of Emotion Activation Studies in PET and fMRI," *NeuroImage* 16, no. 2 (June 2002): 331-48, https://www.sciencedirect.com/science/article/pii/S1053811902910876.

13. Sandra Blakeslee, "A Small Part of the Brain, and Its Profound Effects," *New York Times,* February 6, 2007, https://www.nytimes.com/2007/02/06/health/psychology/06brain.html.

14. Norman Doidge, *The Brain that Changes Itself* (New York: Penguin Books, 2007), xviii-xix.

15. Ibid., 218.

16. Ibid., 220-221.

17. Hanson, *Just One Thing*, 2 (see intro., n. 2).

18. Ibid., 3.

19. Geoffrey L. Cohen and David K. Sherman, "The Psychology of Change: Self-Affirmation and Social Psychological Intervention," *Annual Review of Psychology* 65 (2014): 333, https://ed.stanford.edu/sites/default/files/annurev-psych-psychology_of_change_final_e2.pdf.

20. Hanson, *Just One Thing*, 3.

21. "Cognitive Behavioral Therapy," *Psychology Today*, (blog), accessed January 4, 2019, https://www.psychologytoday.com/us/basics/cognitive-behavioral-therapy.

22. Ben Martin, "In Depth: Cognitive Behavioral Therapy," *Psych Central*, last reviewed April 4, 2018, https://psychcentral.com/lib/in-depth-cognitive-behavioral-therapy/?all=1.

23. Ibid.

24. "Welcome to the Rapid Symptom Response Reduction Track," handout from Kaiser Permanente, 2018.

25. Marianne Williamson, *A Return To Love: Reflections on the Principles of A Course in Miracles* (New York: Harper Collins, 1992), 190-91.

26. Hanson, *Just One Thing*, 3.

27. John D. Sutter, "5 Memorable Quotes from Steve Jobs," CNN, October 5, 2011, https://www.cnn.com/2011/10/05/tech/innovation/steve-jobs-quotes/index.html.

28. Hagerty, "Prayer May Reshape Your Brain (see chap. 12, n. 13).

29. Richard J. Davidson, "The Four Keys to Well-Being," Greater Good, Greater Good Science Center at UC Berkeley, March 21, 2016, https://greatergood.berkeley.edu/article/item/the_four_keys_to_well_being.

30. Ibid.

31. Killingsworth, "Does Mind-Wandering" (see chap. 9, n. 7).

32. Davidson, "The Four Keys."

Chapter Fourteen

1. "2018 World Hunger and Poverty Facts and Statistics," *Hunger Notes,* World Hunger Education Service, revised May 25, 2018, https://www.worldhunger. org/world-hunger-and-poverty-facts-and-statistics/.

2. Helen Keller, "The Open Door Quotes," *Goodreads,* accessed January 4, 2019, https://www.goodreads.com/work/quotes/7276877-the-open-door.

3. *Shine a Light,* directed by Martin Scorsese (Paramount Classics, 2008), 1:17:00.

4. "Giving Thanks Can Make You Happier," *Harvard Health* (blog) *Harvard Health Publishing,* accessed January 4, 2019, https://www.health.harvard.edu/ healthbeat/giving-thanks-can-make-you-happier.

5. Lyubomirsky, *The How of Happiness,* 22 (see chap. 3, n. 4).

6. Hanson, *Just One Thing,* 80 (see intro., n. 2).

7. Luskin, *"Forgiveness,"* 18:50 (see chap. 13, n. 1).

8. Richard C. Mohs, "How Human Memory Works," *HowStuffWorks.com,* May 8, 2007, https://science.howstuffworks.com/life/inside-the-mind/human-brain/human-memory2.htm.

9. Megan E. Speer, Jamil P. Bhanji, and Mauricio R. Delgado, Savoring the Past: Positive Memories Evoke Value Representations in the Striatum, *Neuron* 84, no. 4 (November 19, 2014): 847-56, https://www.ncbi.nlm.nih.gov/pmc/articles/ PMC4254527/.

Chapter Fifteen

Chapter Sixteen

1. Charles Duhigg, "The Power of Habit," TED video, 3:00, published August 18, 2013, https://www.youtube.com/watch?v=OMbsGBlpP30.

2. Ibid., 4:00.

3. Ibid., 14:30.

4. B. J. Fogg, "How to Make Healthy Life Changes from Tiny Habits," WRVO Public Media, audio, 11:05, August 13, 2016, http://www.wrvo.org/post/ how-make-healthy-life-changes-tiny-habits.

5. B. J. Fogg, "Forget Big Change, Start with a Tiny Habit: BJ Fogg at TEDx Fremont," TEDx video, 14:20, published December 5, 2012, https://www.

youtube.com/watch?v=AdKUJxjn-R8.

6. Fogg, "How to Make Healthy Life Changes."

7. Fogg, "Forget Big Change," 15:25.

8. Ibid.

9. B. J. Fogg, "How to Celebrate Tiny Successes," In: Slide Share, https://www.slideshare.net/tinyhabits/dr-bj-fogg-ways-to-celebrate-tiny-successes/1-How_to_Celebrate_Tiny_Successes.

10. *The Free Library*, s.v. *"tiny habits,"* accessed December 5, 2018, http://www.thefreelibrary.com/Tiny+habits%3a+behavior+scientist+BJ+Fogg+explains+a+painless+strategy...-a0346533128.

11. "How Long to Form a Habit?" *Psyblog,* September 21, 2009, https://www.spring.org.uk/2009/09/how-long-to-form-a-habit.php.

12. Andrew S. Grove, *High Output Management* (New York: Vintage Books, 1995), 63.

Jim's Keynotes and Master Classes

Jim McCarthy — TEDx Speaker, Author, internationally recognized Happiness Expert for your conference, convention, or corporate meeting.

Jim McCarthy gets rave reviews on the lecture circuit because of his innovative workshop format and authentic delivery. Audiences deeply appreciate Jim's unique perspective — as a Stanford MBA, internet pioneer, happiness expert, and person living with a cancer diagnosis. His highly interactive talks provide immediate, practical lessons while reinforcing the main goals for your meeting. Bring him to your next event to share his secrets on happiness, purpose, and success. Jim lives and works around the globe.

Happiness:
Create Your Pleasure, Purpose, and Peace

Are the people in your organization happy? What does "happy" even mean for them? This internationally acclaimed keynote helps your team contemplate their careers, legacy, relationships, and meaning — all while contending with nonstop technological and societal disruption. They will walk out with strategies and tactics to overcome obstacles, reduce their stress, enjoy their work, and be happy — right here, right now. Whether they're facing challenges at home or at the office, this talk will help them rethink, refocus, and reenergize.

Speaking Themes:

- Inspiration
- Motivation
- Legacy
- Relationships
- Stress reduction

Participants will:

- Develop science-based, daily practices to overcome stress, anger, fear, and frustration
- Create action plans to make vastly better choices regarding their health, career, family, friends, and community
- Realize the difference between "pleasure" and "meaning," and how they need both to create happiness and peace

Some praise:

"Jim's session turned out to be a high point of our 2-day event. The team deeply appreciated this focus on their well-being, and many folks commented to me on the power of Jim's personal story. I'm very happy we did it and I would recommend it to others."
  – Joe Walowski, VP, Alexa at Amazon

"Jim's Happiness Workshop was a tremendous experience. I highly recommend to others that they do this!"
  – Heidi Roizen, Partner at DFJ Venture Capital

"Simple, yet powerful. It was the perfect closing for our Panama YPO presidential retreat."
  – Jorge Morgan, President and CEO, MMG Bank, Panama

"We brought Jim McCarthy to Kiva to conduct his Happiness Workshop. I was blown away by how he was able to break down very complex ideas and practices into three simple daily routines to incorporate in one's life."
  – Mike Cusenza, Internship Program Manager, Kiva.org

"Jim's Happiness Workshop not only taught us the many benefits of increasing our happiness levels, but he also shared simple, practical methods that we can use every day to achieve this goal. The feedback after the workshop was overwhelmingly positive, and I highly recommend Jim's workshop for anyone looking for a transformational experience."
  – Associate Director and Ph.D., Leading Pharmaceutical Company

Bounce Back!
How to Train Your Brain for Success

Research tells us that a typical human being's thoughts are roughly 80 percent negative. A person's "negativity bias" is bad for their relationships, their career, and their health. On top of that, we all face setbacks, "failure," and even tragedy. This keynote teaches you how to build resilience — ideal for teams facing tough daily challenges.

Speaking Themes:

- Resilience
- Positive thinking
- Leadership
- Teamwork

Participants will:

- Recognize how to reframe disappointments, so they have a mindset of resilience
- Learn how to immediately take control of their thoughts and attitude, in ways validated by neuroscience
- Practice a method to appreciate who they are, what they have, and where they work
- Cultivate a daily practice that keeps them positive and focused on achieving their most important goals

Some praise:

"The work we did in Jim's workshop was an unexpected joy. It helped me to feel renewed gratitude for the life I've been able to live and that

I'm living now."
- Miriam Rivera, Former Trustee, Stanford University;
Cofounder, Stanford Angels & Entrepreneurs

"I organized a workshop for my Young Presidents Organization Chapter and Jim got rave reviews! Jim understood the needs of YPO members and tailored his workshop accordingly. The session provided an excellent opportunity to get to know both oneself and other members. I highly recommend working with Jim. You will remember the material from the session for a long time!"
- Mike Orsak, General Partner, Worldview Technology Partners

"Jim came to Brit + Co to do a condensed version of his workshop. Our employees found the workshop to be extremely engaging, enjoyable, and informative. Jim's portion about daily affirmations truly resonated with our team and will definitely be carried out through our daily practices. He left us wanting more!"
- Ashley Reed, Office and Operations Manager, Brit + Co

"Our team was incredibly engaged in Jim's workshop and people walked away armed with simple and impactful techniques to help create a positive mindset. We're very thankful to Jim for sharing his passion, story, knowledge, and perspective with us."
- Amy Meyer, Chief of Staff and People Operations, 1-Page

Keep Calm:
How to Reduce Your Stress

Are you stressed out? Almost all of us would like to have less anxiety in our lives. Studies prove that relaxed employees are more productive, happier, and less likely to quit. The good news is that your teams can use science-based methods to learn how to de-stress — starting here and now.

Speaking Themes:

- Stress reduction
- Creativity
- Innovation
- Wellness

Participants will:

- Apply scientifically proven methods to improve focus, creativity, and calm
- Practice how to savor the present and improve their relationships with colleagues
- Understand the importance of forgiveness in their professional lives

Some praise:

"Thoroughly enjoyed Jim McCarthy's Happiness Workshop, which introduced new, thought-provoking lessons. Already find myself adopting several of the practices every day. Highly recommended to anyone looking for an impactful and self-reflective session."
– Brian Rumao, Chief of Staff to the CEO, LinkedIn

"If you're looking for someone to come into your company who knows how to help people stop and think about big picture stuff, this guy can do it."
– Jessie Goodpasture, Senior Drug Development Executive

"Thanks to Jim's workshop, a soothing peace of mind has enveloped my home and work life. This transformation has made me become a more productive and insightful employee with my projects, and with my work colleagues."
  – Statistical Programmer / Analyst, Global Pharmaceutical Firm

"Jim McCarthy is a wonderful speaker with an inspirational story. He really helps you think about what's important amidst the daily chaos of work."
  – Breanne Wilson, SEO and Content Strategist, Oracle

Contact Jim to book a talk or interview:
Email: jim@jimmccarthy.com

Keep learning more about how to create your happiness by following Jim McCarthy on Social Media:

Website: jimmccarthy.com
Tedx Talk: https://www.youtube.com/watch?v=x0pulJf7Fl0
LinkedIn: linkedin.com/in/jimmccarthymba/
Facebook: facebook.com/jimmccarthyonhappiness
Instagram: instagram.com/jimmccarthyonhappiness/
Twitter: twitter.com/JimMcCarthyMBA
YouTube: www.youtube.com/channel/UCN_msQIaqqbP0I02afQyUdQ

Post an online review
of *Live Each Day*:

Most people choose their books thorough recommendations and word of mouth. At the same time, independent authors such as Jim McCarthy rely heavily on referrals from readers to spread their message. If you feel that others would benefit from *Live Each Day*, would you mind posting a review on Amazon or Goodreads? It doesn't have to be a lengthy book report — even three or four thoughtful sentences, written off the top of your head, would let others know how this book touched your life in a positive way.

Thank you!

Subscribe to Jim's free email newsletter:

Join thousands of other members of Jim's Happiness Community today. Get exclusive content, special offers and discounts, and the latest news as Jim continues to learn and share what he finds — because happiness is a skill you can develop!

Just go here: www.jimmccarthy.com / subscribe

Thank you!

About Jim

Jim McCarthy teaches people how to create their happiness by blending mindfulness techniques and timeless wisdom with simple, science-based practices. He is a thought-provoking TEDx speaker who has presented his innovative and highly acclaimed keynotes and master classes to organizations of all sizes across the U.S. and internationally.

His talks aren't just inspirational. Audiences take away practical strategies, science-based insights, and daily action plans — because happiness is a skill you can develop. Jim is recognized for his unique perspective — as a Stanford MBA, internet pioneer, and person living with a cancer diagnosis.

ALSO AVAILABLE AS AN EBOOK

For more about Jim and his work visit: www.JimMcCarthy.com

Made in the USA
San Bernardino, CA
07 March 2019